Emperor Penguin

Did You Know?

- Penguins are flightless sea birds.

- The emperor penguin is the largest of the penguins, standing up to 4 feet tall.

- Penguins are good swimmers and use their wings as paddles.

- A penguin's thick layer of blubber helps insulate its body in cold Antarctic waters.

CALIFORNIA

Science

Macmillan
McGraw-Hill

Program Authors

Dr. Jay K. Hackett
Professor Emeritus of Earth Sciences
University of Northern Colorado

Dr. Richard H. Moyer
Professor of Science Education and Natural
  Sciences
University of Michigan–Dearborn

Dr. JoAnne Vasquez
Elementary Science Education Consultant
NSTA Past President
Member, National Science Board
  and NASA Education Board

Mulugheta Teferi, M.A.
Principal, Gateway Middle School
St. Louis Public Schools
St. Louis, MO

Dinah Zike, M.Ed.
Dinah Might Adventures LP
San Antonio, TX

Kathryn LeRoy, M.S.
Executive Director
Division of Mathematics and Science Education
Miami-Dade County Public Schools, FL

Dr. Dorothy J. T. Terman
Science Curriculum Development Consultant
Former K–12 Science and Mathematics Coordinator
Irvine Unified School District, CA

Dr. Gerald F. Wheeler
Executive Director
National Science Teachers Association

Bank Street College of Education
New York, NY

Contributing Authors

Dr. Sally Ride
Sally Ride Science
San Diego, CA

Lucille Villegas Barrera, M.Ed.
Elementary Science Supervisor
Houston Independent School District
Houston, TX

Dr. Stephen F. Cunha
Professor of Geography
Humboldt State University
Arcata, CA

**American Museum
of Natural History**
New York, New York

Contributing Writer

Ellen Grace
Albuquerque, NM

 The American Museum of Natural History in New York City is one of the world's preeminent scientific, educational, and cultural institutions, with a global mission to explore and interpret human cultures and the natural world through scientific research, education, and exhibitions. Each year the Museum welcomes around four million visitors, including 500,000 schoolchildren in organized field trips. It provides professional development activities for thousands of teachers; hundreds of public programs that serve audiences ranging from preschoolers to seniors; and an array of learning and teaching resources for use in homes, schools, and community-based settings. Visit www.amnh.org for online resources.

RFB&D 🎧
learning through listening

Students with print disabilities may be eligible to obtain an accessible, audio version of the pupil edition of this textbook. Please call Recording for the Blind & Dyslexic at 1-800-221-4792 for complete information.

D

The McGraw·Hill Companies

Macmillan/McGraw-Hill

Copyright © 2008 by The McGraw-Hill Companies, Inc. All rights reserved. Except as permitted under the United States Copyright Act, no part of this publication may be reproduced or distributed in any form or by any means, or stored in a database or retrieval system, without prior permission of the publisher.

Science Content Standards for California Public Schools reproduced by permission, California Department of Education, CDE Press, 1430 N Street, Suite 3207, Sacramento, CA 95814.

Send all inquiries to:
Macmillan/McGraw-Hill
8787 Orion Place
Columbus, OH 43240-4027

 is a trademark of The McGraw-Hill Companies, Inc.

Printed in the United States of America

ISBN: 987-0-02-284377-9
MHID: 0-02-284377-9

4 5 6 7 8 9 (027/055) 10 09 08

Scientific Method

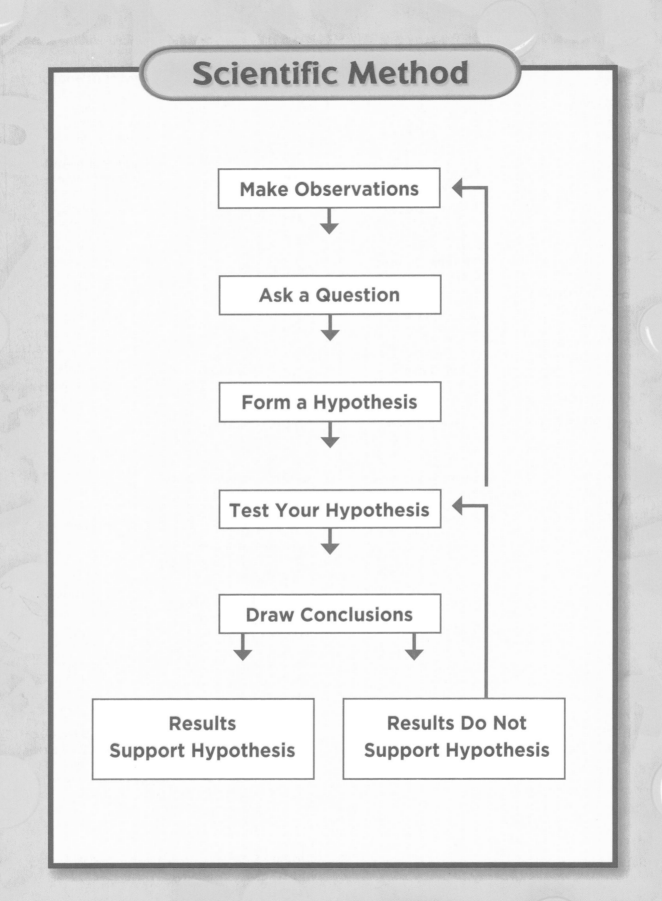

Be a Scientist

What Is Science? 2

Observation................................. 4

Question and Hypothesis 6

Experiment 8

Collecting Data 10

Conclusion................................. 12

Forming a Hypothesis 14

Defining Variables......................... 15

Designing an Experiment 16

Analyzing Data 17

Forming New Questions 18

Students use tools to measure and record data. ▶

v

Life Science

CHAPTER 1

Adaptations in Land Environments 20

Literature: Giant Sequoias 22

Lesson 1 Living Things and Their Needs 24

Inquiry Skill Builder: Compare and Classify . . 34

Lesson 2 Life in the Desert 36

Inquiry Investigation 44

Lesson 3 Life in the Grassland 46

Reading in Science 54

Lesson 4 Life in the Forest 56

Inquiry Investigation 66

Lesson 5 Life in the Arctic Tundra 68

Writing in Science 78

Math in Science 79

Chapter 1 Review and Test Practice 80

CHAPTER 2

Adaptations in Water Environments 84

Literature: Dragons of the Sea 86

Lesson 1 The Water Planet 88

Inquiry Skill Builder: Predict 96

Lesson 2 Life in an Ocean 98

Inquiry Investigation 108

Lesson 3 Life in the Wetlands 110

Reading in Science 118

Writing in Science 120

Math in Science 121

Chapter 2 Review and Test Practice 122

CHAPTER 3

Environments Change 126

Literature: Can We Save the Peregrine Falcon? 128

Lesson 1 Living Things Change Their Environment . . . 130

Inquiry Skill Builder: Record Data. 138

Lesson 2 Changes Affect Living Things 140

Inquiry Investigation 150

Lesson 3 Living Things of the Past 152

Reading in Science 162

Writing in Science 164

Math in Science 165

Chapter 3 Review and Test Practice 166

Once Upon a Woodpecker. 170

Careers in Science 172

Beavers use branches to build dams and lodges in the water. ▶

Earth Science

CHAPTER 4

Our Earth, Sun, and Moon 174

Literature: The Sun and the Moon 176

Lesson 1 Day and Night 178

Inquiry Skill Builder: **Analyze Data** 186

Lesson 2 The Seasons 188

Writing in Science 196

Math in Science 197

Lesson 3 The Moon 198

Inquiry Investigation 206

Reading in Science 208

Chapter 4 Review and Test Practice 210

◀ **During the summer, temperatures are warmer, and there are more hours of daylight.**

CHAPTER 5

Our Solar System 214

Literature: To Space and Back 216

Lesson 1   The Sun and Its Planets 218

Inquiry Skill Builder: Observe 226

Lesson 2   Telescopes: Discovering the
Solar System. 228

Inquiry Investigation 234

Lesson 3   The Stars. 236

Reading in Science 244

Writing in Science 246

Math in Science 247

Chapter 5 Review and Test Practice 248

What a Difference Day Length Makes 252

Careers in Science 254

▼ **The four inner planets are warmer than the other planets because they are closer to the Sun.**

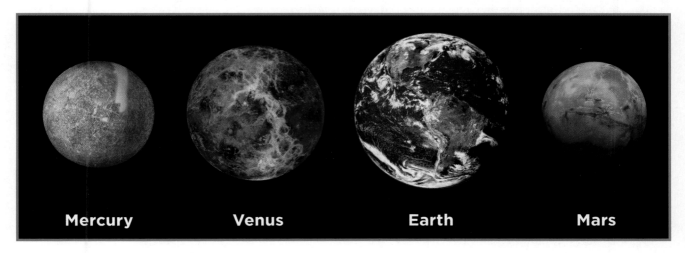

Mercury   **Venus**   **Earth**   **Mars**

Physical Science

CHAPTER 6

Matter. **256**

Literature: Freezing Rain. 258

Lesson 1 Solids, Liquids, and Gases 260

Inquiry Skill Builder: Measure 270

Lesson 2 Building Blocks of Matter 272

Reading in Science 280

Writing in Science 282

Math in Science 283

Lesson 3 Changing Matter 284

Inquiry Investigation 292

Chapter 6 Review and Test Practice 294

CHAPTER 7

Energy **298**

Literature: Wind Power 300

Lesson 1 Energy All Around. 302

Inquiry Skill Builder: Draw Conclusions 312

Lesson 2 Using Energy 314

Reading in Science 322

Writing in Science 324

Math in Science 325

Lesson 3 Energy on the Move 326

Inquiry Investigation 336

Chapter 7 Review and Test Practice 338

CHAPTER 8

Light 342

Literature: Crystal Vision. 344

Lesson 1 How Light Moves 346

Inquiry Skill Builder: Experiment. 354

Lesson 2 Seeing Light and Color 356

 Reading in Science 364

Inquiry Investigation 366

Lesson 3 Shadows 368

Writing in Science 376

Math in Science 377

Chapter 8 Review and Test Practice 378

Ranger Rick The Shocking Story of Electric Eels 382

Careers in Science 384

◀ When a roller coaster is at the top of the track, it has stored energy.

Activities

Life Science

CHAPTER 1

Explore Activities

What do plants need to live? 25

What adaptations help plants survive in a desert? 37

What kinds of animals live in a grassland? 47

Will a plant grow toward light? 57

Does fat help animals survive in cold environments? 69

Quick Labs

Observe Plant Parts 29

Desert Adaptations 41

How Grasses Grow 51

Hiding Out 63

Arctic Adaptations 75

Skill Builders and Investigations

Compare and Classify 34

How does camouflage help some animals survive? 44

How do trees affect light in a rain forest? 66

CHAPTER 2

Explore Activities

Can ocean animals live and grow in fresh water? 89

How do jellyfish and some other water animals move? 99

How do wetlands filter water? 111

Quick Labs

Water Temperatures 93

Plant Growth 103

Wetland Plants and Water Level 115

Skill Builders and Investigations

Predict 96

How does salt affect the way things float in water? 108

CHAPTER 3

Explore Activities

How can worms change their environment? 131

What happens to some plants when there is a flood? 141

How do fossils tell us about the past? 153

Quick Labs

A Beaver's Tools 135

Grassland Ecosystem 147

Fossil Mystery 159

Skill Builders and Investigations

Record Data 138

How do environmental changes affect plants? 150

Earth Science

CHAPTER 4

Explore Activities

How do shadows change?. 179

What happens when seasons change?. 189

How does the Moon's shape appear to change? 199

Quick Labs

A Model of Earth 183

Sunset Times 193

Make a Moon Phase Flip Book . . 202

Skill Builders and Investigations

Analyze Data 186

Why does the Moon's shape appear to change? 206

CHAPTER 5

Explore Activities

How do the planets move through space? 219

How do telescopes help us learn about distant objects? 229

Why do we only see the stars at night?. 237

Quick Labs

Why Do Planets Shine? 221

A Water Lens 231

Make a Constellation. 241

Water drops act like lenses. ▶

Activities

Physical Science

CHAPTER 6

Explore Activities

How do you describe objects? . . . 261

How can you classify matter? 273

How does matter change? 285

Quick Labs

Solids, Liquids, and Gases 265

Model of an Atom 277

Chemical Changes. 289

Skill Builders and Investigations

Measure 270

How can physical and chemical
changes affect matter? 292

CHAPTER 7

Explore Activities

What happens to air as
it is heated? 303

How can you increase the distance
a toy car travels? 315

Do waves carry energy? 327

Quick Labs

Forms of Energy 307

Using Energy 319

How Sounds Are Made. 333

Skill Builders and Investigations

Draw Conclusions 312

How does sound energy move
through different materials? 336

CHAPTER 8

Explore Activities

How does light move? 347

How does light affect
the color you see? 357

How do materials affect light? . . 369

Quick Labs

Movement of Light 351

How Light Affects Your Pupils . . .359

What Causes a Shadow
to Change Size? 373

Skill Builders and Investigations

Experiment 354

How can you mix
colors of light? 366

Reference

California Science Content Standards 386

Science Handbook

Units of Measurement 388

Measure Time 390

Measure Length. 391

Measure Area. 391

Measure Mass 392

Measure Volume 393

Measure Weight/Force 394

Measure Temperature 395

Use a Hand Lens 396

Use a Microscope 397

Use Calculators 398

Use Computers 400

Make Graphs 402

Make Maps 404

Make Tables 405

Make Charts 406

FOLDABLES 407

Glossary 411

Index 425

Safety Tips

In the Classroom

- Read all of the directions. Make sure you understand them. When you see "⚠ **Be Careful,**" follow the safety rules.

- Listen to your teacher for special safety directions. If you do not understand something, ask for help.

- Wash your hands with soap and water before an activity.

- Be careful around a hot plate. Know when it is on and when it is off. Remember that the plate stays hot for a few minutes after it is turned off.

- Wear a safety apron if you work with anything messy or anything that might spill.

- Clean up a spill right away, or ask your teacher for help.

- Tell your teacher if something breaks. If glass breaks, do not clean it up yourself.

- Wear safety goggles when your teacher tells you to wear them. Wear them when working with anything that can fly into your eyes or when working with liquids.

- Keep your hair and clothes away from open flames. Tie back long hair, and roll up long sleeves.

- Keep your hands dry around electrical equipment.

- Do not eat or drink anything during an experiment.

- Put equipment back the way your teacher tells you to.

- Dispose of things the way your teacher tells you to.

- Clean up your work area after an activity, and wash your hands with soap and water.

In the Field

- Go with a trusted adult—such as your teacher, or a parent or guardian.

- Do not touch animals or plants without an adult's approval. The animal might bite. The plant might be poison ivy or another dangerous plant.

Responsibility

- Treat living things, the environment, and one another with respect.

Be a Scientist

The name of this fossil, *Archaeopteryx*, means "ancient wing."

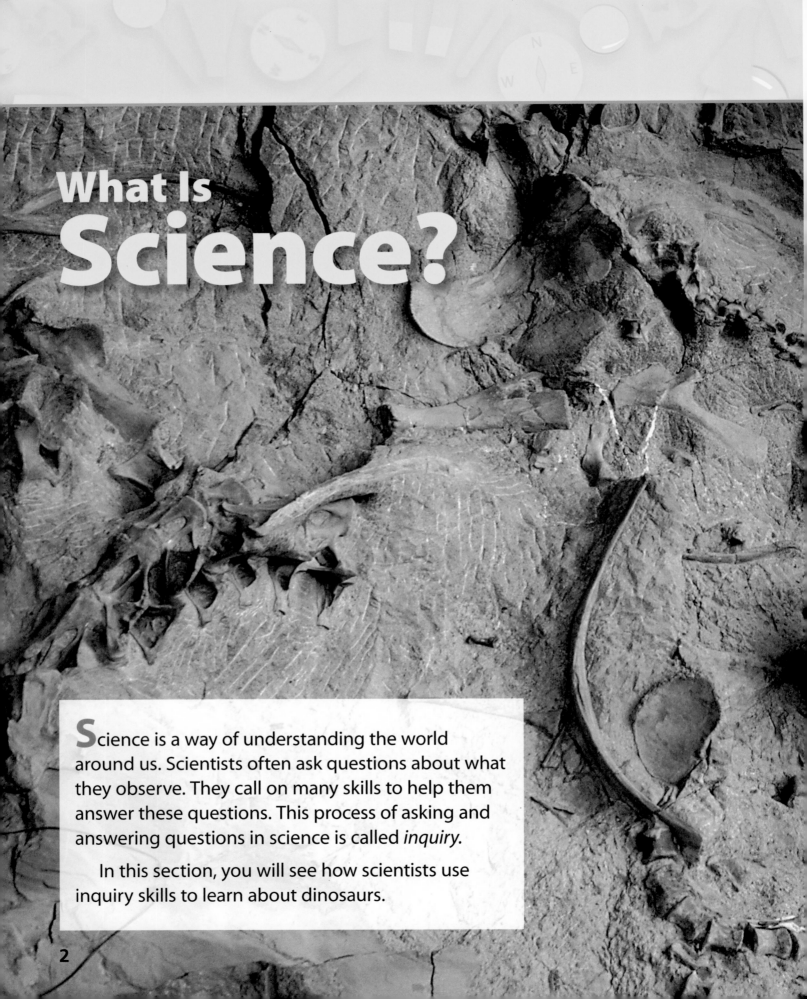

What Is Science?

Science is a way of understanding the world around us. Scientists often ask questions about what they observe. They call on many skills to help them answer these questions. This process of asking and answering questions in science is called *inquiry*.

In this section, you will see how scientists use inquiry skills to learn about dinosaurs.

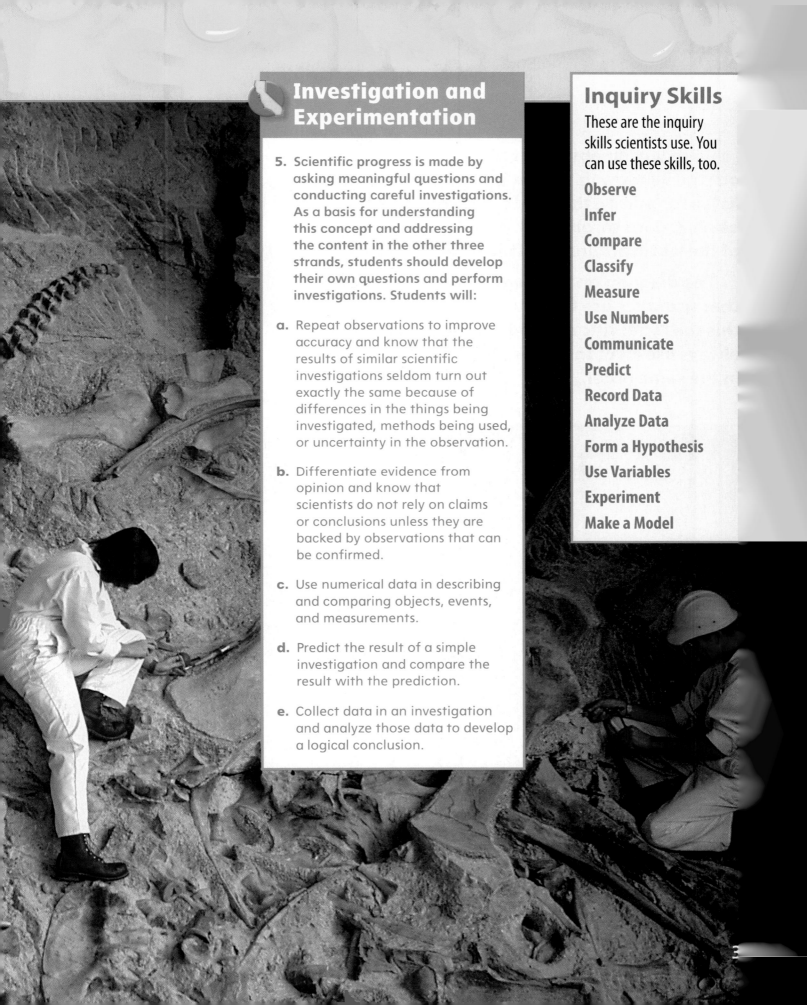

Investigation and Experimentation

5. Scientific progress is made by asking meaningful questions and conducting careful investigations. As a basis for understanding this concept and addressing the content in the other three strands, students should develop their own questions and perform investigations. Students will:

a. Repeat observations to improve accuracy and know that the results of similar scientific investigations seldom turn out exactly the same because of differences in the things being investigated, methods being used, or uncertainty in the observation.

b. Differentiate evidence from opinion and know that scientists do not rely on claims or conclusions unless they are backed by observations that can be confirmed.

c. Use numerical data in describing and comparing objects, events, and measurements.

d. Predict the result of a simple investigation and compare the result with the prediction.

e. Collect data in an investigation and analyze those data to develop a logical conclusion.

Inquiry Skills

These are the inquiry skills scientists use. You can use these skills, too.

Observe

Infer

Compare

Classify

Measure

Use Numbers

Communicate

Predict

Record Data

Analyze Data

Form a Hypothesis

Use Variables

Experiment

Make a Model

Are you an observant person? You might look out the window to see if it is raining. You might even listen for rain on the windowsill. You make observations throughout your day. Observations of the world around us often raise questions.

The diagram on this page shows processes that scientists use to answer questions. Many call this the "scientific method." Scientists don't always use all of the steps. They may not use them in the same order.

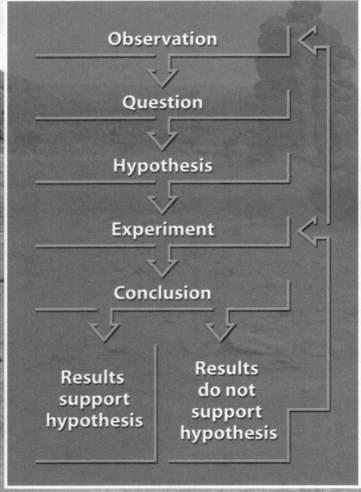

Observation

↓

Question

↓

Hypothesis

↓

Experiment

↓

Conclusion

Results support hypothesis

Results do not support hypothesis

Inquiry Skills

When you make observations, you use these skills.

Observe Use your senses to learn about an object or event.

Classify Place things that share properties together in groups.

Measure Find the size, distance, time, volume, area, mass, weight, or temperature of an object or an event.

Scientists are curious people who observe the world around them and try to understand it. To observe means to use your senses to learn about something. Scientists ask questions about the things they observe. You can too. When you ask questions about the things you see, smell, hear, taste, or feel, you are a scientist.

The scientist in this photo is uncovering dinosaur footprints. What can scientists learn about dinosaurs by observing their footprints?

5

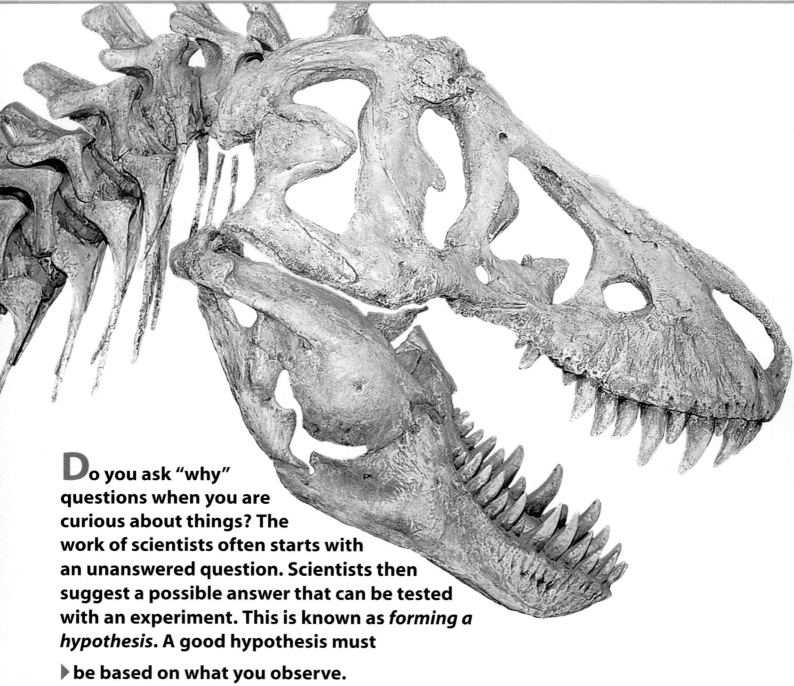

Do you ask "why" questions when you are curious about things? The work of scientists often starts with an unanswered question. Scientists then suggest a possible answer that can be tested with an experiment. This is known as *forming a hypothesis*. A good hypothesis must

▶ be based on what you observe.
▶ be testable by doing an experiment.
▶ be useful in predicting new findings.

   Which of these dinosaurs was a meat eater and which was a plant eater? Form a hypothesis to answer this question.

Inquiry Skills

When you ask questions and form hypotheses, you use these skills.

Infer Form an idea from facts or observations.

Form a hypothesis Make a statement that can be tested to answer a question.

A scientific hypothesis must be testable. That means you must be able to support or disprove your hypothesis by experimenting. When you experiment you do a hands-on activity to test an idea.

Scientists often do research before they experiment. They look in books, scientific journals, or Internet resources for information that other scientists have found. Scientists also know that they cannot rely on someone's opinion or claim unless it has been backed up by observations.

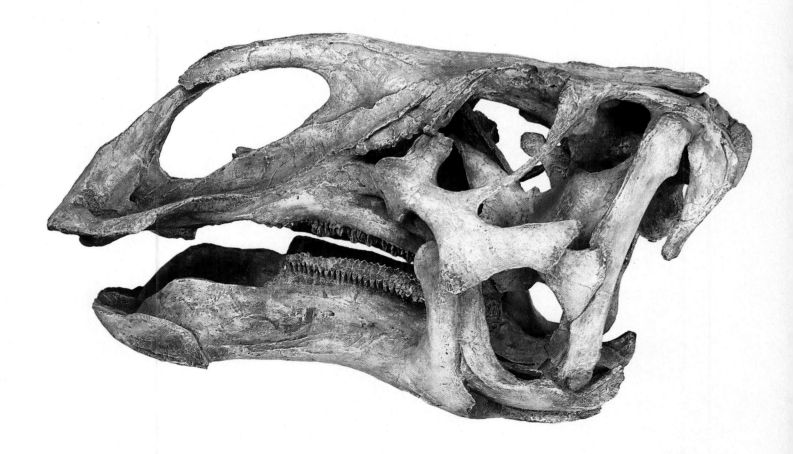

3.IE.5.b. Differentiate evidence from opinion and know that scientists do not rely on claims or conclusions unless they are backed by observations that can be confirmed.

Now it's time to test your hypothesis with an experiment. In experiments you change one variable to see what happens with another variable. For example, you might make a model to find out how the type of soil affects the shape of a dinosaur's footprint. What would happen if you changed both the type of soil and the size of the dinosaur?

Experiments must be able to be repeated, too. This allows scientists to evaluate and compare each other's work. They can check their own work too! So a good experiment must:

▶ change only one variable at a time.
▶ be able to be repeated.

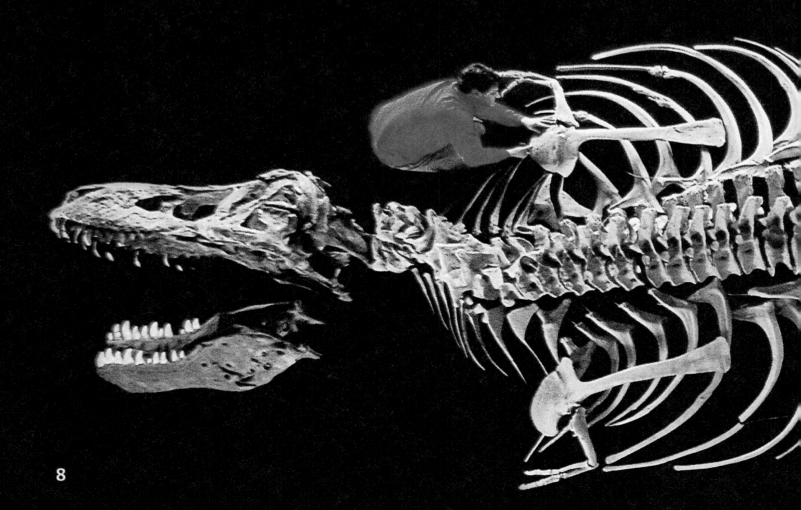

Before you test a hypothesis, you must have a plan. When scientists make a plan, they think about the variables they want to test. A variable is something that can be changed or controlled. It is important to change or control only one variable at a time. Keep all other parts of the experiment the same. That way you will know what caused your results.

After they determine their variables, scientists decide what materials they will need. Then they write a procedure. A procedure is a series of numbered steps that tell what to do first, next, and last.

After scientists have developed their procedure, they predict what will happen when they follow it. To predict means to tell what you think will happen.

Inquiry Skills

When you experiment, you use these skills.

Experiment Perform a test to support or disprove a hypothesis.

Use variables Identify things in an experiment that can be changed or controlled.

Predict State possible results of an event or experiment.

Make a model Make something to represent an object or event.

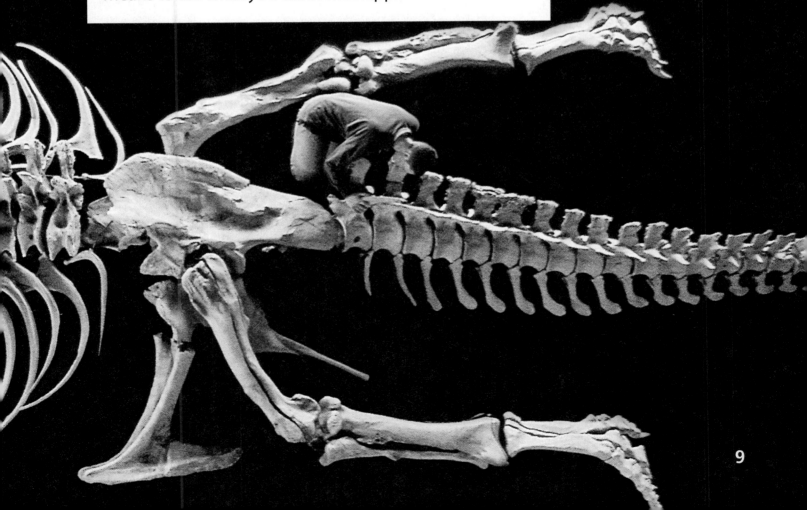

What's one important part of a science experiment? Collecting and recording good data! When data are collected they may then be explained, or interpreted. Collecting and interpreting data often requires working with numbers.

This scientist will measure and record the length and weight of the dinosaur fossil she is studying.

When scientists follow their procedure, they make observations and record data. Data is information. Measurements are a type of data. Scientists use measurements whenever they can to describe objects and events. Scientists measure such things as length, volume, mass, temperature, and time.

Scientists repeat their procedure several times. This helps them know if their results are correct. They often compare their results with other scientists. Other scientists will repeat the procedure to see if they get the same results.

Inquiry Skills

When you collect and interpret data, you use these skills.

Use Numbers Order, count, add, subtract, multiply, and divide to explain data.

Measure Find the size, distance, time, volume, area, mass, weight, or temperature of an object or an event.

Record Data Accurately arrange and store information collected in science investigations.

Analyze Data Use the information that has been gathered to answer questions or solve a problem.

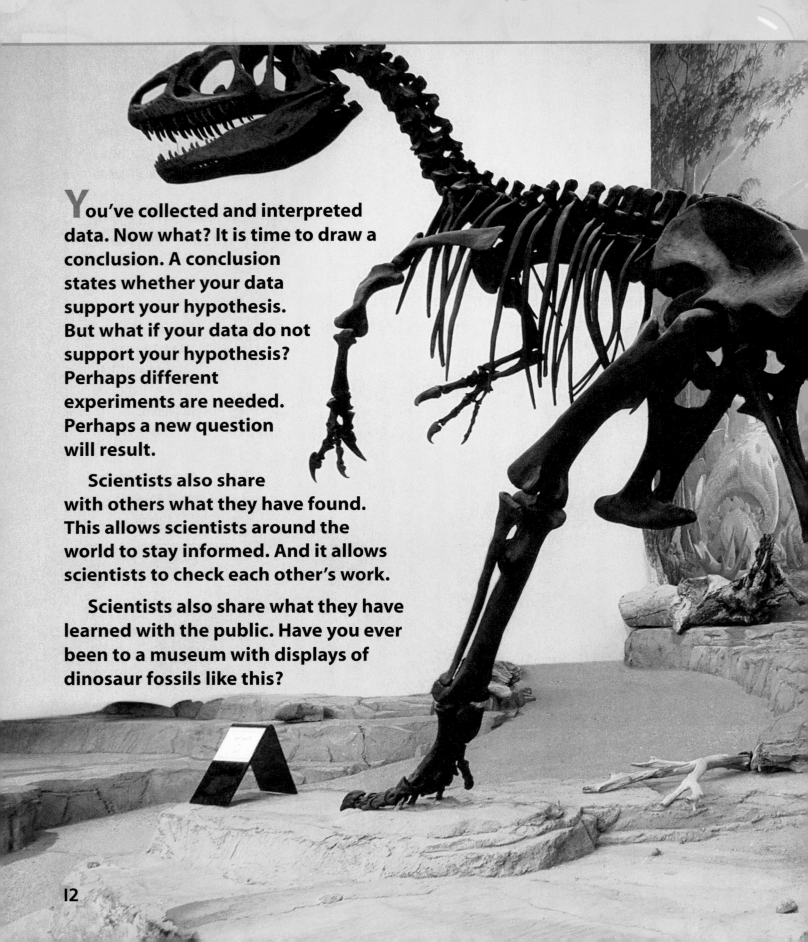

You've collected and interpreted data. Now what? It is time to draw a conclusion. A conclusion states whether your data support your hypothesis. But what if your data do not support your hypothesis? Perhaps different experiments are needed. Perhaps a new question will result.

Scientists also share with others what they have found. This allows scientists around the world to stay informed. And it allows scientists to check each other's work.

Scientists also share what they have learned with the public. Have you ever been to a museum with displays of dinosaur fossils like this?

Inquiry Skills

When you draw conclusions and communicate results, you use this skill.

Communicate Share information.

Scientists organize and analyze their data to see if the results support or disprove their hypothesis. They determine if their prediction matched their results. They draw conclusions and try to explain their results. When you draw conclusions you interpret observations to answer questions.

Sometimes the results of an experiment lead to new questions. These questions can be used to form a new hypothesis and perform new tests. The process starts all over again. This process of asking and answering questions is called the scientific method.

Forming a Hypothesis

Now it's your turn to be a scientist and design a good experiment.

Most science experiments start with an unanswered question. Students wondered how dinosaur footsteps could show how large the animal was. This was their question:

Question

- Does the length of your leg affect the distance between your footsteps?

The students turned the question into a statement that can be tested. This is called a hypothesis. A hypothesis is an "if… then…" statement.

Hypothesis

If the leg is longer, then the distance between the footsteps will be greater.

Defining Variables

Make a plan to test the hypothesis.

The first step is to identify what is being tested and what is not being tested. These are called your *variables*.

Controlled variables are not being tested. These variables remain constant during an experiment.

In this experiment the controlled variables will be:

- The walking pace for each student tested
- The location of the test
- The starting point for the test

The only thing that will change is the factor you are testing. This is the independent variable. Your independent variables will be the length of the leg of each student tested. The dependent variable is what you are measuring. In this experiment the dependent variable is the distance between the footsteps.

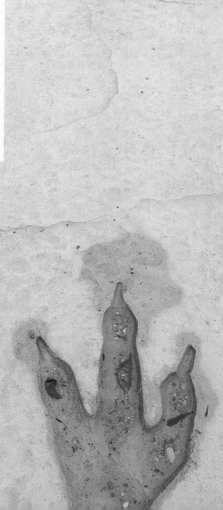

Designing an Experiment

Design an experiment to test the hypothesis. Here is an experiment a group of students designed to test this hypothesis.

Procedure

1. Choose three classmates with different leg lengths. Measure the length from the waist to the ground. Record each length.

2. Predict which student will have the longest footstep.

3. Measure a 3-meter piece of butcher paper. Mark a START line at one end of the paper.

4. Have students take 3 normal steps from the START line. Measure each footstep from heel to heel. Record your measurements in a data chart.

5. Repeat the experiment to verify your results.

6. Was your prediction correct?

Data Chart

Student	Length of leg (cm)	Length of footstep (cm)
Isabel	45	30
Sue	52	49
Jose	50	42

Analyzing Data

In order to communicate the results of an experiment, the data need to be presented in a clear way. These students used the data chart to make a bar graph that shows how the length of the leg relates to the length of the footstep.

Does this graph help others understand the results of the experiment? Why is it important to repeat experiments?

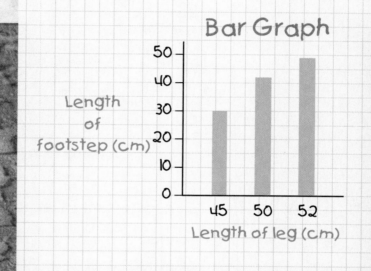

3 IE 5.a. Repeat observations to improve accuracy and know that the results of similar scientific investigations seldom turn out exactly the same because of differences in the things being investigated, methods being used, or uncertainty in the observation. • 3 IE 5.c. Use numerical data in describing and comparing objects, events, and measurements. • 3 IE 5.d. Predict the result of a simple investigation and compare the result with the prediction. • 3 IE 5.e. Collect data in an investigation and analyze those data to develop a logical conclusion.

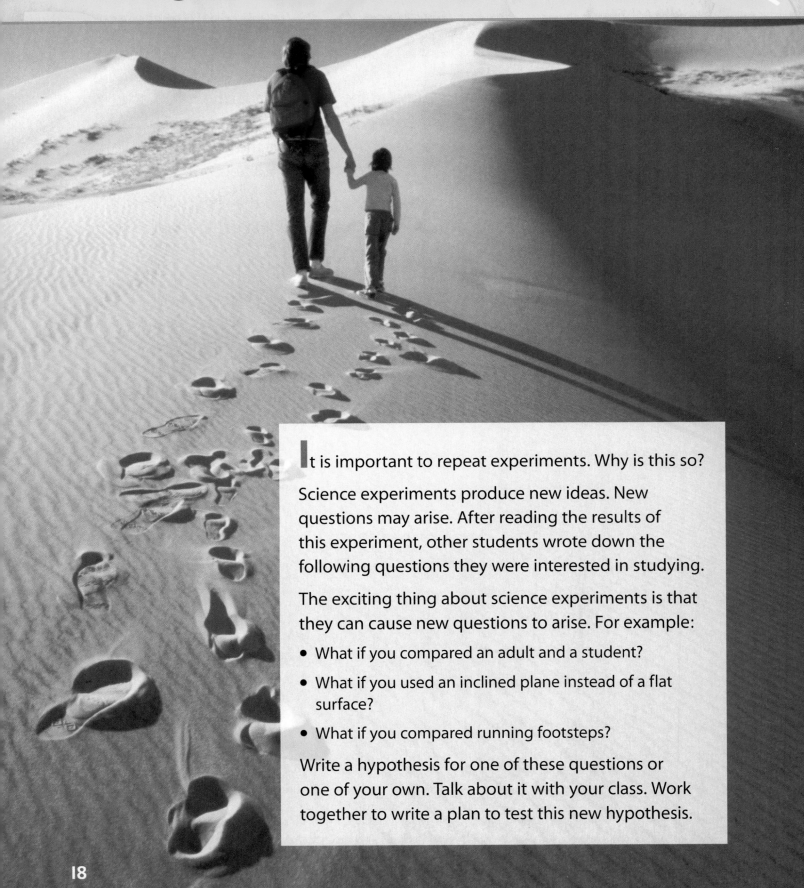

Forming New Questions

It is important to repeat experiments. Why is this so?

Science experiments produce new ideas. New questions may arise. After reading the results of this experiment, other students wrote down the following questions they were interested in studying.

The exciting thing about science experiments is that they can cause new questions to arise. For example:

- What if you compared an adult and a student?

- What if you used an inclined plane instead of a flat surface?

- What if you compared running footsteps?

Write a hypothesis for one of these questions or one of your own. Talk about it with your class. Work together to write a plan to test this new hypothesis.

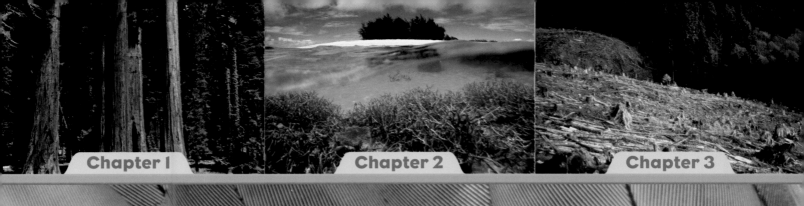

Chapter 1
Chapter 2
Chapter 3

Life Science

Touching a bullfrog will not give you warts.

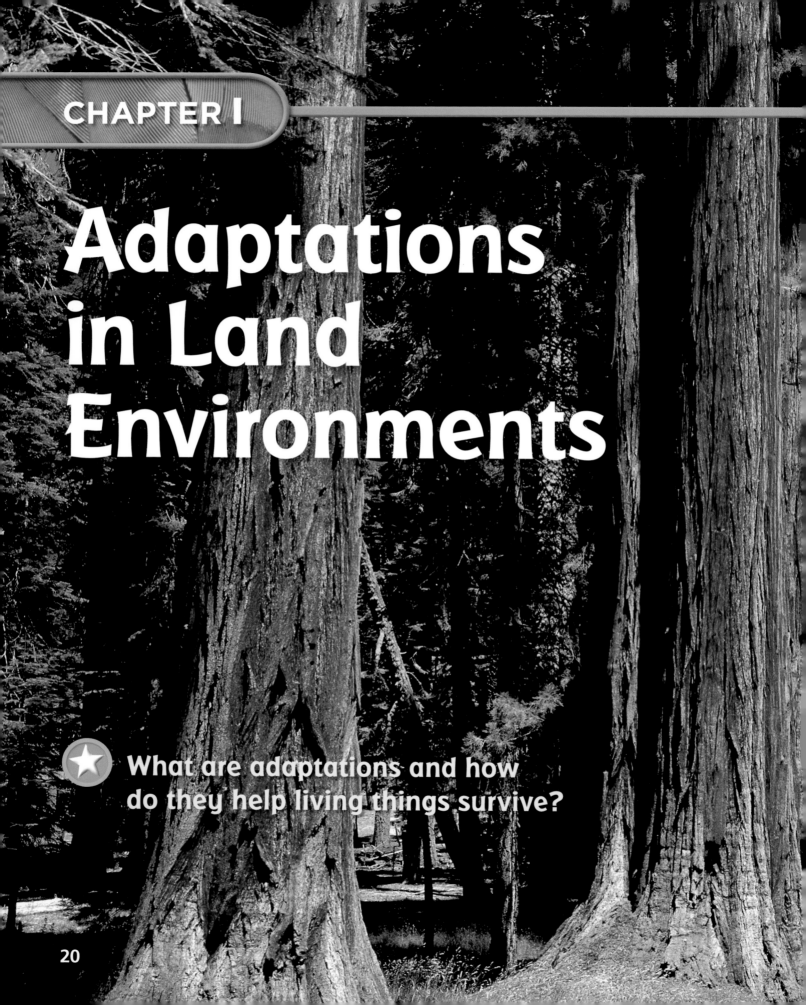

Adaptations in Land Environments

What are adaptations and how do they help living things survive?

Lesson 1

Living Things and Their Needs

PAGE 24

Lesson 2

Life in the Desert

PAGE 36

Lesson 3

Life in the Grassland

PAGE 46

Lesson 4

Life in the Forest

PAGE 56

Lesson 5

Life in the Arctic Tundra

PAGE 68

 3 LS 3. Adaptations in physical structure or behavior may improve an organism's chance for survival.

Literature
Poem

ELA R 3.2.3. Demonstrate comprehension by identifying answers in the text.
ELA W 3.1.1. Create a single paragraph: **a.** Develop a topic sentence. **b.** Include simple supporting facts and details.

giant sequoias

Giant SEQUOIAS

from *Iguanas in the Snow*

by Francisco X. Alarcón

These are the great-great-
great-great-grandparents
of the Sierra Nevada

their many scars tell
of the storms and fires
they have survived

every year without fail
their huge trunks
add another ring

thick in a wet year
with plentiful rains—
thin in a dry one

it takes my whole
family holding hands
for us to give a hug

to the tallest
and oldest tree
in this grove

Write About It

Response to Literature This poem tells us that sequoia trees can survive forest fires. What else have you learned about them from this poem? Write a paragraph about sequoia trees. Think about what you already know about trees and use details from the poem.

LOG ON e-Journal Write about it online @ **www.macmillanmh.com**

Living Things and Their Needs

Look and Wonder

Living things can be found all over Earth. How do living things get what they need to survive?

Building block lesson for 3 LS 3.a. Students know plants and animals have structures that serve different functions in growth, survival, and reproduction. **3 LS 3.b.** Students know examples of diverse life forms in different environments, such as oceans, deserts, tundra, forests, grasslands, and wetlands.

What do plants need to live?

Form a Hypothesis

Do plants need light? Do they need water? Write a hypothesis.

Test Your Hypothesis

1 Label four identical plants as shown.

Light and Water	Light and No Water
No Light and Water	No Light and No Water

2 Observe How do the plants look? Record your observations in a chart.

3 Put the plants labeled *No Light* in a dark place. Put the plants labeled *Light* in a sunny place. Water the plants labeled *Water* every few days.

4 Predict What do you think will happen to each plant?

5 Record Data Look at the plants every few days. Record your observations in your chart.

Draw Conclusions

6 Analyze Data Which plant grew the most after two weeks? Which plant looks the healthiest?

7 What do plants need to live?

Explore More

Experiment What else do plants need to live? How could you find out? Make a plan and try it.

Materials

4 identical plants

measuring cup and water

Step **1** Plants	Day 1	Day 4	Day 8	Day 12
Light and Water				
Light and No Water				
No Light and Water				
No Light and No Water				

3 IE 5.e. Collect data in an investigation and analyze those data to develop a logical conclusion.

Read and Learn

▶ **Main Idea** 3 LS 3.a
3 LS 3.b

Living things get what they need from their environment.

▶ **Vocabulary**

environment, p. 26

biome, p. 26

climate, p. 27

soil, p. 27

humus, p. 27

structure, p. 29

shelter, p. 30

adaptation, p. 32

 **e-Glossary**
@ www.macmillanmh.com

▶ **Reading Skill**

Draw Conclusions

Text Clues	Conclusions

▶ **Technology**

 Explore biomes with the Secret Agents.

Deserts are biomes that have dry climates and sandy soil. Deserts can be hot or cold.

Where do living things live?

Look outside. Do you see any living things? You probably do. Living things live almost everywhere on Earth. They live in any environment (en•VIGH•ruhn•muhnt) where they can meet their needs. An environment is everything that surrounds a living thing.

Environments are made up of both living and nonliving things. Plants and animals are living things. Water, air, and sunlight are nonliving things.

Biomes

Scientists group environments with similar traits into biomes (BIGH•ohmz). A biome is an area of land or water that has certain kinds of living and nonliving things. Deserts, forests, and grasslands are examples of biomes.

Grasslands are biomes that have mainly grasses.

Each biome has a certain kind of climate (KLIGH•mit). **Climate** describes the typical weather conditions of an area over time. Some biomes are cold and dry for most of the year. Some are warm and wet. A biome's climate affects which living things can survive there.

Each biome also has a certain type of soil. **Soil** is a substance that covers the ground. It is made of broken-down rocks and humus (HYEW•muhs). **Humus** is broken-down plant and animal material. Humus adds nutrients to the soil. It soaks up rainwater and keeps the ground moist.

 Quick Check

Draw Conclusions Do all deserts have similar kinds of living things?

Critical Thinking What are some of the living things in a city environment?

How do plants get what they need?

From the tallest redwood tree to the smallest pansy, most plants have the same basic needs. They need water, sunlight, energy from food, and carbon dioxide. Carbon dioxide is a gas found in air. Plants need nutrients, too. *Nutrients* are substances that help living things grow and stay healthy. Plants must get all these things from their environment in order to survive, but they make their own food.

Stems carry food and water throughout the plant. Stems also keep a plant upright so leaves can get sunlight.

Roots take in water and nutrients from the soil. They also keep a plant in place.

Plants have structures that help them get or make what they need. A **structure** is a part of a living thing. Most plants have roots, stems, and leaves. Many plants also have flowers, fruits, and seeds. These parts help plants live, grow, and reproduce. *Reproduce* means to make new plants like themselves.

 Quick Check

Draw Conclusions Why are roots important to plants?

Critical Thinking Why don't plants need to eat?

Leaves take in carbon dioxide from the air. They use energy from the Sun to change carbon dioxide and water into food for the plant.

≡Quick Lab

Observe Plant Parts

❶ Get two plants to observe.

❷ **Observe** Look at the parts of each plant. Does each plant have roots? How about stems and leaves?

❸ **Record Data** Use pictures and words in a chart to describe each plant's parts.

❹ **Compare** How are the parts of these plants alike? How are they different?

basil

carrot

Read a Diagram

How do leaves help plants get what they need?

Clue: Bold words can help you find information.

How do animals get what they need?

Like plants, all animals have the same basic needs. Animals need water, energy from food, and oxygen. Oxygen is a gas found in air and water. Some animals need shelter, too. A **shelter** is a place in which an animal can stay safe.

Animals have structures that help them meet their needs in their environment. Body parts, such as legs, wings, and beaks are examples of animal structures.

Getting Food, Water, and Oxygen

Animals cannot make their own food the way plants can. Instead, they must eat plants or other animals. Legs, fins, and wings help animals move to find food. Beaks and tongues help animals catch and swallow food. They help animals drink water, too.

▲ Some birds use nests for shelter.

A lion's rough tongue helps it get water. ▶

▲ Gills help fish get oxygen.

Structures help animals breathe. Animals breathe to get oxygen. Many animals breathe with lungs. Lungs take in oxygen from the air. Fish breathe by pushing water through their gills. Gills take in oxygen from water.

Finding Shelter and Staying Safe

Some animals use trees or other plants for shelter. Other animals build their own shelters. Birds, for example, build nests as shelters for their young. Birds use their beaks and feet to gather materials and build their nests.

Some animals have structures that help them stay safe. A kangaroo's pouch helps young kangaroos stay safe. A porcupine's sharp quills help it stay safe from other animals.

▲ A young kangaroo develops in its mother's pouch. There it stays safe.

Quick Check

Draw Conclusions Why are legs, fins, and wings important to some animals?

Critical Thinking How might the shape of a bird's beak affect what it eats?

What helps living things survive in their environment?

Living things live in the environment that meets their needs. Redwoods grow along the California coast. Here the cool, damp climate and rich soil are just right for them to grow. Cactuses grow well in Southern California. Here the warm, dry climate and sandy soil are just right for them to grow.

Adaptations (ad•uhp•TAY•shuhns) help living things survive in their environment. An **adaptation** is a special feature or behavior that helps a living thing survive. In the next lessons, you will learn about some adaptations that help living things survive in different environments.

 Quick Check

Draw Conclusions Why can't a cactus grow where redwoods grow?

Critical Thinking Are a bear's sharp teeth an adaptation?

A bear's claws are an adaptation that help it catch fish.

Lesson Review

Summarize the Main Idea

Living things live in different kinds of **environments**. (pp. 26–27)

Plants and animals have **structures** that help them get what they need. (pp. 28–31)

Adaptations help living things survive. (p. 32)

Make a FOLDABLES™ Study Guide

Make a three-tab book. Use it to summarize what you learned.

Think, Talk, and Write

1 **Main Idea** How do living things get what they need from their environments?

2 **Vocabulary** What is climate?

3 **Draw Conclusions** Some soil has very little humus. Would this kind of soil soak up a lot of water or a little?

Text Clues	Conclusions

4 **Critical Thinking** How are an animal's needs similar to a plant's needs? How are they different?

5 **Test Practice** How are biomes grouped?
  A by their size
  B by their living and nonliving things
  C by their structures
  D by the height of the trees

 Writing Link

Write a Paragraph
How do your moving parts help you survive? Make a chart. In one column list your moving parts. In the second column tell how each helps you. Use your chart to write a paragraph.

 Math Link

Make a Bar Graph
List ten plants that live near your school. Then group the plants into categories, such as grasses or trees. Make a graph to show how many of each category live near your school.

Compare and Classify

Earth is a big place. Millions of living things find homes in many different environments. With so many living things and so many environments, what can scientists do to understand life in our world? One thing they do is **compare and classify** living things and their environments.

❶ Learn It

When you **compare**, you look for ways that things are similar or different from each other. When you **classify**, you put things into groups that are alike. Comparing and classifying are useful tools for organizing and analyzing things. It is easier to study a few groups of things that are alike than millions of individual things.

❷ Try It

You learned that scientists **compare and classify** Earth's environments. They compare and classify animals, too. Can you?

▶ To start, observe the animals shown on page 35. Look for things they have in common.

▶ Then use their similarities and differences to group the animals. What trait can you use for grouping the animals? Let's try wings. Which animals have wings? Which animals do not? Make a chart to show your groups.

rhea

wings	no wings

 3 IE 5.e. Collect data in an investigation and analyze those data to develop a logical conclusion.

❸ Apply It

Compare and classify these animals using a different rule.

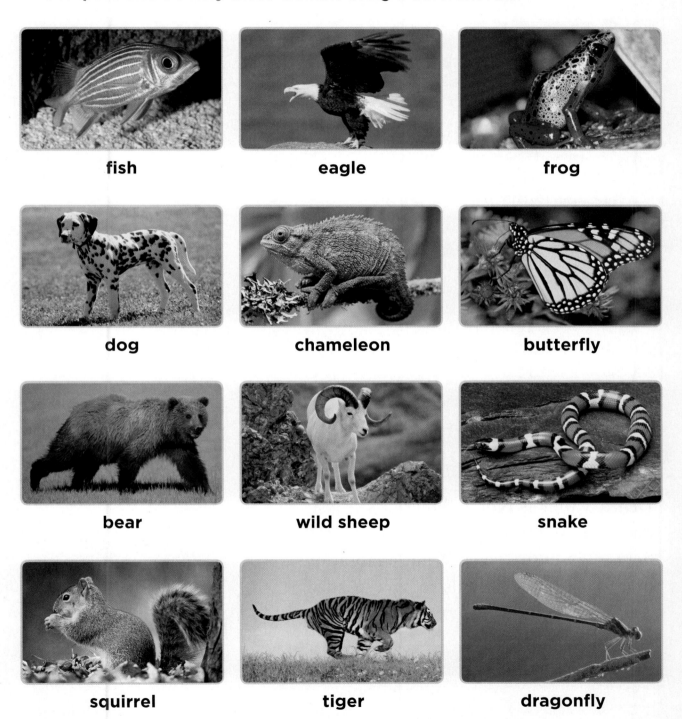

fish

eagle

frog

dog

chameleon

butterfly

bear

wild sheep

snake

squirrel

tiger

dragonfly

Life in the Desert

Look and Wonder

Death Valley is North America's driest desert. Less than two inches of rain fall here in an entire year! What adaptations help plants and animals survive in such a dry place?

3 LS 3.a. Students know plants and animals have structures that serve different functions in growth, survival, and reproduction. **•3 LS 3.b.** Students know examples of diverse life forms in different environments, such as oceans, deserts, tundra, forests, grasslands, and wetlands.

What adaptations help plants survive in a desert?

Make a Prediction

Why can some plants live in dry environments? How do special structures help them survive? Write a prediction.

Test Your Prediction

1 Observe Use a hand lens to observe each plant. What structures do they have? What are their leaves like? What are their stems like?

2 Record Data Make a chart to record your observations. Use words and pictures.

3 Observe Cut a leaf from each plant in half. Use a hand lens to look at the leaves. What are the leaves like inside?

Draw Conclusions

4 Compare How are the plants alike? How are they different?

5 Infer What special structures help the desert plant survive in its hot, dry environment?

Explore More

Experiment Put a leaf from each plant on the windowsill. How do the leaves change?

 3 IE 5.e. Collect data in an investigation and analyze those data to develop a logical conclusion.

Materials

hand lens

two plants

scissors

Step 1

Step 3

▶ **Main Idea**

Deserts have dry climates and sandy soil. Desert plants and animals have adaptations that help them survive.

▶ **Vocabulary**

desert, p. 38

nocturnal, p. 42

camouflage, p. 42

e-Glossary

@ www.macmillanmh.com

▶ **Reading Skill**

Compare and Contrast

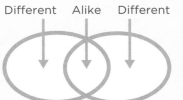

Different   Alike   Different

What is a desert?

A wave of heat blasts your body. You take a deep breath and dry air stings your nose. Dust from the sandy ground covers your shoes. You are in the Sonoran Desert. This is one of the largest deserts in North America.

A **desert** is a biome that has a dry climate. Less than 25 centimeters (10 inches) of rain falls in a desert each year. Several centimeters of rain may fall all at once within a few days. Then for months there is no rain at all.

Saguaro National Park is in the Sonoran Desert. ▶

Temperatures in a desert vary widely between day and night. During the day, the Sun's heat warms the land and air. After the Sun sets, the temperature drops quickly. The desert is much cooler at night than in the day.

The soil in a desert is mostly sand. There is little humus to soak up rain water. Rain water trickles down through the desert sand. It goes deeper than most plants' roots can reach.

 Quick Check

Compare and Contrast How do a desert's daytime and nighttime temperatures compare?

Critical Thinking What are three key features that describe deserts?

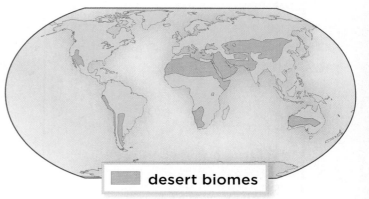

desert biomes

What adaptations help desert plants?

Some plants can grow in deserts. Other plants cannot. Plants that grow in deserts have adaptations that help them survive with little water. Special roots help them take in water. Special leaves and stems help them store water. Spines and thorns protect them from thirsty animals. The diagram below shows some of these adaptations.

Adaptations of Desert Plants

mesquite tree

Small leaves help conserve water.

Thorns protect the tree from hungry animals.

These **long roots** grow deep underground where they can find stored water.

saguaro cactus

Spines help protect a cactus from animals. They also collect water.

Waxy skin helps seal in water.

Shallow roots can quickly soak up the little rain that falls.

Thick stems help store water.

Read a Diagram

What adaptations help desert plants survive?

Clue: Look at the picture and read the captions.

LOG ON *Science in Motion* Watch desert plant adaptations @ **www.macmillanmh.com**

▲ Succulents, such as this aloe, are common desert plants. Their waxy skin and thick leaves are adapted to store lots of water.

≡Quick Lab

Desert Adaptations

1 **Make a Model** Wet two paper towels. Then wrap one in wax paper. This models a plant that has waxy skin. Use the uncovered towel to model a plant that does not have waxy skin.

2 Place your models in a sunny window.

3 **Compare** How do the paper towels feel later in the day?

4 **Draw Conclusions** How does waxy skin help desert plants survive?

✓ Quick Check

Compare and Contrast How are the roots of a mesquite tree similar to the roots of a cactus? How are they different?

Critical Thinking A prickly pear cactus has shallow roots, spines, and waxy skin. Could it survive in a desert? Explain your answer.

prickly pear cactus ▶

What adaptations help animals?

Desert animals can survive in the desert because of their adaptations. Here are just a few of their many adaptations.

Sleeping the Day Away

Can you imagine sleeping all day and going to school at night? Except for going to school, this is what many desert animals do. Rattlesnakes and coyotes, among others, are nocturnal (nahk•TURN•uhl). **Nocturnal** means they sleep during the day. They come out at night when it is cooler.

Keeping Cool

Large ears and thin bodies help animals, such as the desert jackrabbit, stay cool. These special features are adaptations that help animals lose extra body heat.

Blending In

Some desert animals can hide in plain site. Their body coverings blend in with their environment. Blending in is an adaptation called **camouflage** (KAM•uh•flahzh). Camouflage helps animals stay safe.

▲ Rattlesnakes are nocturnal.

▲ A jackrabbit's long ears help it stay cool.

▲ Can you see the frog? Camouflage helps it blend in with the rock.

✔ Quick Check

Compare and Contrast How are desert animals and plants similar?

Critical Thinking Could an animal with thick fur survive in a hot desert?

Lesson Review

Summarize the Main Idea

A **desert** is a biome that has a dry climate and dry, sandy soil.
(p. 38–39)

Desert plants have special roots, stems, and leaves that help them take in and store water.
(p. 40–41)

Desert animals have adaptations that help them stay safe and cool.
(p. 42)

Make a FOLDABLES™ Study Guide

Make a pyramid fold. Use it to summarize what you read about deserts and desert plants and animals.

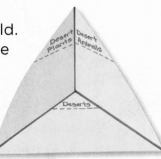

Think, Talk, and Write

1 **Main Idea** What adaptations help desert plants and animals survive?

2 **Vocabulary** What is a desert like? Talk about it.

3 **Compare and Contrast** How are a cactus's adaptations similar to a mesquite tree's? How are they different?

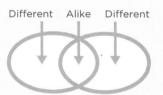

Different   Alike   Different

4 **Critical Thinking** Buffalo have thick, dark coats. They eat mainly grasses. Could a buffalo survive in a desert? Explain your answer.

5 **Test Practice** Deserts are biomes with

  A cold climate and frozen soil

  B wet climate and marshy soil

  C dry climate and sandy soil

  D hot climate with lots of rainfall

 Writing Link

Writing a Story
Write a story about life in the desert. Use information from this lesson to help set the scene. Remember to include a beginning, a middle, and an end.

 Math Link

Make a Chart
Use the Internet to find the average temperature for each month in Death Valley. Record the information in a chart. Write a sentence to describe Death Valley's climate.

Be a Scientist

Materials

yellow paper

brown paper

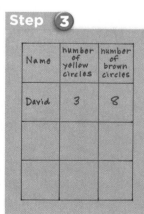

stopwatch

Inquiry Structured

How does camouflage help some animals survive?

Form a Hypothesis

How does camouflage help animals stay safe? Record your hypothesis. Start with "If an animal has camouflage, then . . ."

Test Your Hypothesis

1 Cut out 20 yellow circles and 20 brown circles.

2 **Experiment** Spread out the circles on the paper to model animals with and without camouflage. Then ask a classmate to pick up as many circles as he or she can in 10 seconds.

Step 2

3 **Record Data** How many of each color circle did your classmate pick up? Use a chart to record the results.

4 Repeat steps 1 and 2 with two other classmates.

Step 3

Name	number of yellow circles	number of brown circles
David	3	8

Draw Conclusions

5 **Analyze Data** Did your classmates pick up more yellow or brown circles? Which circles were harder to find?

6 How might camouflage help animals survive?

How do pale colors help some animals survive?

Form a Hypothesis

Pale body coverings help desert animals stay cool. Why is this true? Write a hypothesis.

Test Your Hypothesis

Design a plan to test your hypothesis. Use the materials shown. Write the steps you plan to follow.

Materials

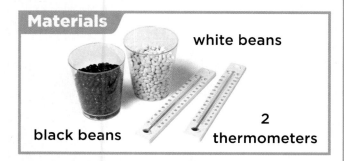

white beans

black beans

2 thermometers

Draw Conclusions

Did your results support your hypothesis? Why or why not? Share your results with your classmates.

What other questions do you have about desert plants and animals? Talk with your classmates about questions you have. How might you find the answers to your questions?

Remember to follow the steps of the scientific process.

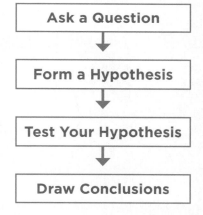

Ask a Question

↓

Form a Hypothesis

↓

Test Your Hypothesis

↓

Draw Conclusions

3 IE 5.c. Use numerical data in describing and comparing objects, events, and measurements. •**3 IE 5.e.** Collect data in an investigation and analyze those data to develop a logical conclusion.

Life in the Grassland

Look and Wonder

Long-necked giraffes, speedy cheetahs, and watchful zebras live in Africa's Serengeti Plain. What is the Serengeti? How do these animals find food and stay safe?

3 LS 3.a. Students know plants and animals have structures that serve different functions in growth, survival, and reproduction. •**3 LS 3.b.** Students know examples of diverse life forms in different environments, such as oceans, deserts, tundra, forests, grasslands, and wetlands.

What kinds of animals live in a grassland?

Make a Prediction

Why do animals live in a grassland? Write your prediction.

Test Your Prediction

1 Use research materials to learn about an animal that lives in a grassland biome.

2 **Record Data** Make a picture fact card for your animal. Draw or tape a picture of the animal on the card and label it. On the other side, write the name of the grassland biome. List three facts you learned about it.

3 **Compare** Trade fact cards with your classmates. Do your animals live in the same grassland biome?

4 **Classify** Group the animals according to their grassland biomes.

Draw Conclusions

5 What are some important things that animals find in grassland biomes?

6 What are some reasons you think animals live in a grassland?

Explore More

What would happen to a grassland after a month of no rain? How does rainfall affect grassland animals?

 3 IE 5.d. Predict the outcome of a simple investigation and compare the result with the prediction.

Materials

large index cards

color pencils

tape

Step **2**

Zebra

Savanna
1. tall grass
2. always warm
3. Serengeti Plain

Step **3**

Read and Learn

Main Idea 3 LS 3.a 3 LS 3.b

Grasses are the main type of plant in a grassland biome. Plants and animals that live in a grassland have structures and behaviors that help them survive.

Vocabulary

grassland, p. 48

temperate, p. 49

tropical, p. 49

LOG ON e-Glossary
@ www.macmillanmh.com

Reading Skill

Compare and Contrast

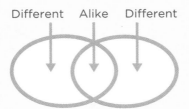

Different   Alike   Different

▲ The prairies of North America are temperate grasslands.

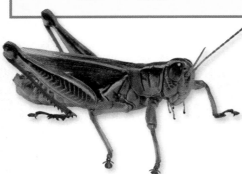

▲ Grasshoppers have back legs built for jumping.

What is a grassland?

Miles of green grass stretch out before you. Wildflowers bloom. The air is warm against your skin. Grasshoppers jump. A green snake slithers. Suddenly, the wind blows and thousands of blades of grass make a quiet swishing sound. You are in the grasslands of North America.

A **grassland** is a biome that is covered with grasses. Grass is everything to a grassland. Grass is food for animals. Grass is like a blanket that keeps in warmth and moisture. Grass is both a hiding place and a shelter from the wind and cold. Grass holds down soil that would otherwise blow away in the wind.

There are two types of grasslands. Temperate grasslands are one type. **Temperate** means the environment has a mild climate and four seasons. Temperate grasslands have soil that is rich in humus. The North American *prairies* are temperate grasslands.

Tropical grasslands are the second type of grasslands. **Tropical** means the environment is near the equator and is warm all year round. Tropical grasslands have a rainy season and a dry season. They usually have more trees and poorer soil than temperate grasslands. The *savanna* grasslands of Africa's Serengeti Plain are tropical grasslands.

Both temperate and tropical grasslands get about 25 to 75 centimeters (10 to 30 inches) of rain each year. With so little rain, the land can dry out. Fires can start easily. Fires form regularly in grasslands.

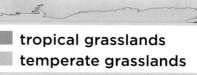

tropical grasslands
temperate grasslands

✓ Quick Check

Compare and Contrast How are temperate and tropical grasslands different?

Critical Thinking What kind of grasslands are in North America?

The savannas of Africa are tropical grasslands.

What adaptations help grassland plants survive?

Different grasslands have different kinds of grasses. However, nearly all grassland grasses are adapted to grow well in dry conditions.

Grasses have deep roots. The roots work like a sponge, soaking up moisture and storing nutrients. When a fire burns, everything above ground is destroyed. Down below, the roots survive. They hold on to their moisture and nutrients.

After a fire, new stalks can grow from the roots. The old, dead grass becomes part of a new layer of soil. Over time, the soil gets richer and richer.

Most grasses are adapted to grow from the bottom up. This helps them survive and grow after animals graze on the tops of the plants.

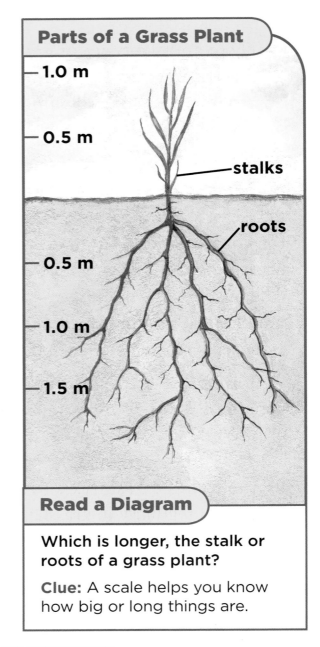

Parts of a Grass Plant

- 1.0 m
- 0.5 m
- **stalks**
- **roots**
- 0.5 m
- 1.0 m
- 1.5 m

Read a Diagram

Which is longer, the stalk or roots of a grass plant?

Clue: A scale helps you know how big or long things are.

◄ Fire may burn the grass above the soil, but deep roots are not harmed. This means grass can grow back quickly after a fire.

Trees that grow in tropical grasslands also have adaptations that help them survive. The baobab tree grows in Africa's savannas. It grows leaves only during the wet season. It loses its leaves during the dry season. This adaptation helps it conserve water.

The baobab's thick trunk is adapted to store water during the long, dry season. Its bark is fire resistant, making it well adapted to survive grassland fires.

 Quick Check

Compare and Contrast How are tropical grassland grasses and trees alike?

Critical Thinking Could a cactus survive in a grassland? Why?

Baobab trees have bark that resists fire.

≡ Quick Lab

How Grasses Grow

1. Put some sand or pebbles in the bottom of a plastic cup. Add potting soil almost to the top. Sprinkle grass seeds over the soil. Water the soil. Place the cup in a sunny spot.

2. **Record Data** Record when you planted the grass on a calendar.

SUN.	MON.	TUES.	WED.	THURS.	FRI.	SAT.
	1	2	3	4	5	6
7	8	9	10	11	12	13

3. **Observe** Check your grass seeds each day. Keep the soil moist. Record your observations on the calendar.

4. **Compare** Carefully uproot some grass. Measure the grass and the roots. Which is longer? Was the grass easy to pull out? Why or why not?

What adaptations help animals survive in grasslands?

Many kinds of animals live in grasslands. All of them have adaptations that help them survive.

Flat Teeth

Some grassland animals have flat teeth adapted for eating grass. Zebras bite off the tough tops of grasses. Antelopes eat the stems closest to the ground.

Burrows

Small animals can hide easily. Prairie dogs dig burrows, or holes, in the ground. They come out only during certain hours of the day.

Speed

Cheetahs can catch prey by running fast. African cheetahs can run at a speed of up to 112 kilometers (70 miles) per hour.

▲ Prairie dogs can escape danger quickly by hiding in their burrows.

✔ **Quick Check**

Compare and Contrast Compare how different animals survive in grasslands.

Critical Thinking Some grassland animals travel in herds. How might this help them stay safe?

Zebras bite grass easily with their flat teeth. ▼

African cheetahs have flexible spines that help them run very fast. ▼

Lesson Review

Summarize the Main Idea

A **grassland** is a biome covered with grasses. (pp. 48–49)

Grassland plants have adaptations that help them survive in dry conditions and fires. (pp. 50–51)

Grassland animals have special structures and behaviors that help them survive. (p. 52)

Make a  Study Guide

Make a pyramid fold. Use it to summarize what you read about grasslands.

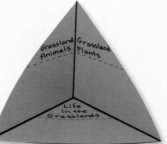

Think, Talk, and Write

1 **Main Idea** What are grasslands?

2 **Vocabulary** What word describes grasslands that are warm year-round?

3 **Compare and Contrast** How are grasslands and deserts alike? How are they different?

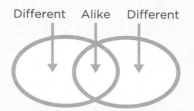
Different   Alike   Different

4 **Critical Thinking** The world's fastest running land animals live in grasslands. Explain why speed is an important adaptation for grassland animals.

5 **Test Practice** Tropical grasslands are found mostly
   A near the North Pole
   B near the equator
   C in North America
   D in Antarctica

 **Writing Link**

Write a Report
Use research materials to find out more about cheetahs. Why do the people of Africa value this animal? What must be done to protect the cheetah?

 Math Link

Multiply and Divide
If a cheetah runs for four minutes at a speed of 105 kilometers per hour, how many kilometers has the cheetah run?

Reading in Science

Meet Ana Luz Porzecanski

Grasslands, known as *pampas*, are common in South America. That is where Ana Luz Porzecanski, a scientist at the American Museum of Natural History, grew up.

Ana studies the birds of the pampas. Some of the birds she studies are called *tinamous*. Their brown and grey feathers help them blend in with the tall grass and other shrubs and bushes. This camouflage helps them hide from predators like foxes and hawks that eat the birds or their eggs.

How does Ana find tinamous if they are so well hidden? She listens for their songs. Each species of tinamou has a different song. Sometimes she has to sing or play a recording of their song to get the birds to answer back. It takes time, patience, and a little luck.

The tinamous are hard to see, but their shiny green, turquoise, and purple eggs really stand out. Ana wants to know why the eggs are so colorful. Why do you think the tinamous have such colorful eggs?

▲ Ana is an ornithologist. That's a scientist who studies birds.

AMERICAN MUSEUM OF NATURAL HISTORY

ELA R 3.2.6. Extract appropriate and significant information from the text, including problems and solutions.

Compare and contrast

▶ explains how things are alike

▶ explains how things are different

▶ uses compare words, such as *like* and *both*, and contrast words, such as *unlike* and *but*

Tinamou eggs are colorful. ▶

Write About It

Compare and Contrast Work with a partner to compare the tinamou with another animal you read about in this chapter. List ways the animals are alike and different in a Venn diagram. Then use your diagram to write about the animals.

LOG ON **e-Journal** Write about it online @ **www.macmillanmh.com**

Life in the Forest

Look and Wonder

Under the shade of tall trees, how do plants grow on the forest floor?

3 LS 3.a. Students know plants and animals have structures that serve different functions in growth, survival, and reproduction. •**3 LS 3.b.** Students know examples of diverse life forms in different environments, such as oceans, deserts, tundra, forests, grasslands, and wetlands.

Will a plant grow toward light?

Make a Prediction

Plants need sunlight to survive. If something is blocking the light, how will a plant respond?

Test Your Prediction

1. Cut a hole in one end of a shoe box.

2. Cut two dividers from the cardboard as tall as the shoe box but an inch shorter than its width.

3. Tape the dividers upright along the inside of the box. The first divider should be attached to the same side as the hole that was cut into the box in step 1. The other divider should be on the other side.

4. Put your plant in the end of the box opposite the hole. Then put the lid on the box and turn the hole toward bright sunlight.

5. **Observe** Every three or four days, remove the lid to water your plant and observe its growth. Do this for several weeks.

Draw Conclusions

6. How does the plant change after a few weeks? How does it get the light it needs?

7. **Infer** How might this be similar to what happens on the forest floor?

Explore \ More

Observe plants around your school. Are they getting direct sunlight? Are they in shade from a tree or building? How do they get the light they need?

 3 IE 5.d. Predict the outcome of a simple investigation and compare the result with the prediction.

Materials

scissors   large shoe box

heavy cardboard

masking tape

small potted plant

Step 4

Step 5

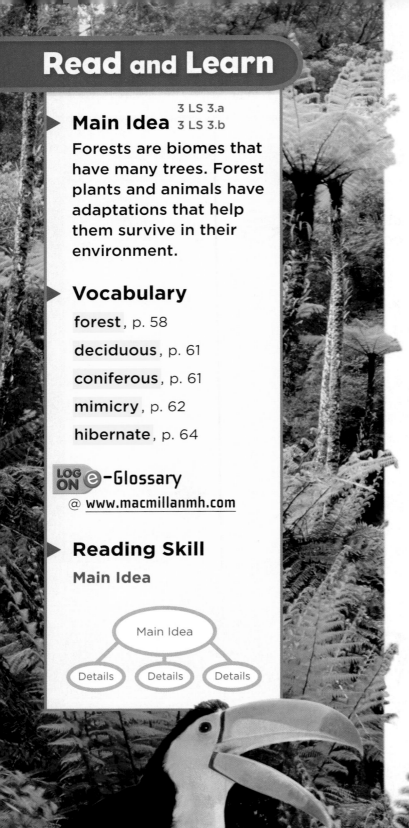

Main Idea 3 LS 3.a 3 LS 3.b

Forests are biomes that have many trees. Forest plants and animals have adaptations that help them survive in their environment.

Vocabulary

forest, p. 58

deciduous, p. 61

coniferous, p. 61

mimicry, p. 62

hibernate, p. 64

LOG ON e-Glossary
@ www.macmillanmh.com

Reading Skill

Main Idea

Main Idea

Details   Details   Details

What is a forest?

It is dark and damp. Tall trees surround you. Raindrops drip from overhead. The hot, moist air feels heavy around you. Insects buzz. Birds sing. You are in the Amazon Rain Forest.

A **forest** is a biome that has many trees. Different types of forests can be found in different parts of the world.

Tropical Rain Forests

A *tropical rain forest* is a forest biome found near the equator. Tropical rain forests are green, rich forests. They have more kinds of living things than any other land biome.

Tropical rain forests are hot and wet. About 200 to 460 centimeters (80 to 180 inches) of rain falls here in a single year. The temperature usually stays between 20°C and 34°C (68°F and 93°F) all year round.

Tropical rain forests are hot, wet forest biomes near the equator.

The soil in a tropical rain forest is not very rich in plant nutrients. This is because nutrients are quickly absorbed by rain-forest plants. The nutrients are only in a thin, top layer of soil. Hard clay lies below.

Temperate Forests

A *temperate forest* is a forest biome found in North America, Europe, and Asia. Unlike tropical rain forests, temperate forests have four seasons: winter, spring, summer, and fall. Temperatures and rainfall change from season to season. Winters are cold and dry. Summers are warm and wet. About 76 to 127 centimeters (30 to 50 inches) of rain fall each year.

The soil in a temperate forest is rich in humus. Humus helps keep the soil moist. It also supplies nutrients for plants to grow.

 Quick Check

Main Idea What are two types of forests?

Critical Thinking Compare a tropical rain forest to a temperate forest.

■ temperate forest
■ tropical rain forest

Temperate forests are forest biomes that have four seasons.

The Rain Forest

The forest's tallest trees reach the **emergent layer.**

Tree branches and leaves form the **canopy.**

Smaller trees and plants grow in the **understory.** This layer doesn't get much light.

The **forest floor** is dark and damp.

What adaptations help forest plants survive?

Forest plants grow in layers. The plants in each layer are adapted to grow toward the light. They also have other adaptations that help them survive.

Tropical Rain-Forest Plants

Many tropical trees grow very tall. Their branches spread out in the canopy or emergent layer. Although tall, many of these trees have shallow roots. Buttresses help support their tall size. *Buttresses* are special root structures that spread out from the trunk.

Trees and smaller plants that grow in the canopy or understory often have leaves with drip tips. This adaptation helps them lose extra rainwater.

Very little sunlight reaches the understory and forest floor. Most plants that grow here have very large leaves. This adaptation helps plants soak in as much sunlight as possible.

Read a Diagram

What are the layers of a rain forest?

Clue: Bold words can help you find information.

Temperate Forest Plants

The tall trees of the temperate forest are deciduous (di•SI•juh•wuhs) or coniferous (coh•NI•fuh•ruhs). **Deciduous** trees lose their leaves in fall as the temperature gets cooler. The leaves grow back in spring and summer. This adaptation helps them conserve energy during the cold winter. **Coniferous** trees make cones instead of flowers. Coniferous trees are often called evergreens. They stay green all year. Their thin, needle-like leaves are tough and waxy. This adaptation helps them conserve water during the cold, dry winters.

▲ A pine cone holds the seeds of a coniferous tree.

✔ Quick Check

Main Idea What are some adaptations of forest plants?

Critical Thinking Could temperate forest trees survive in a tropical rain forest? Explain.

Leaves on deciduous trees change from green to yellow, orange, and red in the fall. They fall off, then grow back in spring.

How do animals survive in a tropical rain forest?

The rain forest is one of the world's richest biomes. Many kinds of animals swing, swoop, dart, and jump in the canopy. Each kind of animal has adaptations that help it survive.

Warning Colors

How does this bright-colored frog stay safe in the rain forest? You would think predators would notice its bright colors and attack. Predators do notice the bright colors. But the frog's brilliant colors are a warning that say, "I'm poisonous!" So predators stay away.

▲ The poison arrow frog's bright colors warn predators to stay away.

Blending In

Can you find the mantis in the photograph on the right? The orchid mantis is well disguised. It stays safe in its environment by looking like the flower of an orchid. This adaptation is called mimicry (MI•mi•kree). **Mimicry** is when one living thing imitates another living thing in color or shape.

Mimicry helps this orchid mantis stay safe. ▼

Getting Away

What if you were stuck on a branch with a predator closing in? If you were an iguana, you would fall. Iguanas can fall 18 meters (60 feet) or more from a high branch without getting hurt. Iguanas often sit on tree limbs that hang over water. When an enemy comes, they just drop into the water!

An iguana's long tail helps it balance in the high branches of a tropical rain forest.

☰ Quick Lab

Hiding Out

1 **Make a Model** Fold a piece of colored construction paper in half. Draw a butterfly outline. Cut out two butterflies.

2 Select a piece of fabric or wrapping paper to be your butterfly habitat.

3 Draw two large spots or "eyes" on one butterfly's wings. Color the other butterfly to look like the habitat.

4 **Observe** Place your butterflies on the habitat. Which one can you find quickly? Which one looks like it does not belong there?

5 **Infer** Why would blending in help a butterfly stay safe? Would having large spots or other markings help protect a butterfly? Why do you think so?

✓ Quick Check

Main Idea What are some adaptations of tropical rain-forest animals?

Critical Thinking How might an animal's appearance protect it from predators?

How do animals survive in a temperate forest?

Temperate forest animals have adaptations that help them survive the changing seasons. They also have adaptations that keep them safe.

Surviving the Winter

When the weather gets cool in fall, some animals eat extra food. They store energy for the winter, when food is harder to find. Some animals also grow thicker coats to keep them warm during winter.

Some animals hibernate (HIGH•buhr•nayt). **Hibernate** means to go into a deep sleep that lasts through the winter. The animals live off energy stored in their bodies.

Staying Safe

Skunks and porcupines have unusual ways to stay safe. Skunks spray a stinky chemical if an enemy gets too close. It also stings the predator's eyes. Porcupines have needle-like quills that they raise when an enemy comes near. If the attack continues, the enemy gets stuck with sharp quills!

▲ Dormice hibernate during the winter.

▲ A porcupine's sharp quills help it stay safe.

 Quick Check

Main Idea How do adaptations help animals in temperate forests?

Critical Thinking Why do some animals hibernate?

Skunks spray a smelly chemical to keep predators away. ▼

Lesson Review

Summarize the Main Idea

A **forest** has mostly trees. Tropical rain forests and temperate forests are types of forests. (pp. 58–59)

Forest plants have special structures that help them survive. (pp. 60–61)

Forest animals have adaptations that help them grow and survive. (pp. 62–64)

Make a FOLDABLES™ Study Guide

Make a pyramid fold. Use it to summarize what you read about forests.

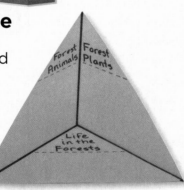

Think, Talk, and Write

1 Main Idea How are tropical rain forests different from temperate forests? In what ways are these two types of forests similar?

2 Vocabulary What is mimicry?

3 Main Idea What adaptations help plants and animals survive the cold winters in a temperate forest?

4 Critical Thinking Many of the fruits you eat come from tropical rain forests. What is it about tropical rain forests that allows fruits to grow?

5 Test Practice All of the following are layers of the rain forest EXCEPT

A emergent

B submergent

C canopy

D understory

Writing Link

Write a Paragraph
Rain forests are disappearing. Research and find out why. Look up ways we can help save rain forests. Then write a paragraph.

Health Link

Do Research
Find out about healthful products that come from the rain forest. Write a short paragraph about one of these natural wonders.

Be a Scientist

Materials

brown and green
construction paper

masking tape

ruler

scissors

cardboard

lamp

How do trees affect light in a rain forest?

Form a Hypothesis

Rain forest trees can grow as high as 60 m (197 ft). The trees' branches spread wide to form the canopy. How does the thickness of the canopy affect the amount of light that reaches the forest floor? Write a hypothesis. Begin with, "If the rain forest canopy is thick, then . . ."

Test Your Hypothesis

1. **Make a Model** Use 6 sheets of brown paper to create 6 tubes of different heights. These model tree trunks.

Step 1

2. Draw 3 circles with a diameter of about 8 cm on green paper. Draw 3 more circles with 4 cm diameters. Cut out the circles. These represent tree branches.

3. **Use Variables** Tape the circles to the tree trunks. Arrange the trees onto a piece of cardboard so that the trees are close to each other and form a thick canopy.

4. **Experiment** Shine a lamp down onto your forest. How much light reaches the forest floor? Record your observations.

Step 3

5. **Use Variables** Repeat steps 3 and 4 several times. Vary the thickness of the canopy by placing the trees closer or farther apart.

Draw Conclusions

6 How does the thickness of the canopy affect the amount of light that reaches the forest floor?

7 **Infer** How do trees affect plants that grow on the forest floor?

How do trees affect rain water?

Form a Hypothesis

Does the canopy affect the amount of water that reaches the forest floor? Write a hypothesis.

Test Your Hypothesis

Design an experiment to see if the canopy affects the water that reaches the forest floor. Decide on the materials you will use. Then write the steps you will follow. Record your results and observations.

Draw Conclusions

Did your experiment support your hypothesis? Why or why not?

What else would you like to learn about rain forests? For example, what happens to plants in the understory if a tree is cut down? Design an experiment to find out about new questions you have.

Remember to follow the steps of the scientific process.

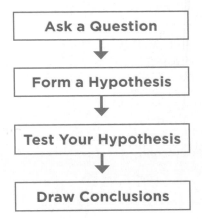

Ask a Question
↓
Form a Hypothesis
↓
Test Your Hypothesis
↓
Draw Conclusions

3 IE 5.d. Predict the outcome of a simple investigation and compare the result with the prediction.

Life in the Arctic Tundra

Look and Wonder

Did you know that a polar bear's hair is hollow? Hollow hair helps it absorb heat from the Sun. What other adaptations help animals survive in cold environments?

3 LS 3.a. Students know plants and animals have structures that serve different functions in growth, survival, and reproduction. **•3 LS 3.b.** Students know examples of diverse life forms in different environments, such as oceans, deserts, tundra, forests, grasslands, and wetlands.

Does fat help animals survive in cold environments?

Form a Hypothesis

Does fat help animals stay warm? Does fat keep animals cool? Write a hypothesis. Start with "If an animal has extra fat, then . . ."

Test Your Hypothesis

1 Use a paper towel to spread vegetable fat over one of your index fingers. Try to coat your finger completely with fat.

2 **Predict** What will happen when you put both index fingers in a bowl of ice water?

3 **Experiment** Ask a partner to time how long you can keep each index finger in the ice water. Record the data in a chart.

4 Trade roles with your partner and repeat steps 1 through 3.

Draw Conclusions

5 **Analyze Data** Did your observations match your prediction? What happened when you put both fingers in the ice water?

6 How does fat help animals survive in cold places?

Explore More

Experiment How does thick fur help animals survive in cold environments? Form a hypothesis. Then make a plan to test it.

 3 IE 5.d. Predict the outcome of a simple investigation and compare the result with the prediction.

Materials

vegetable fat

paper towel

ice water   stopwatch

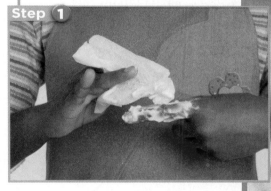
Step 1

Step 3

Main Idea 3 LS 3.a
3 LS 3.b

The arctic tundra is a cold biome with little rainfall. Tundra plants and animals have adaptations that help them survive.

Vocabulary

arctic tundra, p. 70

permafrost, p. 71

blubber, p. 74

migrate, p. 76

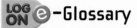 **e-Glossary**
@ www.macmillanmh.com

Reading Skill

Draw Conclusions

Text Clues	Conclusions

What is an arctic tundra?

You've reached Denali National Park. The air is so cold it burns your lungs. A biting-cold wind whips across your face. The ground is frozen and hard beneath your feet. This is the arctic tundra.

The **arctic tundra** is the cold biome above the Arctic Circle. Winters here are long and dark. In the middle of winter, the Sun never rises. Temperatures can drop to −60°F (−15°C) and several feet of snow fall. Few plants are able to survive here in winter. Many animals leave for warmer places.

In the six to ten weeks of summer, the Sun never sets. It is light during both the day and night.

In winter, the arctic tundra is cold and dark. These caribou move south to find a warmer environment. ▼

With heat from the Sun, the snow melts. The melted snow cannot soak into the ground. A layer of permafrost keeps it from draining. **Permafrost** is soil that is always frozen. The land becomes soggy with pools of water.

As temperatures rise, the top few inches of soil thaw. Small plants grow in the wet ground. The arctic tundra comes to life as animals return to feed and nest.

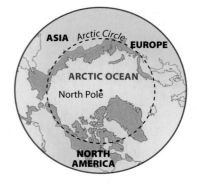

 Quick Check

Draw Conclusions Why is there permafrost in the arctic tundra?

Critical Thinking How is the arctic tundra similar to the desert? How is it different?

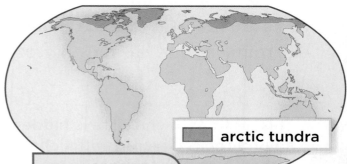

arctic tundra

In summer, the arctic tundra becomes soggy with melted snow. ▼

Read a Map

Where in the world is the arctic tundra?

Clue: A map key can help you understand the information on a map.

What adaptations help arctic plants?

About 1,700 different kinds of plants can grow in the arctic tundra. Arctic plants have adaptations that help them survive in their cold, icy environment.

Shallow Roots

One adaptation that helps arctic plants survive is small, shallow roots. All of the plants that live in the arctic tundra have shallow roots, or no roots at all. Shallow roots are necessary for surviving in an environment that has mostly frozen soil.

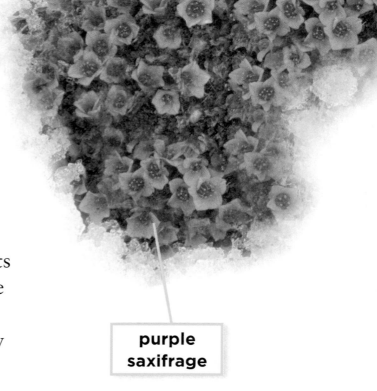

purple saxifrage

This arctic tern chick stays hidden among rocks covered with lichen. Lichen is similar to moss.

lichen

Short and Small

Small size is another adaptation that helps plants survive here. Most arctic plants grow close to the ground. They rarely reach more than one foot tall. This adaptation protects plants from the cold and wind.

Growing Together

Many arctic plants grow close together in tight clumps that look like cushions. Arctic forget-me-nots are an example. Growing together is an adaptation that protects plants from wind and freezing temperatures. Plants that grow this way are called *cushion plants.*

Dark Colors

A deep red or pink color helps many plants, such as dwarf fireweed, survive in the arctic tundra. Their dark color is an adaptation that helps them absorb sunlight. It also helps attract birds and other animals that they depend on to spread their seeds and reproduce.

 Quick Check

Draw Conclusions Could a banana tree live in the arctic tundra? Explain your answer.

Critical Thinking How does color help some plants survive in the arctic tundra?

arctic forget-me-not

dwarf fireweed

What adaptations help arctic animals?

A variety of animals make their home in the arctic tundra. Arctic animals have adaptations that help them survive in cold, snowy environments.

Staying Warm

Polar bears, musk oxen, and many other arctic animals have thick fur coats. They also have a thick layer of blubber. **Blubber** is fat. Thick coats and fat help animals stay warm. Arctic animals usually have larger bodies and thicker fur than their relatives in other biomes. They also have smaller ears and shorter legs. All these adaptations help them absorb and conserve heat.

A thick fur coat and layer of blubber help polar bears and musk oxen stay warm in the cold arctic tundra.

The lynx's wide, furry feet are perfect for running in the snow.

Wide Paws and Strong Claws

The lynx, snowshoe hare, and polar bear, among many tundra animals, have wide, furry feet. This helps them run in the snow. Wide feet work like snowshoes. They keep animals from sinking in the snow. Long, strong claws give animals extra grip. They keep animals from sliding on slippery ice.

 Quick Check

Draw Conclusions Why do most rain-forest animals have thinner fur coats than arctic animals?

Critical Thinking How do special feet help some animals survive in the tundra?

Quick Lab

Arctic Adaptations

1. **Observe** What do you notice about the arctic and desert foxes' features? What are their coats and bodies like?

2. **Compare** How are the animals alike? How are they different?

3. **Infer** How do the arctic fox's features help it survive in the arctic tundra?

arctic fox

desert fox

What are some other arctic animal adaptations?

Canada geese, tundra swans, and caribou are a few arctic animals that migrate (MIGH•grayt). To **migrate** means to move to another place. Animals migrate when their home environment can no longer meet their needs. In winter the arctic becomes too cold for plants to grow. Animals that eat plants move south where food is easier to find. When temperatures rise in the arctic in spring, plants begin to grow again. Animals can then return home.

The arctic hare and fox, among others, change color from season to season to stay camouflaged. Camouflage helps animals like the hare stay safe from animals that hunt them. It helps animals like the fox hunt without being seen.

▲ Many Canada geese migrate south into parts of the United States.

▲ arctic fox in winter

 Quick Check

Draw Conclusions How does color help some animals survive?

Critical Thinking Why do some animals migrate?

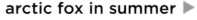
arctic fox in summer ▶

Lesson Review

Summarize the Main Idea

The **arctic tundra** is a cold, dry biome above the Arctic Circle. (pp. 70–71)

Arctic plants have adaptations that protect them from the cold and wind. (pp. 72–73)

Arctic animals have adaptations that help them survive in cold, snowy environments. (pp. 74–76)

Make a FOLDABLES™ Study Guide

Make a pyramid fold. Use it to summarize what you read about the arctic tundra.

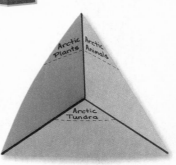

Think, Talk, and Write

1 Main Idea What adaptations help arctic plants and animals survive?

2 Vocabulary What is the arctic tundra like? Write about it.

3 Draw Conclusions Why can't trees grow in the arctic tundra?

Text Clues	Conclusions

4 Critical Thinking Could an arctic animal live in a hot desert? Explain your answer.

5 Test Practice An arctic fox's white fur is an example of

A mimicry

B migration

C camouflage

D hibernation

 Writing Link

Writing That Compares
Describe your favorite arctic animal. What adaptations help it to survive? Compare this animal to a forest animal. Write how the animals are alike and how they are different.

 Social Studies Link

Do Research
Few people live in the arctic tundra, but some Inuit live in areas where they can fish and hunt for food. Write a list of questions that you could ask someone who lives in the tundra. Research the Inuit to find the answers.

Describe Where You Live

In this chapter, you went on a trip to different environments around the world. Now tell about where you live. Describe the sights and sounds of your community. What plants and animals live around you? What is the climate like?

A good description

▶ includes describing words to tell how something looks, sounds, feels, smells, or tastes

▶ uses details to create a picture for the reader

▶ groups together details in an order that makes sense

Write About It

Descriptive Writing Write a description in your science journal about your environment. Use the first paragraph on page 70 as a model for your writing.

 LOG ON ⓔ-Journal Write about it online @ **www.macmillanmh.com**

 ELA W 3.2.2. Write descriptions that use concrete sensory details to present and support unified impressions of people, places, things, or experiences.

Estimating the Area of Leaves

Most plants in the tundra are very small. This is an adaptation that helps them survive. What are plants like in your environment? Are they big and tall? What kind of leaves do they have?

How to estimate area

▶ First, trace a flat object on a piece of graph paper.

▶ Then, estimate the area by counting the number of squares it covers. Count any square that is more than half covered.

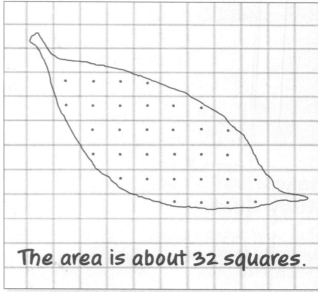

The area is about 32 squares.

 Solve It

Collect the leaves of some plants from your environment. Compare their sizes. Estimate their areas.

 MA MG 3.1.2. Estimate or determine the area and volume of solid figures by covering them with squares or by counting the number of cubes that would fill them.

Summarize the Main Ideas

Living things get what they need from their environment. (pp. 24–33)

Desert plants and animals have adaptations that help them conserve water. (pp. 36–43)

Grassland plants and animals have adaptations that help them survive in grasslands. (pp. 46–53)

Forest plants and animals have adaptations that help them survive in forests. (pp. 56–65)

Arctic plants and animals have adaptations that help them survive freezing temperatures. (pp. 68–77)

Make a FOLDABLES Study Guide

Glue your lesson study guides together as shown. Use your study guide to review what you have learned in this chapter.

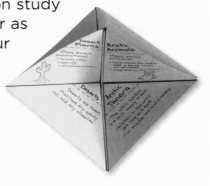

Fill each blank with the best word from the list.

adaptation, p. 32   environment, p. 26

camouflage, p. 42   grasslands, p. 48

deciduous, p. 61   migrate, p. 76

desert, p. 38   mimicry, p. 62

1. Everything that surrounds a living thing makes up its _____. 3 LS 3.b

2. Animals use _____ to blend in with their environment. 3 LS 3.a

3. A _____ has a dry climate and sandy soil. 3 LS 3.b

4. Trees that lose their leaves in fall are called _____. 3 LS 3.a

5. The spines of a cactus are an example of an _____. 3 LS 3.a

6. When animals _____ they leave their homes in winter for a warmer environment and then return home in summer. 3 LS 3.b

7. Zebras, horses, and other grazing animals live mostly in _____. 3 LS 3.b

8. An adaptation in which one living thing looks like another is called _____. 3 LS 3.a

LOG ON e-Review Summaries and quizzes online @ www.macmillanmh.com

Discuss or write about each of the following.

9. Compare and Contrast How do adaptations protect the animals shown below from enemies? 3 LS 3.a

porcupine

poison arrow frog

10. Descriptive Writing Describe a desert. 3 LS 3.b

11. Compare Compare the animals shown below. What special structures help them survive? 3 LS 3.a

grasshopper

musk oxen

12. Critical Thinking What might happen to rain-forest plants if their environment suddenly became cold and dry? 3 LS 3.b

Answer each of the following in a complete sentence.

13. Why do grasses grow well in grasslands? 3 LS 3.b

14. What adaptations help polar bears survive in the arctic tundra? 3 LS 3.a

15. How do the three adaptations shown in the diagram help a cactus survive in the desert? 3 LS 3.a

spines

thick stem

shallow roots

 What are adaptations and how do they help living things survive? 3 LS 3

CHAPTER 1

Make a Biome Book

- Make a book about a biome you would like to visit. Include information about the climate and soil in this biome.

- Tell about the plants and animals that live there. Explain what adaptations help the plants and animals survive in their environment.

- Include a cover for your book and illustrate each page with pictures.

Examples of Biomes

grassland

desert

arctic tundra

forest

82

1 How do a plant's roots help it get what it needs? 3 LS 3.a

A They take in sunlight.

B They take in carbon dioxide.

C They take in food.

D They take in water.

2 Where do animals with flat teeth for grazing mainly live? 3 LS 3.a

A desert

B grassland

C forest

D tundra

3 The chart shows information Ms. Smith's class collected about Death Valley.

Death Valley, California	
Climate	• hot and dry • 2-15 inches of rainfall each year
Soil	• dry and sandy
Plants	• prickly pear cactus • barrel cactus
Animals	• coyote • collared lizard • cactus wren

Death Valley, California is in what kind of biome? 3 IE 5.e

A desert

B grassland

C forest

D arctic tundra

4 Caribou live in the arctic tundra. They spend most of the summer eating small plants.

What do they do in winter when plants are hard to find? 3 LS 3.b

A eat meat instead of plants

B hibernate

C migrate

D change color

5 What kinds of plants are mainly found in forests? 3 LS 3.b

A grasses

B trees

C cushion plants

D cactuses

6 Where would you be most likely to find animals with thick fur and a lot of blubber? 3 LS 3.a

A desert

B grassland

C forest

D arctic tundra

CHAPTER 2

Adaptations in Water Environments

 What adaptations help living things survive under water?

Lesson 1

The Water Planet

PAGE 88

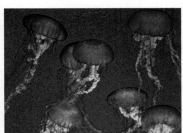

Lesson 2

Life in an Ocean

PAGE 98

Lesson 3

Life in the Wetlands

PAGE 110

 3 LS 3. Adaptations in physical structure or behavior may improve an organism's chance for survival.

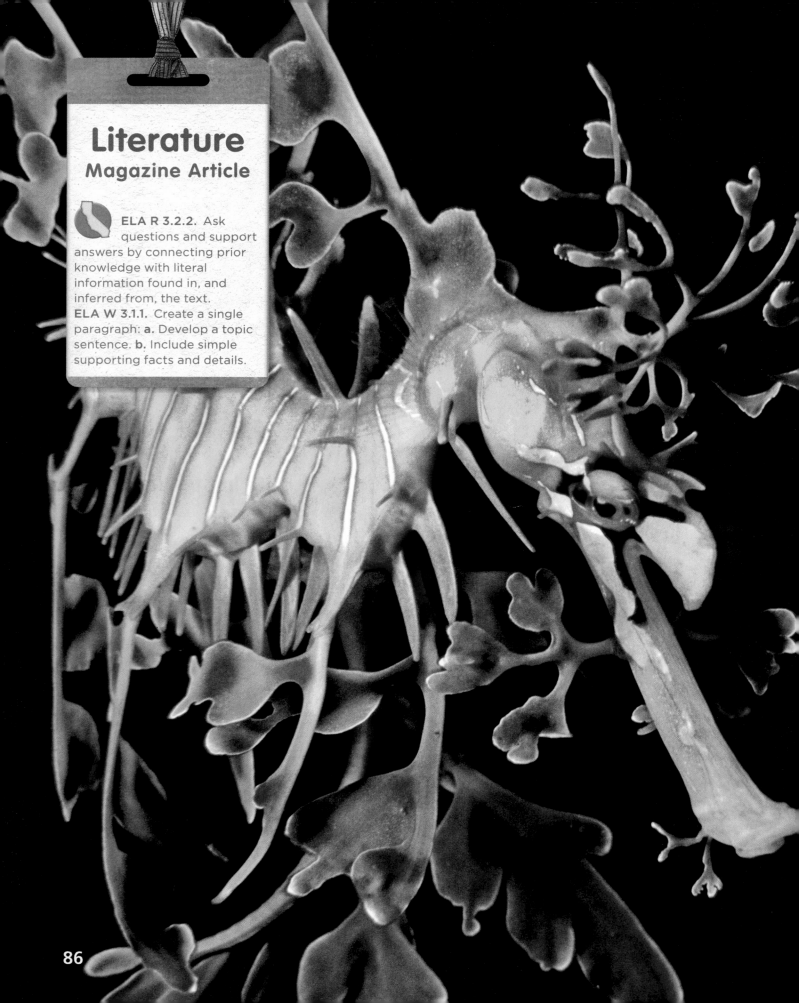

Literature
Magazine Article

ELA R 3.2.2. Ask questions and support answers by connecting prior knowledge with literal information found in, and inferred from, the text.
ELA W 3.1.1. Create a single paragraph: **a.** Develop a topic sentence. **b.** Include simple supporting facts and details.

Dragons of the Sea

by Elizabeth Schleichert

Hi. That dude with the stunning headdress and cool, matching outfit in the photo at left is me, Lennie. We *leafy seadragons* are the best-dressed fish around. Yep, that's right. We're fish—seahorse cousins, as a matter of fact. . . . Where would you find us? In the ocean off southern Australia. . . .

leafy seadragon

Predators have a hard time finding us because we look so much like seaweed swaying in the current. Being camouflaged helps us get a meal too. Baby shrimp and other tasty treats drift past us. We often reach out and suck them right up with our long, tube-like snouts. So our strange looks *really* work for us!

Write About It

Response to Literature In this article, you learned that looking like seaweed keeps leafy seadragons safe in their environment. What special structures do you have that keep you safe? For example, how does your nose protect you? Do some research. Write a report about how your body keeps you safe.

LOG ON **e-Journal** Write about it online @ **www.macmillanmh.com**

The Water Planet

Look and Wonder

Green sea turtles live in oceans throughout the world. Can all water plants and animals live in all water environments?

Building block lesson for 3 LS 3.a. Students know plants and animals have structures that serve different functions in growth, survival, and reproduction.
•3 LS 3.b. Students know examples of diverse life forms in different environments, such as oceans, deserts, tundra, forests, grasslands, and wetlands.

Can ocean animals live and grow in fresh water?

Form a Hypothesis

Can brine shrimp grow in fresh water and salt water?

Test Your Hypothesis

1. Fill each jar with 480 mL of water. Put two tablespoons of sea salt in one jar. Label the jars *Fresh Water* and *Salt Water*.

Step 1

2. Add one teaspoon of brine shrimp eggs to each jar.

3. **Observe** Watch what develops in each jar over the next few days. Use a hand lens.

Draw Conclusions

4. Can ocean animals live and grow in a freshwater environment?

5. **Infer** Are oceans freshwater or saltwater environments?

Explore More

Experiment Does temperature affect the hatching of brine shrimp eggs? Design an experiment to find out.

 3 IE 5.e. Collect data in an investigation and analyze those data to develop a logical conclusion.

Materials

2 jars

measuring cup and water

measuring spoons

sea salt

brine shrimp eggs

hand lens

Step 3

Main Idea 3 LS 3.a
3 LS 3.b

Earth's water environments differ in their salt content, depth, and temperature.

Vocabulary

saltwater environment, p. 91

freshwater environment, p. 91

brackish environment, p. 91

depth, p. 92

LOG ON e-Glossary
@ www.macmillanmh.com

Reading Skill

Summarize

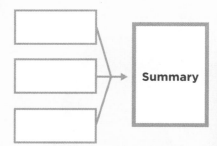

Summary

Technology

SCIENCE QUEST Explore biomes with the Secret Agents.

What is a water environment?

If you could look at Earth from space, you would see a blue, watery world. Almost three quarters of our planet is covered by water.

Oceans, lakes, ponds, rivers, streams, and wetlands make up Earth's water environments. These environments are different from one another in many ways. One of the biggest differences is in the amount of salt the water in each environment has.

Earth's Water

 = salt water (970 buckets)

 = fresh water in rivers, lakes, streams and ponds (3 buckets)

 = fresh water in ice and underground sources (27 buckets)

If Earth's water supply were poured into 1,000 buckets, only 30 buckets would contain fresh water. The rest would be salt water.

▲ Earth is called the water planet. From space you can see that most of Earth's surface is covered with water.

Read a Diagram

Is most of Earth's water salt water or fresh water?

Clue: Compare the buckets of salt water and fresh water.

Saltwater environments have water that is very salty. Oceans and seas are saltwater environments. Saltwater environments are also called *marine environments*.

Freshwater environments have water that contains almost no salt. The water you drink is fresh water. Most lakes, ponds, rivers, and streams are freshwater environments.

Brackish environments have a mixture of fresh and salt water. The environment where a river meets the ocean is brackish. Many marine animals lay eggs and raise their young in this environment.

✔ *Quick Check*

Summarize What are three types of water environment?

Critical Thinking What is the most likely source for the water you drink?

How are water environments different from each other?

You know that water environments differ in the amount of salt they have. There are other differences, too.

Depth

Water environments have different depths. Depth describes how deep something is. It measures the distance from the water's surface to the floor below. Oceans can be thousands of meters deep. Ponds can have depths of just a few meters. Most water plants and animals live near the surface.

Sunlight

Water environments get different amounts of sunlight. Near the surface, sunlight shines through the water. Green plants and algae get enough light to grow. As water gets deeper, less sunlight shines through. Deep water is dark. Plants cannot grow in very deep water. Few animals live there.

▲ Snorkelers swim near the surface of the water. Here there is plenty of sunlight for them to observe marine life.

In the deep sea, divers must use a light to observe marine life. They must wear wet suits to stay warm in the cold water. ▶

Temperature

Water environments have different temperatures, too. Near the equator, tropical waters stay warm all year. In temperate environments, water gets cold during winter.

Water depth can affect water temperature. Near the surface, where the sunlight heats the water, the water is warmer. In deep water, where there is little sunlight, the water is colder.

The ocean bottom is extremely cold and dark. Scientists must use submarines to study it. ▼

≡ Quick Lab

Water Temperatures

① Fill two jars each with 200 mL of water. Label one jar *Sunlight* and put it in a sunny place. Label the other jar *No Sunlight* and put it in a very dark place.

② **Observe** After a few hours, measure the water temperature in each jar with a thermometer. Which jar is warmer?

③ **Draw Conclusions** The two jars model two parts of the ocean. What are those parts? How are they different?

④ **Infer** Where do you think most animals live in the ocean?

✔ Quick Check

Summarize Describe three ways water environments are different from each other.

Critical Thinking Which is probably colder, water that is 100 meters deep or water that is 1,000 meters deep?

What plants and animals live in water environments?

Different kinds of plants and animals live in different water environments. Each kind lives where it can best meet its needs. Each has adaptations that help it survive. For example, water lilies live in freshwater ponds. Air spaces inside their leaves help them float.

Tropical fish live in the warm salt water of tropical oceans. Here they can find food, lay their eggs, and stay safe. These fish could not survive in fresh water, or in deep, cold ocean environments.

 Quick Check

Summarize Why do different plants and animals live in different water environments?

Critical Thinking Could a tropical fish live in Arctic waters? Why or why not?

▲ Water lilies float in freshwater ponds. Their roots are buried in the muddy soil below.

▲ Many kinds of fish live in the sunny, shallow water of coral reefs.

Whales live in oceans. They have a coat of blubber, or fat, under their skin that keeps them warm in cold water. ▶

Summarize the Main Idea

Three kinds of **water environments** are: salt water, fresh water, and brackish water. (pp. 90–91)

Depth, **sunlight**, and water **temperature** affect water environments. (pp. 92–93)

Water plants and animals have **adaptations** that help them survive in water environments. (p. 94)

Make a FOLDABLES™ Study Guide

Make a layered-look book. Use it to summarize what you learned about water environments.

Water Environments

Depth, Sunlight, and Temperature

Adaptations

The Water Planet

Think, Talk, and Write

1 **Main Idea** How are oceans different from freshwater environments? How are the two environments similar?

2 **Vocabulary** What are brackish environments? Where are they found?

3 **Summarize** What are some adaptations that help plants and animals survive in water environments?

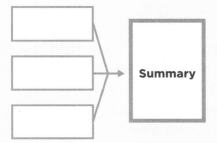

Summary

4 **Critical Thinking** Can all freshwater animals survive in salt water? Explain.

5 **Test Practice** Brine shrimp live in

A salt water

B ponds

C fresh water

D lakes

Writing Link

Write a Report
Use research materials to learn how an oil spill can harm water plants and animals. Then write a report.

Art Link

Draw a Water Biome
Draw an underwater world. Include living things adapted to the environment.

Focus on Inquiry Skills

Predict

You just learned about saltwater and freshwater environments. Which do you think freezes faster, salt water or fresh water? To find answers to questions like this, scientists **predict** what they think will happen. Next, they experiment to find out what does happen. Then, they compare their results with their prediction.

① Learn It

When you **predict**, you state the possible results of an event or experiment. It is important to record your prediction before you do an experiment, record your observations as you experiment, and record the final results. Then you have enough data to figure out if your prediction was correct.

② Try It

Predict what will happen when you freeze fresh water and salt water. Write your prediction on a chart like the one shown on page 97. Then do an experiment to test your prediction.

▶ Pour 125 mL of water into a plastic container. Label this container *Fresh Water*.

▶ Pour 125 mL of water into another plastic container. Add 1 tablespoon of salt and stir with a spoon. Label this container *Salt Water*.

▶ Place both containers into the freezer. Check them every 15 minutes. Draw or write your observations.

Now answer these questions: Which freezes faster, fresh water or salt water? Was your prediction correct?

Which Freezes Faster?	
My Predictions	
observations of **fresh water**	
observations of **salt water**	
results	

❸ Apply It

Now that you have learned to think like a scientist, make another prediction. Do you **predict** that salt water or fresh water will evaporate faster? Plan an experiment to find out if your prediction is correct.

3 IE 5.d. Predict the outcome of a simple investigation and compare the result with the prediction.

Life in an Ocean

Look and Wonder

These strange life-forms are jellyfish. They have no brains, bones, or eyes. They have poisonous tentacles that capture food. How are their bodies adapted to move through water?

3 LS 3.a. Students know plants and animals have structures that serve different functions in growth, survival, and reproduction. •**3 LS 3.b.** Students know examples of diverse life forms in different environments, such as oceans, deserts, tundra, forests, grasslands, and wetlands.

How do jellyfish and some other water animals move?

Materials

balloon

Purpose

To model how jellyfish and some other ocean animals are adapted to move through water

Procedure

Step 1

① **Make a Model** Blow up a balloon. Hold the end of the balloon tight so the air cannot escape. The balloon models the hollow, bell-shaped body of a jellyfish. The air is like water that fills into the jellyfish's body.

② **Predict** What do you think will happen when you let go of the balloon?

③ **Experiment** Let go of your balloon. What happens as "water" is pushed out of a "jellyfish's body"?

⚠ **Be Careful.** Make sure you do this away from other students.

Draw Conclusions

④ How does a jellyfish move through the ocean? How does this adaptation help a jellyfish survive in its water environment?

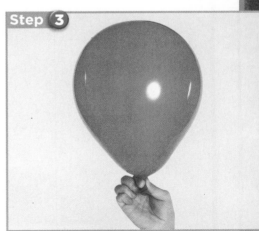

Step 3

Explore More

How do other animals move through the ocean? Do research to find out.

 3 IE 5.d. Predict the outcome of a simple investigation and compare the result with the prediction.

Read and Learn

► **Main Idea** 3 LS 3.a
3 LS 3.b

The ocean is Earth's largest environment. Ocean plants and animals have adaptations that help them survive in this environment.

► **Vocabulary**

ocean, p. 101

algae, p. 102

gills, p. 104

LOG ON e-Glossary
@ www.macmillanmh.com

► **Reading Skill**

Compare and Contrast

Different   Alike   Different

Coral reefs are found in the warm, shallow waters of tropical oceans.

What is an ocean like?

Bubbles rise from your snorkel. Before your eyes is a world of color and beauty. A coral reef is like no other place on Earth. It is a ridge of colorful fish, sponges, and other forms of ocean life. Its shallow waters are warm and clear. Its maze of coral can be millions of years old. The coral reef is a highlight of Earth's largest environment—the ocean.

An **ocean** is a large body of salt water. Earth has five oceans that are all connected. These are the Atlantic, Pacific, Indian, Arctic, and Southern Oceans. The Pacific Ocean is the largest. It covers more than 166 million square kilometers (64 million square miles), or about one-third of the planet.

Billions of living things are found in Earth's oceans. Almost all ocean life forms live in shallow waters that are 100 meters deep (about 328 feet) or less. Yet, most of the world's oceans have a depth of 1,500 meters (4,920 feet) or more. The bottom of the ocean is too cold and dark to support much life.

✔ Quick Check

Compare and Contrast How is the bottom of the ocean different from the top of the ocean?

Critical Thinking Are coral reefs found in tropical or temperate environments?

Eelgrass is often mistaken for algae, but it is really a flowering plant.

How do plants survive in the ocean?

Few true plants are adapted to survive in the ocean. Eelgrass is one of them. Most of the ocean's "plants" are not true plants. They are **algae** (AL•jee). Algae are plantlike living things. Just like plants, they use water, carbon dioxide gas, and sunlight to make their own food. Just like plants, they give off oxygen—the gas we breathe.

Two main kinds of algae are found in the ocean. One kind has rootlike structures that attach to the ocean bottom. These algae can only live in shallow water where they get enough sunlight to grow. The other kind does not have roots. They drift near the sunlit surface of the water. Both kinds of algae have adaptations that help them survive in the ocean's salty water.

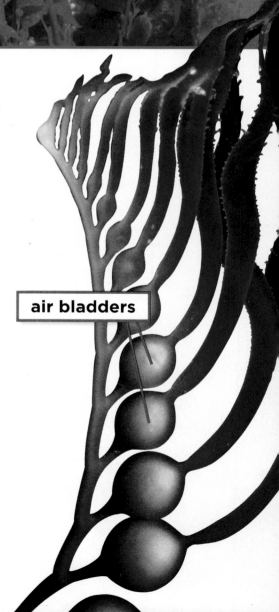

air bladders

Kelp forests grow tall toward the water's sunlit surface.

Kelp Forests

Algae grows very quickly. A type of algae called kelp can group together and grow to huge sizes. Kelp forests in the Pacific Ocean can reach heights of 30 meters (98 feet). Kelp has leaflike structures that take in sunlight. It also has balloonlike structures called *air bladders* that help it float. Kelp grows in clear, shallow water. Animals such as sea urchins and sea otters live in kelp forests.

◀ Kelp looks similar to a land plant, but it has adaptations that help it survive in water.

☰ *Quick Lab*

Plant Growth

1. Get two self-sealing plastic bags. Place a paper towel in each plastic bag. Add 60 mL of water to one bag. Label it *Fresh Water*. Add 60 mL of water and 1 teaspoon of salt to the other bag. Label it *Salt Water*.

2. Punch a line of staples about 3 cm from the bottom of each bag. Drop 5 bean seeds into each bag. Hang the bags on a wall or a window.

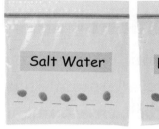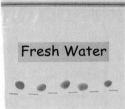

3. **Compare** Do plants grow in both water environments?

4. **Draw Conclusions** Do plants need special adaptations to survive in salt water?

 ## *Quick Check*

Compare and Contrast How are ocean plants and land plants similar? How are they different?

Critical Thinking Where does some of the oxygen we breathe come from?

Breathing and Moving

1. Water enters the fish's mouth.

2. Structures in the gills then take in oxygen from the water.

3. Fins help the fish steer as it swims.

4. A fish moves forward by waving its muscular tail back and forth.

Read a Photo

How are fish specially adapted to life under water?

Clue: Match each body part with its numbered caption.

How do animals survive under water?

Of all the animals in the ocean, fish are the most numerous. Ocean animals have adaptations that help them live in their environment.

Breathing

Like people, fish need oxygen to breathe. Fish use a body part called **gills** to get oxygen from water. The gills are located on both sides of the fish just behind its head. Water comes into the fish's mouth, then passes through the gills. The gills take in oxygen as the water passes out.

Moving

A fish's body is shaped to move easily through water. Fish have strong tails to help them move forward. Fins help them steer.

Crabs are related to spiders. Like spiders, they walk along the ground. ▼

Staying Safe

The ocean is a wild place. Many animals interact in a constantly changing environment. Small fish feed on plants, and large fish eat smaller fish. Still larger animals, such as sharks and whales, rule the underwater animal kingdom. How do animals stay safe in this environment?

The stingray has a sharp and poisonous tail. Waving its flat body, the stingray swims quickly along the ocean floor. If a stingray senses danger, in just a few seconds it will cover itself with some sand. Its skin is the same color as the sand. This *camouflage* is a way that the stingray and some other ocean animals stay safe under water.

 Quick Check

Compare and Contrast How are land animals different from ocean animals?

Critical Thinking How do ocean animals move through the water? Give some examples.

The color of the stingray's skin is similar to the ocean floor. This helps it blend in and stay safe.

How do animals survive in the very deep ocean?

Deep, deep down, near the bottom of the ocean, it is extremely cold and dark. Only animals with special adaptations can live there. Look at the photo of the viperfish. Its giant eyes help it find food even in the dark. The giant squid, another deep ocean animal, has eyes as big as volleyballs. On land, animals that hunt at night have big eyes, too. This adaptation is helpful in environments where there is little light.

The angler fish, on the other hand, has small eyes. It has poor vision. It has a different adaptation that helps it get food. It has a growth on top of its head that lights up. Other animals are attracted to the light. When they swim close to the light, the angler fish attacks. Both the viperfish and the angler fish have very sharp teeth.

▲ The viperfish opens its jaws wide to capture fish swimming by.

▲ The angler fish has a lighted "fishing pole" to attract prey.

 Quick Check

Compare and Contrast How do animals that hunt at night compare with animals that hunt near the bottom of the ocean?

Critical Thinking Would large eyes be a necessary adaptation for animals that live near the surface of the water? Why?

Tube worms have a hard-shelled tube that protects them from predators. ▶

Lesson Review

Summarize the Main Idea

The **oceans** are Earth's largest environment. Oceans cover about one-third of the planet. (pp. 100–101)

Ocean plants have special adaptations that help them survive in the ocean. (pp. 102–103)

Ocean animals have body parts that help them live under water. Some live in the **very deep ocean**. (pp. 104–106)

Make a FOLDABLES™ Study Guide

Make a four-door book. Use it to summarize what you learned about life in oceans.

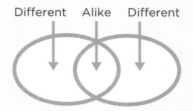

Oceans | Ocean Plants
The Deep Ocean | Ocean Animals

Think, Talk, and Write

1. **Main Idea** Why is most ocean life found near the surface?

2. **Vocabulary** What is the main function of gills on a fish?

3. **Compare and Contrast** What are some differences between shallow water and deep water environments?

Different   Alike   Different

4. **Critical Thinking** Why is kelp important to animals under water and on land?

5. **Test Practice** What is one way an animal stays safe in the ocean?
   A waterproof skin
   B camouflage
   C hibernation
   D breathing

 Writing Link

Write a Summary
Write about an underwater environment in your own words. Be sure to mention plants and animals you learned about. Include important facts and details.

 Math Link

Measure Volume
If you place an object in a container, the change in the water's measurement is the volume of the object. John puts a rock into a beaker, and the water level rises from 250 mL to 320 mL. What is the volume of the rock?

Be a Scientist

Materials

2 mixing bowls

measuring cup
and water

spoon

sea salt

1 fresh egg

How does salt affect the way things float in water?

Form a Hypothesis

Animals that live in Earth's oceans move around easily. Does salt water affect the way things move or float? Form a hypothesis. Begin with, "If water is salty, then . . ."

Test Your Hypothesis

1. **Measure** Label one bowl *Fresh Water* and the other bowl *Salt Water*. Pour 400 mL of water into each bowl.

2. **Measure** Pour $\frac{1}{8}$ cup of sea salt into the bowl labeled *Salt Water*. Stir.

3. **Observe** Carefully place a fresh egg in the fresh water bowl. Record what happens in a chart.

Step 1

Bowl	What I Observed
Fresh Water	
Salt Water	

Step 2

4. **Observe** Take the egg out and gently place it in the salt water bowl. Record what you observe in your chart.

Step 4

Draw Conclusions

⑤ Analyze Data Does the egg float in fresh water? In salt water?

⑥ Infer How does salt affect the way animals move in the oceans?

Inquiry **Guided**

Does salt water affect plants?

Form a Hypothesis

What effect does salt water have on some plants? Write your answer in the form "If water has salt, then . . ."

Test Your Hypothesis

Design an experiment to investigate what happens to lettuce when it absorbs fresh water and salt water. Write the steps you will follow.

Materials

sea salt

water

lettuce

2 plastic bowls

Draw Conclusions

Do your results support your hypothesis? Why or why not? Share your thoughts with your classmates.

Inquiry **Open**

What other questions do you have about animals and plants that live in the ocean? Talk with your classmates about questions you have. Make up the steps you will follow to answer your questions. Write a list of the materials you will use in your investigation.

Remember to follow the steps of the scientific process.

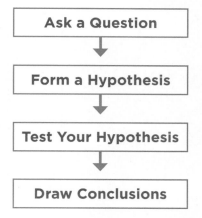

Ask a Question

↓

Form a Hypothesis

↓

Test Your Hypothesis

↓

Draw Conclusions

 3 IE 5.e. Collect data in an investigation and analyze those data to develop a logical conclusion.

Life in the Wetlands

Look and Wonder

Can you guess what is the most important part of a wetland? The grasses and plants of a wetland help clean the water that passes through. Wetlands are also home to a variety of birds and wildlife.

3 LS 3.a. Students know plants and animals have structures that serve different functions in growth, survival, and reproduction. **•3 LS 3.b.** Students know examples of diverse life forms in different environments, such as oceans, deserts, tundra, forests, grasslands, and wetlands.

How do wetlands filter water?

Purpose

To find out how a wetland cleans the environment

Procedure

1. Spread modeling clay in one-half of the pan to represent land. Have the land slope down into the empty part of the pan.

2. **Observe** Use the watering can to pour clean water over the land. This represents a heavy rain. How quickly does the heavy rain flood the low part of the land?

3. **Observe** Remove the water. Place the carpet over the clay. The carpet represents wetland grasses. Then once again use the watering can to create "heavy rain." How quickly does the water from the heavy rain flow to the low part of the land this time?

4. **Predict** Remove the water. Try the experiment again using muddy water. What do you predict will happen?

Draw Conclusions

5. What can a model teach us about a real wetlands environment?

Explore More

What other filters can you think of? Design an experiment that shows how they work.

 3 IE 5.e. Collect data in an investigation and analyze those data to develop a logical conclusion.

Materials

modeling clay

aluminum pan

watering can

strip of carpeting

clean water

muddy water

Step 2

Main Idea 3 LS 3.a
3 LS 3.b

Wetlands are places where the soil is wet for most of the year. Wetland plants and animals have adaptations that help them survive in their environment.

Vocabulary

wetland, p. 112

marsh, p. 114

swamp, p. 114

bog, p. 114

amphibian, p. 116

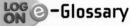
LOG ON ⓔ-Glossary
@ www.macmillanmh.com

Reading Skill

Predict

What I Predict	What Happens

What are wetlands?

Your paddle slows down. The trunks of tall trees tower above you. The dark, muddy water is still. Frogs croak and insects buzz. An egret quietly looks for fish. You are in the wetlands.

Wetlands are environments where water covers the soil for most of the year. The water in a wetland may be salt water, fresh water, or a mixture of salt and fresh water. Because wetland soil is usually covered by water, it does not hold much oxygen. Only plants that have adaptations for growing in this kind of soil can survive in wetlands.

Wetlands are found all over the world, except in Antarctica. They usually form along the edge of a water body where land and water meet.

This great egret finds everything it needs to survive in the wetlands of Florida's Everglades.

Wetlands Help the Environment

Fertilizers and chemicals from farming can harm ponds, lakes, and rivers. Wetlands slowly filter and clean the water.

The plants and soil of a wetland act like sponges absorbing water. When oceans, rivers, ponds, or lakes overflow, the extra water is absorbed by a wetland. This helps prevent land environments from flooding.

Wetlands also filter and clean the environment. They absorb chemicals that can leak into water. As the water flows through wetlands, it is filtered by the plants and soil. The water is cleaned by this natural process.

✓ Quick Check

Predict If a wetland near a river were replaced with farmland, what could happen after heavy rains?

Critical Thinking Why is it important to preserve wetlands?

Read a Diagram

How do wetlands clean the environment?

Clue: Look at the difference between the two pictures.

LOG ON *Science in Motion* Watch how wetlands clean the environment @ **www.macmillanmh.com**

Grasses and reeds grow in a marsh.

Bogs have wet, spongy ground covered in moss.

What kinds of plants live in wetlands?

There are different kinds of wetlands. Each one has different kinds of plants. **Marshes** are wetlands where grasses and reeds grow. There are no trees in marshes. **Swamps** are wetlands with trees and shrubs. Cypress and willow trees grow well in swamps. **Bogs** are freshwater wetlands that are filled with moss and rich soil. Moss is a small, leafy plant.

Plants that grow in wetlands have adaptations that help them survive in their wet environment. For example, some marsh plants have special tubes in their stems. These tubes carry oxygen from the leaves to the roots.

Mangroves are swamp trees. These trees have giant, woody roots that grow above the water line. The roots take oxygen directly from the air. Mangrove roots are home to shellfish and many small animals.

Mangrove trees drop seeds shaped like little sticks into the water. Seeds may float for months. In time, the sharp end of a seed touches down on fertile land. Then a new plant begins to grow.

 Quick Check

Predict How well would a cactus grow in a swamp?

Critical Thinking How are marshes and swamps similar? How are they different?

≡ *Quick Lab*

Wetland Plants and Water Level

1 Place four moist sponges in a flat pan. Each sponge acts like a wetland to soak up water. Pour 1 liter of water into the pan, covering the sponges.

2 **Observe** Mark the level of water in the pan.

3 Pour the water out of the pan and wring out the sponges. Repeat steps 1 and 2 using only one sponge.

4 **Compare** How is the water level different in each situation? If wetlands are destroyed, what can happen to non-wetland environments?

The roots of mangrove trees are adapted to take in oxygen from the air.

What kinds of animals live in wetlands?

Many kinds of animals live in wetlands. Here they find food, water, and shelter. Each has adaptations that help it survive.

Amphibians (am•FIB•ee•enz) are especially suited for life in the wetlands. Amphibians are animals that spend part of the time in water and part of the time on land. Frogs are amphibians. They are adapted to breathe through their wet skin.

Herons are wetland birds. They are adapted to hunt in wetlands. They stand motionless and wait for prey. When the time is right, the heron snaps its long beak to catch frogs, insects, mice, or lizards.

Walking catfish live in wetland ponds. A pond may disappear during a dry season. When this happens, the catfish moves over land to another body of water. The fish uses its fins as "legs." It uses a special body part that holds air to breathe on land for short periods of time.

▲ This bullfrog must return to the water often to keep its skin wet.

▲ This walking catfish can survive out of water for a short while.

 Quick Check

Predict Some wetland frogs are disappearing. How might this affect wetland birds?

Critical Thinking Why should people preserve wetlands?

This great blue heron uses its excellent eyesight to hunt. ▶

Lesson Review

Summarize the Main Idea

Wetlands are places where the soil is wet for most of the year. (pp. 112–113)

Three types of wetlands are marshes, swamps, and bogs. Each has different **wetland plants**. (pp. 114–115)

Wetland animals have adaptations that help them live in wet environments. (p. 116)

Make a FOLDABLES™ Study Guide

Make a three-tab book. Use it to summarize what you learned about wetlands.

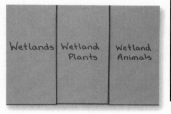

Wetlands | Wetland Plants | Wetland Animals

Think, Talk, and Write

1 **Main Idea** Describe three types of wetlands.

2 **Vocabulary** What is the difference between a swamp and a marsh?

3 **Predict** What happens to wetlands during a storm?

What I Predict	What Happens

4 **Critical Thinking** Why do birds need wetlands during long migrations?

5 **Test Practice** Which of the following is not a type of wetland?
  A marsh
  B swamp
  C dune
  D bog

 Math Link

Wetlands Plan
In 1993, there were about 450,000 acres of wetlands in California. The government plans to add 225,000 acres of wetlands by 2010. If the plan is successful, how many acres of wetlands will there be in 2010?

 **Social Studies Link**

Design a Map
Draw or trace a map of California. What are three kinds of water environments found in your state? Show them on your map.

Mail Call

buckeye butterfly

Scientists at the American Museum of Natural History work to protect endangered habitats around the world. They collect stories from people around the world to learn about these environments.

TO: American Museum of Natural History
FROM: Tommy
SUBJECT: Save the Mangroves!

Dear Museum Scientists,

My name is Tommy. I live on the coast of Florida, near a mangrove swamp. My mom is a tour guide who shows people the amazing creatures that live in the mangroves. I am writing to you because I am worried about what is happening near my home. The mangroves are home to many animals, including storks, butterflies, snakes, and crabs. Mangrove roots provide shelter for fish and shrimp. The mangroves also protect the coast from wind, waves, and floods.

Lately many new neighborhoods are being built. This construction is replacing many mangroves with stores, homes, marinas, airports, and parking lots. What will happen to the animals that call the mangroves home? There must be a way for us and the mangroves and animals to live together.

Tommy

AMERICAN MUSEUM of NATURAL HISTORY

mangrove land crab

When you predict,

▶ you use what you know to tell what you think might happen in the future

 Write About It

Predict What might happen to the wetlands near Tommy's home if people continue to fill them and build new neighborhoods? Write a letter back to Tommy explaining why it is important to save wetlands. Tell ways you think we can help protect them.

LOG ON **e-Journal** Write about it online @ **www.macmillanmh.com**

The wood stork and mangrove water snake make their home in Florida's mangrove swamps.

 ELA R 3.2.4. Recall major points in the text and make and modify predictions about forthcoming information.

A Wetlands Story

In this chapter, you have learned about life in the wetlands. Now suppose that you are visiting a wetland environment. How would you describe this place? What plants and animals would you see?

A good story

► has a beginning, a middle, and an end

► has a plot with a problem that needs to be solved

► has characters who do things and a setting where the events take place

► uses descriptive words and details to tell about the characters, setting, and action

► often has dialogue

▲ Wetlands are an important natural habitat for plants, animals, and people.

 Write About It

Fictional Narrative Write a story about a field trip to the wetlands. Who goes? How do you get there? What does the tour guide say? Use all the parts of a good story in your writing.

 e-Journal Write about it online @ **www.macmillanmh.com**

 ELA W 3.2.1. Write narratives:
a. Provide a context within which an action takes place.
b. Include well-chosen details to develop the plot.
c. Provide insight into why the selected incident is memorable.

Earth's Water

Dr. Peter Gleick of the Pacific Institute in Oakland, California, studies fresh water on Earth and all the ways it is used. He looks at how much fresh water is available compared to ice and sea water. People use fresh water for drinking, cooking, washing, and gardening. Farmers use it for their animals and crops.

Look at the chart below. The 100-square grid represents all the water on Earth.

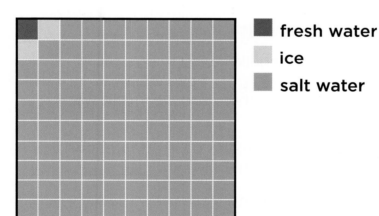

■ fresh water
■ ice
■ salt water

Fractions of water

▶ Use the number 100 as the denominator and 1 as the numerator: $\frac{1}{100}$ = 1 part fresh water in 100 parts water shows fresh water as a fraction of all the water

▶ Write a fraction showing 2 parts of 100; the amount of ice as part of all the water = $\frac{2}{100}$

▶ Use 100 as the denominator to show 97 parts of 100 to represent sea water as a fraction = $\frac{97}{100}$

 ## Solve It

Look at the shoes of everyone in the classroom. Count how many have laces, how many are fastened with something other than laces, and how many are slip-on shoes. Represent your data in fraction form.

 MA NS 3.3.0. Students understand the relationship between whole numbers, simple fractions, and decimals.

Summarize the Main Ideas

Earth's water environments differ in salt content, depth, and temperature. (pp. 88–95)

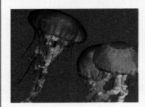

Ocean plants and animals have special adaptations that help them survive in salt water. (pp. 98–107)

Wetland plants and animals have adaptations that help them survive in wet environments. (pp. 110–117)

Make a FOLDABLES™ Study Guide

Tape your lesson study guides on a piece of paper as shown. Use your study guide to review what you have learned in this chapter.

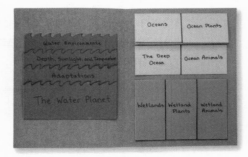

Fill each blank with the best word from the list.

algae, p. 102

bog, p. 114

brackish environment, p. 91

freshwater environments, p. 91

gills, p. 104

marsh, p. 114

saltwater environment, p. 91

swamp, p. 114

1. Wetland plants, such as reeds and grasses, grow mainly in a _____. 3 LS 3.b

2. An ocean is a _____. 3 LS 3.b

3. Fish use special organs called _____ to get oxygen. 3 LS 3.a

4. A _____ is a freshwater wetland filled with spongy moss and rich soil. 3 LS 3.b

5. Plantlike living things called _____ have adaptations that help them survive in salt water. 3 LS 3.a

6. Water lilies have adaptations that help them live in _____. 3 LS 3.b

7. Wetland trees grow mainly in a _____. 3 LS 3.b

8. A _____ is a water environment that is a mixture of fresh and salt water. 3 LS 3.b

Discuss or write about each of the following.

9. Predict What do you think would happen if a fish that lived in a freshwater environment was placed in an ocean? Give reasons for your answer. 3 LS 3.a

10. Explanatory Writing Write a paragraph explaining how kelp and eelgrass are alike and how they differ. 3 LS 3.a

11. Predict What might happen to some ocean animals if kelp forests disappeared? Explain. 3 LS 3.b

underwater kelp forest

12. Critical Thinking Would you find the animals shown below living in the same water environment? Tell why or why not. 3 LS 3.b

bullfrog   jellyfish

Answer each of the following in a complete sentence.

13. Why is water temperature near an ocean's surface warmer than the temperature of deep water? 3 LS 3.b

14. How do fish get the oxygen they need from water? 3 LS 3.a

15. What are the three main kinds of wetlands? How do they differ? 3 LS 3.b

16. What kind of adaptation does a plant need to live in a marsh? 3 LS 3.a

marsh

 What adaptations help living things survive under water? 3 LS 3

Make a Water Environment Book

- Make a book about one of Earth's water environments. Include information about the salt content, depth, and temperature.

- Tell about the plants and animals that live there. Explain what adaptations help the plants and animals survive in their environment.

- Include a cover for your book and illustrate each page with pictures.

saltwater environment

freshwater environment

wetlands

1 Herons and frogs live in a wetland. The chart shows the number of frogs between 1995 and 2004. What might explain the decrease in the number of frogs? 3 IE 3.c

Year	Number of Frogs
1995	200
2000	150
2004	100

A Fewer herons live in the wetland.

B More herons are in the wetland.

C The herons stopped eating frogs.

D The frogs moved to a desert.

2 How do wetlands help the environment? 3 LS 3.b

A They filter and hold water.

B They collect water and sunlight.

C They have fresh and salt water.

D They are pretty and quiet.

3 Which type of plants can be found in a freshwater environment? 3 LS 3.b

A cacti

B water lilies

C palm trees

D sagebush

4 Which feature allows kelp to float? 3 LS 3.a

A rootlike structures

B leaflike structures

C clumping together

D balloonlike structures

5 Look at the drawing below.

Which pair of animals live in the environment shown above? 3 LS 3.b

A salmon and ducks

B stingrays and sea stars

C eels and eelgrass

D frogs and catfish

6 Which animals live in a freshwater environment? 3 LS 3.b

A whales

B starfish

C frogs

D octopuses

7 A mangrove tree takes in oxygen through its 3 LS 3.a

A trunk.

B roots.

C flowers.

D seeds.

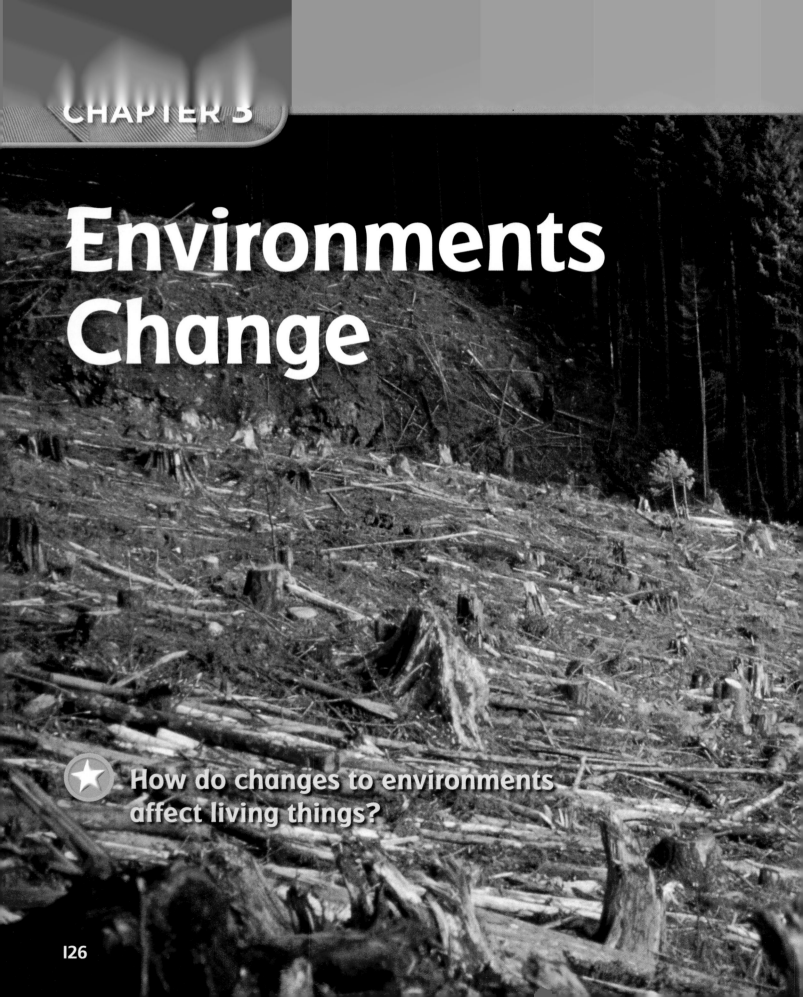

Environments Change

How do changes to environments affect living things?

Lesson 1

Living Things Change Their Environment

PAGE 130

Lesson 2

Changes Affect Living Things

PAGE 140

Lesson 3

Living Things of the Past

PAGE 152

3 LS 3. Adaptations in physical structure or behavior may improve an organism's chance for survival.

Literature
Nonfiction Book

ELA R 3.3.4. Determine the underlying theme or author's message in fiction and nonfiction text. **ELA W 3.1.1.** Create a single paragraph:
a. Develop a topic sentence.
b. Include simple supporting facts and details.

peregrine falcon

Can We Save the Peregrine Falcon?

by David Dobson

Peregrine falcons . . . were quite common in the United States until about 1950, but over the next 20 years they died out almost completely. Most people blame DDT, a chemical used to kill harmful insects. DDT was eaten by the insects, which were eaten by small birds, which were then eaten by the peregrine falcons. The poison made falcon eggshells very thin and easy to break, so peregrines became unable to produce any young. The falcons have been doing much better since DDT has been banned. . . .

Some peregrine falcons have found ways to live with people. They have traded tall trees and cliffs, where they usually build their nests, for tall buildings in cities. In cities the falcons can find plenty of pigeons and other birds to eat.

 Write About It

Response to Literature This book tells us that peregrine falcons almost died out. What is the author trying to tell us about environmental changes? Write a paragraph about environmental changes. Include what we can do to protect the environment.

 **-Journal** Write about it online @ **www.macmillanmh.com**

Living Things Change Their Environment

Look and Wonder

Leaves fall from trees and cover the forest floor. In time, the leaves disappear. Have you ever wondered what happens to fallen leaves? What makes them disappear?

3 LS 3.c. Students know living things cause changes in the environment in which they live: some of these changes are detrimental to the organism or other organisms, and some are beneficial.

How can worms change their environment?

Purpose

To find out how one living thing changes its environment

Procedure

Materials

moist soil

leaves

plastic container

stones

worms

① Put soil in the plastic container. Then put small stones and leaves on top of the soil. This models the forest floor.

② Place live worms on the "forest floor."

③ **Predict** What will the worms do? Make a short list of the things you might see the worms do.

④ **Observe** Check the worms, soil, leaves, and stones every three to four days. Keep the tank moist. How do the worms change their environment? Record your observations.

Draw Conclusions

⑤ How do worms change the environment in which they live?

Explore More

How do other living things change their environments? Make a plan to test your ideas. Then try your plan.

Step ①

Step ②

 3 IE 5.e. Collect data in an investigation and analyze those data to develop a logical conclusion.

How do living things change their environment?

Every living thing changes its environment in some way. Some living things make small changes. A spider spins a web. A bird builds a nest. A squirrel buries an acorn. All these actions change the environment in small ways.

Living things can also change their environment in more noticeable ways. Bacteria, worms, and fungi live in the soil. They break down leaves and other dead plant material. They help add nutrients back to the soil. These living things make big changes that help the environment.

Competition (kahm•pi•TISH•uhn) can be a major cause of change. **Competition** is the struggle among living things for food, water, and other needs.

A Changing Environment

Grass and other small plants sprout in warm, moist soil. They change this bare environment as they grow.

As more plants grow, other living things move to the environment. These living things use the plants for food and shelter.

As grass begins to grow, it takes in nutrients and water from the soil. It changes the environment as it meets its needs. In time, animals eat the grass for food. These animals change the environment as they meet their needs. When shrubs and trees begin to grow, they compete for space, light, and water. The trees block sunlight from reaching the smaller plants. The smaller plants may die. In this way environments change as living things compete to meet their needs.

 Quick Check

Predict How would a forest change if a big tree fell?

Critical Thinking How do you change your environment?

Read a Diagram

How does this environment change over time?

Clue: Arrows help show a sequence.

LOG ON *Science in Motion*
Watch how environments change @ **www.macmillanmh.com**

When shrubs take root, more animals move to the environment. The plants and animals compete to meet their needs.

In time, trees grow and the environment continues to change.

How does a beaver change its environment?

Beavers are master builders. They cut down small trees and plants with their strong teeth. Then they pile up these materials to build dams in streams. Dams block water from flowing through streams. They cause deep pools of water to form in which beavers can build lodges. Lodges are shelters that are made from trees, shrubs, and mud. Beavers use lodges for protection and to raise their young.

▲ Beavers cut down trees with their strong front teeth.

Beavers use branches to build dams and lodges in the water. ▼

When beavers build lodges and dams, they change the environment in many ways. Sometimes they change large areas of land and water. Large beaver dams can cause land to flood. Plants on flooded land can die. The homes of other plants and animals can be washed away. Dams also harm plants and animals that depend on flowing water.

Changes that beavers make can also help some living things. When beavers cut down trees, they make space for smaller plants to grow. Their dams can cause wetlands to form. Wetlands are home to many plants and animals.

✔ Quick Check

Predict If trees were not available, would beavers still build dams?

Critical Thinking Does a beaver help or harm the environment?

Quick Lab

A Beaver's Tools

1 Get several photos of beavers.

2 **Observe** Look at the parts of the beaver's body. Which parts help it to swim, chew wood, and stay warm in cold water?

3 **Communicate** Make a chart to show how each body part helps a beaver meet its needs.

Body Part	Purpose
sharp teeth	
flat tail	
webbed hind feet	
front paws	
fur	

A beaver dam creates a pool of deep water ▶

Trash in the United States

$\frac{1}{10}$

$\frac{3}{10}$

$\frac{6}{10}$

■ trash burned at combustion facilities

■ trash recycled or composted

■ trash in landfills

Read a Chart

Where does our trash go?

Clue: Each section of the pie chart represents a fraction.

WE RECYCLE

How do people change their environment?

People cause more changes to the environment than any other living thing. Some changes are harmful. For example, people produce trash in their daily lives. Most Americans produce about 2.1 kilograms (4.5 pounds) of trash each day. Where does all this trash go? Many towns and cities put the trash they collect in landfills. Landfills can cause pollution (puh•LEW•shuhn). **Pollution** is what happens when harmful materials get into the air, water, or land.

What can we do to protect the environment? One easy thing we can do is practice the 3 *R*s—reduce, reuse, and recycle. **Reduce** means to use less of something. **Reuse** means to use something again. **Recycle** means to turn old things into new things. When you practice the 3 *R*s, you produce less trash and help the environment.

✔ Quick Check

Predict What might happen if you produce less trash?

Critical Thinking Name some things you can reuse.

Summarize the Main Idea

Living things change their environment. (pp. 132–133)

Beavers change the environment in both harmful and helpful ways. (pp. 134–135)

WE RECYCLE

People can help the environment by practicing the 3 *R*s. (p. 136)

Make a FOLDABLES™ Study Guide

Make a three-tab book. Use it to summarize what you learned about environments and change.

Living Things Change Their Environment

Beavers Change the Environment

People Can Help the Environment

Think, Talk, and Write

1 **Main Idea** What are some ways in which plants and animals change their environment?

2 **Vocabulary** What is it called when living things struggle to get what they need?

3 **Predict** What might happen if people keep polluting the environment?

What I Predict	What Happens

4 **Critical Thinking** What are some things you could reduce your use of?

5 **Test Practice** **Beavers build**
   A lodges
   B dens
   C nests
   D hives

 Math Link

Make a Pie Chart
Keep track of the trash you throw away. Make a pie chart that shows one week of trash from your home. Include paper, metal, plastic, and food scraps.

 **Art Link**

Make a Poster
Make a poster about the things people can do to help the environment. Include things you learned from this lesson as well as things you aleady knew.

Record Data

You read that most Americans change their environment daily by producing about 2 kg (4 lbs) of trash each! We can never completely get rid of trash, so it is up to everyone to cut down on trash. Do students in your school practice the 3 *R*s? Find out the same way scientists do: gather and **record data**.

❶ Learn It

When you **record data**, you write or draw facts that have been collected through measuring, counting, and experimenting. It is usually easier to study information if you organize it on a chart or graph. Often, scientists gather and record data by asking questions or by having people fill out surveys. You can do it, too.

❷ Try It

In this activity, you will gather and **record data** about how much trash is thrown out by students in your school. You cannot survey the whole school, but you can do a mini-survey.

▶ Choose five students to survey in the lunchroom.

▶ Ask each student questions about how many pieces of trash from lunch he or she threw away today. Ask about the containers they used. Will anything be reused?

3 IE 5.e. Collect data in an investigation and analyze those data to develop a logical conclusion.

▶ Record each student's data on a chart like the one shown.

Student's Name	Pieces Reused	Pieces Recycled	Pieces Thrown Away	Total Pieces of Trash

Now answer these questions:

▶ Did every student throw out some trash or packaging material?

▶ Were you surprised by the data you recorded?

▶ How many pieces of trash did these five people create from just one lunch?

❸ Apply It

Now combine your data with those of your classmates. Record this larger data. Then make a bar graph to show the results.

Do you predict these same students will throw out more or less trash tomorrow? Plan another survey to collect and **record data**. Compare those results to your first result just as scientists do!

Changes Affect Living Things

Look and Wonder

Rain. Rain. More rain. When it rains too much, everything gets wet. What happens to living things when there is a flood?

 3 LS 3.d. Students know when the environment changes, some plants and animals survive and reproduce; others die or move to new locations.

What happens to some plants when there is a flood?

Make a Prediction

What happens to plants when they get too much water? Write a prediction.

Test Your Prediction

1 Label three plants *A*, *B*, and *C*. Water plant A once a week with 30 mL of water. Water plant B every day with 60 mL of water. Water plant C every day with 120 mL of water.

2 **Predict** What will happen to the plants after three weeks? Record your prediction.

3 **Record Data** Observe your plants every few days. Measure how tall they grow. Record how they look with words and pictures.

4 **Observe** After three weeks, check the plants carefully. What do you observe?

Draw Conclusions

5 How do the plants look after three weeks? Which plant looks the healthiest? Which plant received the right amount of water?

6 **Infer** What happens to some plants when there is a flood?

Explore More

Experiment Stop watering plant C for a week. How does the plant change?

 3 IE 5.d. Predict the outcome of a simple investigation and compare the result with the prediction.

Materials

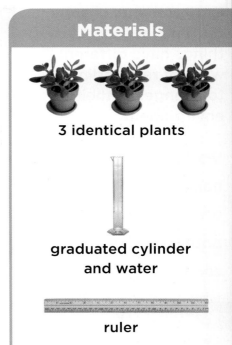

3 identical plants

graduated cylinder and water

ruler

Step 1

Step 3

Read and Learn

Main Idea 3 LS 3.d

Environments change for many reasons. Living things have different ways of responding to changes in their environment.

Vocabulary

habitat, p. 144

ecosystem, p. 146

population, p. 146

community, p. 146

LOG ON e-Glossary
@ www.macmillanmh.com

Reading Skill

Cause and Effect

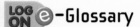

| Cause | → | Effect |

Technology

SCIENCE QUEST Explore how environments change with the Secret Agents.

Wild flowers in Anza Borrego State Park, California, quickly bloom after a spring rain.

What are some ways environments change?

You know that living things change their environment. Weather and other things can also change environments. Lightning might start a grassland or forest fire. Too much rain might cause flooding.

Some changes last a short time. A summer drought can turn a green meadow brown. Spring rain can make a desert bloom with flowers. Other changes have long-lasting effects. Earthquakes, storms, and volcanic eruptions can cause sudden changes in an environment. The damage from such changes may last for years.

◄ Desert marigolds are among the many flowers that bloom in deserts.

Some living things can recover from harmful changes in their environment. Grassland grasses have roots that store food and moisture. The grasses survive and grow back quickly after a fire. However, trees in a forest may take hundreds of years to grow back after a fire.

People often cause permanent changes. When large trees in old forests are cut down, those trees are gone forever. Rivers and lakes polluted by trash or chemicals may not recover unless people clean them up.

 Quick Check

Cause and Effect What are some things that can cause sudden changes in an environment?

Critical Thinking Why do grasses survive a fire better than trees?

In 1980 Mount St. Helens, a volcano in Washington, erupted. The eruption knocked down or scorched trees in nearly 230 square miles of forest. The environment is slowly changing as new living things start to grow again.

How do changes affect plants and animals?

Plants and animals have adaptations that help them survive in their environments. Zebras have flat teeth for chewing grass. Fish have gills that help them get oxygen from water. What would happen to these living things if their environment suddenly changed? What would happen to a zebra if its habitat became too dry for a long time? A **habitat** is a living thing's home. What would happen to the living things in a pond if their habitat dried up?

▲ Animals, such as this springbok, depend on watering holes.

When an environment changes, the plants and animals adapted to that environment can be harmed. If the changes last a long time, some animals may move to a new habitat. Some plants and animals have adaptations that help them survive change. Other plants and animals find a way to survive by changing their behavior. Living things that are not able to travel or change might die.

When there is no rain for a long time in the savanna, grasses can dry up. Watering holes can dry up, too. Zebras and other animals move to a new habitat where they can find food and water. Frogs burrow in the mud. They will come out when rain falls again. Grasses and most fish cannot move. If their habitat stays dry for too long, they may die.

▲ Many frogs are adapted to burrow and survive underground when their environment becomes dry.

 Quick Check

Cause and Effect What environmental changes might cause an animal to move to another place?

Critical Thinking What might happen to an elephant if its habitat suddenly becomes cold?

◀ Animals migrate, or move to another place, in search of food, water, and shelter as their habitat goes through seasonal changes.

How do living things depend on each other?

The living things in an environment depend on each other to meet their needs. Frogs depend on insects for food. Birds depend on plants for food and safety. Living things that depend on each other are part of an ecosystem. An **ecosystem** is all the living and nonliving things that interact in an environment. Ecosystems can be any size. They can be as small as a puddle or as large as an ocean.

Many populations of plants and animals live in an ecosystem. A **population** is all the members of a single type of living thing in an ecosystem. For example, all the prairie dogs in a grassland make up a population. Changes to one population can affect the whole community. A **community** is all the different populations in an ecosystem. Grasses, prairie dogs, and eagles are all part of a prairie community.

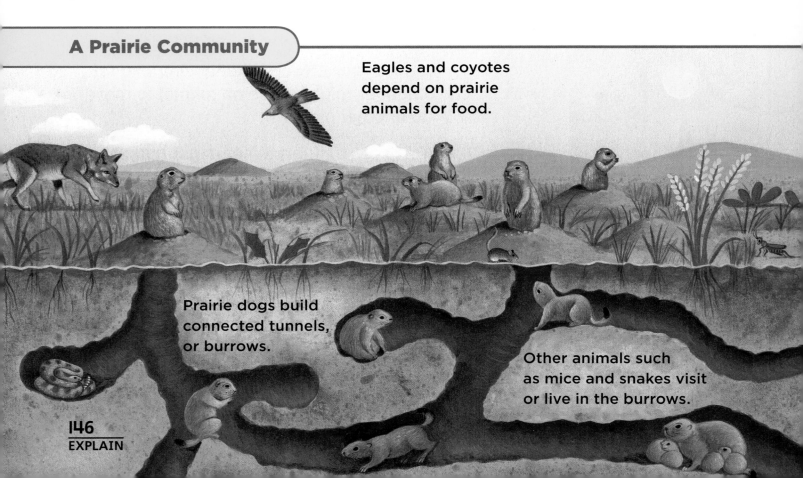

A Prairie Community

Eagles and coyotes depend on prairie animals for food.

Prairie dogs build connected tunnels, or burrows.

Other animals such as mice and snakes visit or live in the burrows.

In some prairie ecosystems, prairie dogs build tunnels and burrows. Other prairie animals, such as burrowing owls and mice, also make their homes in these burrows. Eagles and black-footed ferrets eat some of the animals that live in the burrows. When a prairie dog population disappears, their burrows collapse. Many kinds of animals lose a source of food and shelter.

 Quick Check

Cause and Effect What might happen to an ecosystem if a population disappears?

Critical Thinking What changes might harm an ecosystem?

Quick Lab

Grassland Ecosystem

1. Make five character cards. Label the cards: prairie dog, burrowing owl, snake, eagle, coyote.

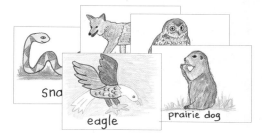

2. Paste the cards on a large sheet of paper.

3. Draw arrows from each card to show how the organisms depend on each other.

4. **Infer** What would happen if prairie dogs disappeared?

5. **Infer** What would happen if eagles disappeared?

If drought kills the grass, prairie dogs lose their source of food.

Without prairie dogs, other prairie populations such as eagles and coyotes will lose a source of food.

The whole prairie ecosystem can be harmed by environmental change.

Read a Diagram

What happens when prairie dogs leave a prairie ecosystem?

Clue: A before-and-after diagram shows change.

◀ Glassy-winged sharpshooters can destroy grape plants.

What happens when new living things move in?

Sometimes new living things enter an ecosystem. Seeds can be carried to an ecosystem by wind. Animals searching for food and water may move in. People can also bring in new plants and animals. New plants and animals can upset the balance in an ecosystem. For example, glassy-winged sharpshooters moved to California from the southeastern United States. They eat California's grape plants and carry a disease that makes grape leaves dry up. The photos show some ways new plants and animals have affected California's ecosystems.

▲ Eucalyptus trees were once planted to prevent soil erosion. They grew quickly and crowded out native trees. They also burn easily, and help wildfires spread. Now they are being removed and replaced with native trees.

✔ Quick Check

Cause and Effect What can happen if a new animal moves into an ecosystem?

Critical Thinking Why can it be harmful to bring new plants into an ecosystem?

People once raised red foxes for their fur. When the fur trade stopped, these animals were released into the wild. They compete with native animals for food and space. ▶

Lesson Review

Summarize the Main Idea

 **Environments can change** in many ways. Some changes last a short time. Others last a long time. (pp. 142–143)

When environments change, **living things may be harmed**. Some may move; others may die. (pp. 144–145)

 Changes to one **population** of living things can affect other populations. (pp. 146–148)

Make a FOLDABLES™ Study Guide

Make a three-tab book. Use it to summarize what you learned.

Ways Environments Can Change

Ways Living Things Are Affected by Change

What Happens When One Population Changes

Think, Talk, and Write

1 **Main Idea** What are some ways in which environmental changes affect the living things in an environment?

2 **Vocabulary** Explain what a population is and give one example.

3 **Cause and Effect** Tell three ways a place could be affected if a very dry season killed most of the plants.

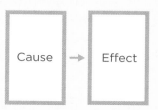

Cause → Effect

4 **Critical Thinking** Why should people take special care when they change a natural environment by building or farming? Explain.

5 **Test Practice** In the prairie dog ecosystem, prairie dogs
- **A** eat eagles
- **B** dig tunnels
- **C** catch fish
- **D** hunt coyotes

 Writing Link

Write an Essay
Find out about an environment that has recently changed in California. Then make a cause-and-effect chart. List what caused the environment to change and what happened as a result. Use your chart to write an essay.

 Social Studies Link

Research Mount St. Helens
Use research materials to find out what the environment was like before Mount St. Helens erupted. Find out how the environment has changed since the eruption. Make a poster or write a report.

Be a Scientist

Materials

aluminum pans

soil

2 cactus plants

2 grass plants

2 African violets

watering can

ruler

How do environmental changes affect plants?

Form a Hypothesis

Changes in the environment affect living things differently. A change may cause one plant to die, but may not affect others. What happens to the plants shown when their environment gets more or less rain than usual? Start with "If the amount of water a plant gets changes, then . . ."

Test Your Hypothesis

1 Fill both pans with the same amount of soil. Label one pan *Flood* and the other pan *Drought*.

2 **Use Variables** Plant one of each kind of plant in each pan.

3 Water plants in the *Flood* pan daily. Do not water plants in the *Drought* pan.

4 **Record Data** Monitor the growth of each plant. Draw and record the growth of each plant over two weeks.

Draw Conclusions

5 **Communicate** What happened to the plants in the *Flood* pan? What happened to the plants in the *Drought* pan?

Step 1

Step 2

Step 3

6 **Infer** Which plants could survive during a drought? Which could survive during a flood?

7 **Infer** Why did the environmental changes affect the plants differently?

How does shade affect plants?

Form a Hypothesis

What happens to plants if large trees grow above them and create shade? Write a hypothesis. Start with "If plants become shaded, then . . ."

Test Your Hypothesis

Design an experiment to investigate the changes that shade will make to a plant. Decide on the materials you will use. Write out the steps you will follow. Record your results and observations.

Draw Conclusions

Did your results support your hypothesis? Why or why not? What if shade came from a building instead of large trees? Would the same things happen?

What other questions do you have about living things and environmental change? Design an experiment to answer your questions. Your experiment must be organized to test only one variable, or item being changed. Your experiment must be written so that another group can complete the experiment by following your instructions.

Remember to follow the steps of the scientific process.

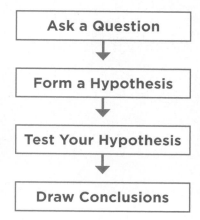

Ask a Question

↓

Form a Hypothesis

↓

Test Your Hypothesis

↓

Draw Conclusions

3 IE 5.b. Differentiate evidence from opinion and know that scientists do not rely on claims or conclusions unless they are backed by observations that can be confirmed.

Living Things of the Past

Look and Wonder

Many fossils are buried in layers of rock and soil. Scientists use tools and brushes to dig them out. What clues to life long ago are found in these fossils?

 3 LS 3.e. Students know that some kinds of organisms that once lived on Earth have completely disappeared and some of those resembled others that are alive today.

How do fossils tell us about the past?

Purpose

To find out how fossils can tell us about the past

Procedure

1. Use the measuring cup to mix a little glue with water.

2. Pour a thin layer of colored sand into a paper cup. Add a "fossil" object. Cover the object with sand of the same color. Add a little water and glue to "set" this layer.

3. Repeat Step 2 with different objects and different colors of sand two more times. Allow all three layers to dry.

4. **Observe** Trade cups with another group. Carefully peel the paper cup away from the layers of sand. Find the fossils.

5. **Record Data** Record in a table the order in which each fossil object was found.

Draw Conclusions

6. **Analyze Data** Which "fossil" was buried first? Last?

7. **Infer** What can layers of rock and soil tell us about fossils and Earth's past?

Explore More

How else could you model a fossil? Make a plan and try it.

 3 IE 5.e. Collect data in an investigation and analyze those data to develop a logical conclusion.

Materials

measuring cup and water

glue

colored sand

paper cup

"fossil" objects

brush

Step 4

Step 5	
Layer	Fossil
top	
middle	
bottom	

▶ **Main Idea** 3 LS 3.e

We can study fossils to learn about ancient plants and animals and their environments.

▶ **Vocabulary**

extinct, p. 154

fossil, p. 156

LOG ON ℮-Glossary

@ www.macmillanmh.com

▶ **Reading Skill**

Draw Conclusions

Text Clues	Conclusions

What can happen if the environment suddenly changes?

Did you know that mammoths once lived in North America? They were closely related to elephants that live in Africa and Asia today. What happened? Why did the mammoths disappear?

Ten thousand years ago, North America was in an ice age. Sheets of ice covered much of the United States. Large animals, such as mammoths and saber-toothed cats, lived in this cold environment. Then, the climate changed. Temperatures began to rise and the ice started to melt. The plants that mammoths ate disappeared. The mammoths started to die. In time, mammoths became extinct. **Extinct** means there are no more of that type of living thing alive.

◀ Scientists think hunting is one reason woolly mammoths disappeared. Climate change is another reason.

Responding to Change			
Change	Living Thing	What Might Happen	Why
warmer climate	saber-toothed cat	becomes extinct	unable to find food; unable to survive in warm climate
volcanic eruption	short-tailed albatross	survives	flies to new environment
colder climate	bear	survives	grows thicker fur

Climate change may cause populations to become extinct. Disease and human activities may also cause populations to become extinct. When a new population moves into an ecosystem a whole community can be in danger. Some populations can survive sudden changes such as these. Other populations cannot.

Read a Chart

What happened to the saber-toothed cat when its environment changed?

Clue: Headings help you find information.

 Quick Check

Draw Conclusions What are some reasons that some living things became extinct?

Critical Thinking Higher temperatures are causing glaciers to melt. What might happen to polar bears?

How can we learn about things that lived long ago?

We can learn about plants and animals that lived long ago by studying fossils. **Fossils** are the remains of living things. Some fossils give clues about a living thing's size and shape. A large fossil tooth or jaw tells us that the animal was probably very large. Other fossils can tell us what an animal ate. Sharp teeth tell us the animal was probably a meat eater. Flat teeth tell us the animal was probably a plant eater. Fossils can also teach us how an animal moved. Foot and leg bones help us learn if the animal could run or climb. Fossils with wings teach us that the animal could fly.

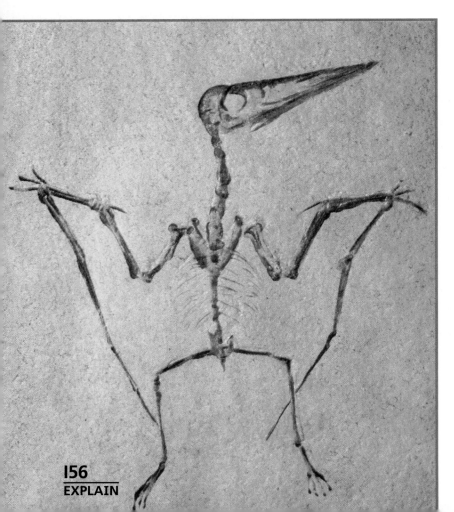

This megalodon tooth (right) is much larger than a great white shark tooth (left). This tells us megalodons were very large.

◀ Some dinosaur fossils give clues that some dinosaurs were related to modern birds.

Fossils can tell us how Earth and living things have changed over time. Many fish fossils are found on land. This tells us millions of years ago, that part of the land was covered by water. Over time, the sea floor rose and changed. There are now layers of rocks and soil where water once was. Fossil layers give clues about Earth's history. Fossils found closest to the surface are usually youngest. Fossils deeper in the ground are oldest.

▲ This woolly mammoth fossil was found in ice. Its heavy fur helps us know mammoths lived in cold environments.

 Quick Check

Draw Conclusions What can you conclude about a fossil with lungs?

Critical Thinking Why is studying fossils an important science?

This fossil of a fish came from a water environment. This fossil of a plant came from a land environment.

How are living things today similar to those that lived long ago?

We can learn a lot about ancient animals by comparing them to today's animals. For example, woolly mammoths lived long ago during the ice age. They looked and acted much like today's elephants, with a few important differences.

Mammoths were like elephants in size, but they grew very large tusks. Mammoth tusks could be as long as 5 meters (about 16 feet). Mammoths had a dense layer of hair that helped them survive cold climates.

elephant

woolly mammoth

frilled lizard

dilophosaurus

Mammoths, like elephants, lived in groups. Their flat teeth were suited for eating grass, woody shrubs, and tree bark. They needed to eat about twice their weight in food each day!

Some dinosaurs resemble lizards that are alive today. The frilled lizard has a tuft of skin around its neck. To frighten its enemies, the lizard can spread its frill to show its colored scales. Would you infer that some dinosaurs used their body parts for defense?

Most scientists believe that horseshoe crabs are the closest living relative of the trilobite. Trilobites are marine animals that have long been extinct. Horseshoe crabs resemble trilobites. They probably ate similar food and moved underwater using similar body parts.

 Quick Check

Draw Conclusions Did trilobites live on land or in water? Explain.

Critical Thinking What clues would you look for to find out about the history of your school grounds?

Quick Lab

Fossil Mystery

① **Observe** Look at the photo of a trilobite fossil. Does it look like any animal alive today?

trilobite

② **Compare** Look at the photo of a horseshoe crab. Horseshoe crabs live near the ocean. Is the trilobite similar to a horseshoe crab?

horseshoe crab

③ **Infer** What environment was home to the trilobite? How did it move?

④ **Draw Conclusions** How can you learn about animals from the past by looking at today's animals?

Have some animals stayed the same over time?

Some animals have stayed about the same for millions of years. Crocodiles, shrimp, and cockroaches are a few examples. Ancient fossils of these animals look the same as the animals living today. These animals have adaptations that have helped them survive through change.

▲ Some shrimp are adapted to survive changing amounts of salt in water. This has helped them survive for over 100 million years.

Many fossil crocodiles (top) look like the crocodiles that are alive today (bottom).

✓ Quick Check

Draw Conclusions What features of the crocodile's body and behavior have helped it survive?

Critical Thinking How are some animals that lived long ago similar to animals that live today?

Summarize the Main Idea

Some animals become **extinct** when their environment suddenly changes. (pp. 154–155)

Fossils tell us about animals and environments of the past. (pp. 156–157)

Some fossils look like plants and animals that are **alive today**. (pp. 158–160)

Make a FOLDABLES™ Study Guide

Make a three-tab book. Use it to summarize what you learned about living things of the past.

Extinct

Fossil Record

Past and Present Life on Earth

Think, Talk, and Write

1 **Main Idea** What can happen to living things when their environment suddenly changes?

2 **Vocabulary** What is a fossil?

3 **Draw Conclusions** What are some reasons an animal may become extinct?

Text Clues	Conclusions

4 **Critical Thinking** Why do people study fossils?

5 **Test Practice** Trilobites are animals that
   A lived in forests, deserts, and farms
   B were hunted by humans
   C were sea creatures that lived millions of years ago
   D were related to mammoths

 Writing Link

Write a Report
Use research materials to learn about woolly mammoths. When did they live? What was their environment like? Write a report to share what you learn.

+6 Math Link

Estimate
The bottom layer of a fossil bed contained a trilobite that was 400 million years old. The top layer had a 300 million year old trilobite. In between the two layers was a third layer that contained a fish fossil. What would you estimate the age of the fish to be?

Looking at DINOSAURS

Dinosaurs were once common on Earth. Many dinosaurs became extinct millions of years ago. New evidence is helping scientists to find out how these dinosaurs lived and why they might have disappeared. Take a look at how our ideas about dinosaurs have changed based on new evidence.

1842

1923

1995

Dinosaurs Don't Drag Their Tails

The *T. rex* skeleton at the American Museum of Natural History is changed to show the predator standing on two feet with its head low and tail off the ground. This is based on studies of fossils, dinosaur tracks, and how different animals move.

Dinosaurs Are Named

British scientist Richard Owen names the group of large, extinct reptiles "dinosauria," from Greek words meaning "fearfully great lizard." Before that, people thought these strange bones came from dragons or giants!

Dinosaur Nests Are Found

American scientists Roy Chapman Andrews and Walter Granger find dinosaur nests in the Gobi desert in China. The nests prove that dinosaurs laid eggs and did not give birth to live babies.

AMERICAN MUSEUM OF NATURAL HISTORY

ELA R 3.2.3. Demonstrate comprehension by identifying answers in the text.

Dinosaurs Have Feathers

A team of Chinese and American scientists finds a 130-million-year-old fossil dinosaur covered from head to tail with primitive feathers. Now most scientists agree that birds are living dinosaurs!

Cause and effect

▶ The *cause* tells why something happened.

▶ The *effect* is what happened because of the cause.

▶ Clue words such as *because*, *if*, *then*, and *in order* describe a cause-and-effect relationship.

2000

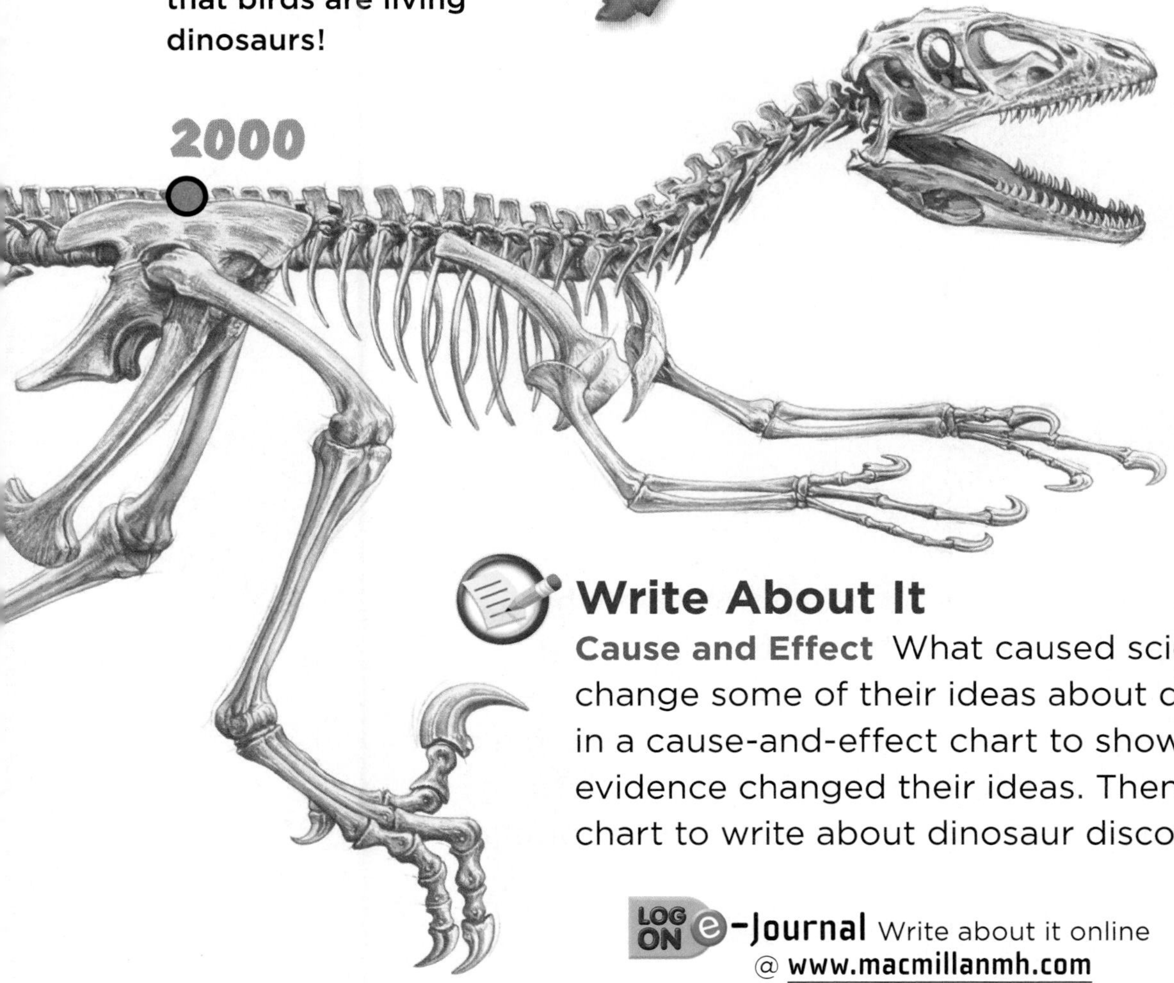

Scientists continue to find new fossils and use new tools to discover more about dinosaurs.

Write About It

Cause and Effect What caused scientists to change some of their ideas about dinosaurs? Fill in a cause-and-effect chart to show how new evidence changed their ideas. Then use your chart to write about dinosaur discoveries.

LOG ON e-Journal Write about it online
@ **www.macmillanmh.com**

Amber Fossils

Millions of years ago, an insect landed on some tree resin. Because the resin was sticky, the insect became trapped. As more resin oozed from the tree, it covered the insect. Over time, the resin became hard and turned into amber. The insect was preserved in the amber. By looking at insects preserved in amber, scientists can see what insects from the past looked like.

An expository paragraph

▶ has a topic sentence that tells the main idea

▶ includes facts and details that back up the main idea

▶ uses connecting words such as *because*, *therefore*, *so*, and *as a result* to go from one idea to the next

▶ draws a conclusion based on facts

◀ **This is an insect fossil preserved in amber.**

 ## Write About It

Expository Writing Write a paragraph. Tell what scientists can learn from looking at footprints of animals that lived long ago. Include facts and details. Use words such as *because* and *so* to go from one idea to the next. At the end of your paragraph, tell what conclusions scientists can draw from looking at fossil footprints.

 @-Journal Write about it online @ **www.macmillanmh.com**

 ELA W 3.1.1. Create a single paragraph:
a. Develop a topic sentence.
b. Include simple supporting facts and details.

Using Expanded Notation

Some kinds of animals that are alive today could become extinct. The California condors were saved from extinction. Scientists worked to find ways to help them survive.

Look at the information in the chart. It shows some species that have been saved from extinction.

How to use expanded notation

▶ First, identify the place value for each digit.

▶ Then, write out each value in an addition sentence.

The increase in snow leopards is 5,105. Written in expanded notation:
5,105 = 5,000 + 100 + 0 + 5

The increase in California condors is 183. Written in expanded notation:
183 = 100 + 80 + 3

Name of Animal	Year of Original Count	Original Count	2005
snow leopard	1960	1,000	6,105
California condor	1986	17	200
California bighorn sheep	1995	100	250
giant panda	1965	1,000	1,817
humpback whale	1966	20,000	35,105

 Solve It

Find out the population of students at your school. Write the number in expanded notation. Then find out if the population has increased or decreased since last year. Write the difference in expanded notation.

▲ California condor

 MA NS 3.1.5. Use expanded notation to represent numbers (e.g., 3,206=3,000+200+6).

Summarize the Main Ideas

Living things change the environment in ways that may be helpful or harmful. (pp. 130–137)

When their environment changes, living things may be harmed. Some survive through changes, others die. (pp. 140–149)

Some living things become extinct when their environment changes quickly. We can learn about them by studying fossils. (pp. 152–161)

Make a **FOLDABLES**™ Study Guide

Tape your lesson study guides on a piece of paper as shown. Use your study guide to review what you have learned.

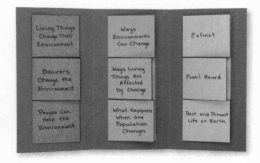

Fill each blank with the best word from the list.

community, p. 146   **fossil**, p. 156

competition, p. 132   **pollution**, p. 136

ecosystem, p. 146   **population**, p. 146

extinct, p. 154   **recycle**, p. 136

1. All the living and nonliving things that share an environment are part of an _____. 3 LS 3.d

2. When living things struggle for the resources they need, _____ occurs. 3 LS 3.c

3. Prairie dogs are a _____ found in some prairie ecosystems. 3 LS 3.d

4. When harmful materials get into air, water, or land, _____ happens. 3 LS 3.c

5. A _____ is the remains of a living thing that lived long ago. 3 LS 3.e

6. All the living things in an ecosystem make up a _____. 3 LS 3.d

7. When a group of organisms die out, they become _____. 3 LS 3.e

8. When you make something new from old things, you _____. 3 LS 3.c

LOG ON **e-Review** Summaries and quizzes online @ **www.macmillanmh.com**

Discuss or write about each of the following.

9. **Cause and Effect** What might have caused the animal shown in the photo to become extinct? 3 LS 3.e

woolly mammoth

10. **Persuasive Writing** A builder wants to cut down a forest to make room for a mall. Write a letter to the builder explaining how his actions will harm the environment. 3 LS 3.c

11. **Record Data** Suppose you were studying how changes in watering holes affect animal populations. Describe how you would obtain and record your data. 3 LS 3.d

watering hole

12. **Critical Thinking** What are two things that might happen when a population cannot meet its needs from its environment? 3 LS 3.d

Answer each of the following in a complete sentence.

13. How can a beaver's dam both help and harm the environment? 3 LS 3.c

14. What are three ways that people can help the environment? 3 LS 3.c

15. How might the change shown in the photo affect plants and animals that live in the environment? 3 LS 3.d

flood

16. Why do we study fossils? 3 LS 3.e

 How do changes to environments affect living things? 3 LS 3

CHAPTER 3

Make a Postage Stamp

- Design a postage stamp about the environment. You can use the 3 *R*s, or draw an ecosystem, animal, or plant that needs to be protected.

- Write a notice for your local newspaper, introducing the stamp.

- Tell why people should protect the environment.

168

1 Some dinosaur fossils have structures that look like wings. What might you infer about these animals? 3 LS 3.e

A They lived in water.

B They could fly.

C They were large.

D They ate fish.

2 Competition is a struggle for resources. Which three resources do living things compete for? 3 LS 3.c

A food, water, and space

B food, water, and air

C food, water, and fuel

D space, air, and fuel

3 Mrs. Carroll's class studied worms. They did an experiment to test how much a worm ate in a week. The students got different results from their experiments. What should they do? 3 IE 5.a

A get new worms

B read more books about worms

C ask a gardener about worms

D do their experiment again

4 What would happen if prairie dogs were removed from a grassland? 3 LS 3.d

A Rabbits would have more places to make their homes.

B Coyotes would have more food.

C Eagles would have less food.

D The soil would have more nutrients.

5 Which environmental change is too slow to notice? 3 LS 3.c

A spiders spinning a web across leaves

B birds gathering materials and building a nest

C bacteria breaking down leaves

D a squirrel hiding an acorn

6 In the drawing of a rain forest below, trees have been cut down.

What will happen on the forest floor? 3 LS 3.d

A There will be no change.

B Animals will not notice a change.

C New plants will grow in the sunlight.

D Roots of vines will grow up the new trees.

7 Which of the following is an example of a present-day animal and an ancient animal that look alike? 3 LS 3.e

A a mammoth and a tiger

B a hummingbird and an eagle

C an elephant and a mammoth

D a dragon and a lizard

Once Upon a Woodpecker

Tap! Rap-tap-tap! Do you hear that drumming sound? Oh, look, there's a woodpecker tapping on that dead tree. Let's move closer for a better look. If we're quiet, we can watch the woodpecker at work.

Woodpeckers have some amazing adaptations that help them survive. See how hard the bird is hammering on the tree trunk? Strong muscles in its neck put power behind each blow. These muscles also work as shock absorbers, so the woodpecker doesn't get a headache!

A pileated woodpecker hammers on a tree trunk. ▶

Can you see the woodpecker's toes? Unlike most birds, a woodpecker has two toes pointing forward and two toes pointing backward. That helps it hold onto the side of a tree. The woodpecker gets an even better grip by propping its stiff tail feathers against the trunk.

Watch how the woodpecker stops and tilts its head. It's listening for the sounds of insects inside the tree. It uses its strong beak to chop a hole and find a tunnel an insect has made. But how will it get that tasty snack out of the tunnel? The woodpecker sticks out its extra-long tongue to spear the insect. A barb on the tip of its tongue works like a fishhook to reel in the meal. Look out, bugs! You can't hide from the well-adapted woodpecker.

▲ A pileated woodpecker listens for the sounds of insects inside the tree.

▲ A pileated woodpecker spears insects with its tongue.

 3 LS 3 Adaptations in physical structure or behavior may improve an organism's chance for survival. **ELA R 3.2.5.** Distinguish the main idea and supporting details in expository text.

Careers in Science

Wildlife Manager

Do you like to learn about plants and animals? Do you want to help keep environments clean and healthy? Then one day you might become a wildlife manager.

Wildlife managers help take care of animals and their environments. They keep track of the plants and animals in places such as wildlife sanctuaries. They look for ways to help wildlife. They also teach people about wildlife and why it is important to take care of environments.

To become a wildlife manager, you must care about environments and living things. Plan to study science in high school and college. You will also need a degree in a field such as biology or environmental science.

▲ Animal rescue workers measure a Tasmanian devil.

▲ A park ranger places a satellite collar on a polar bear to track its movements.

Here are some other Life Science careers:
- veterinarian or veterinary technician
- emergency medical technician
- animal rescue worker
- florist
- park ranger

LOG ON e-Careers @ www.macmillanmh.com

Chapter 4

Chapter 5

Earth Science

The Sun is the only star in our solar system.

Our Earth, Sun, and Moon

 How do Earth and the Moon move through space?

Lesson 1

Day and Night

PAGE 178

Lesson 2

The Seasons

PAGE 188

Lesson 3

The Moon

PAGE 198

 3 ES 4. Objects in the sky move in regular and predictable patterns.

Literature
Poem

ELA R 3.3.5. Recognize the similarities of sounds in words and rhythmic patterns (e.g., alliteration, onomatopoeia) in a selection. **ELA W 3.2.2.** Write descriptions that use concrete sensory details to present and support unified impressions of people, places, things, or experiences.

The Sun

and the Moon

by Elaine Laron

▲ moonrise in Joshua Tree National Park

The Sun is filled with shining light
It blazes far and wide
The Moon reflects the sunlight back
But has no light inside.

I think I'd rather be the Sun
That shines so bold and bright
Than be the Moon that only glows
With someone else's light.

 Write About It

Response to Literature The poet uses rhyme, rhythm, and vivid words to tell how she feels about the Sun and Moon. Write a poem about the Sun and Moon. Show how they are different. Use words that create a strong impression and show how you feel.

LOG ON **e-Journal** Write about it online @ **www.macmillanmh.com**

sunset in the Serengeti

Day and Night

Look and Wonder

Have you ever watched the Sun rise? Bright light appears on the horizon. Slowly, the Sun rises and night becomes morning. The Sun's light casts long shadows. How do shadows change during the day?

3 ES 4.e. Students know the position of the Sun in the sky changes during the course of the day and from season to season.

How do shadows change?

Form a Hypothesis

How does the location of the Sun in the sky affect the length of shadows on the ground? How does it affect the position of the shadows? Write a hypothesis.

Test Your Hypothesis

1 Work in pairs outside on a sunny morning. Use the chalk to mark an *X* on the ground. Have your partner stand on the *X*.

2 Trace your partner's shadow.

3 Measure Use the measuring tape to find the length of the shadow. Record your results in a table. Draw a sketch.

4 Predict How do you think the shadow will change during the day?

5 Observe Repeat steps 2 and 3 at midday and in the afternoon on the same spot. How does the shadow change?

Draw Conclusions

6 Compare Use the data in your table to answer these questions. When is the shadow very long? When is the shadow very short?

7 Infer What causes the shadows to change position and length?

Explore More

How can you find out in which month the Sun's position appears highest in the sky? Lowest?

 3 IE 5.d. Predict the outcome of a simple investigation and compare the result with the prediction.

Materials

chalk

measuring tape

Step **2**

| Step **3** | |
Time	Length of Shadow
Morning	
Midday	
Afternoon	

Main Idea 3 ES 4.e

The position of the Sun in the sky appears to change during the day. Earth's rotation causes day and night.

Vocabulary

horizon, p. 180

rotate, p. 182

axis, p. 184

sphere, p. 184

LOG ON e-Glossary

@ www.macmillanmh.com

Reading Skill

Summarize

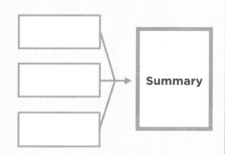

Technology

 Explore day and night with the Secret Agents.

The Sun seems to rise in the east and set in the west. Looking at these pictures, you are facing south. ▶

How does the Sun's position in the sky seem to change?

Each day the Sun seems to move across the sky in a giant arc. In the morning the Sun appears low on the eastern horizon (huh•RIGH•zuhn). At midday, it appears high overhead. In the evening, it appears low on the western horizon. The **horizon** is an imaginary line where the land seems to meet the sky.

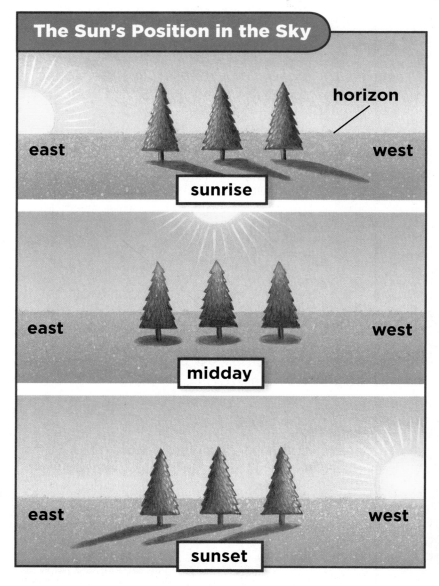

The Sun's Position in the Sky

horizon

east   west

sunrise

east   west

midday

east   west

sunset

▲ At midday, the Sun is high overhead and shadows are short.

▲ As the Sun begins to set, shadows get long.

The Sun and Shadows

Have you ever noticed how shadows change during the day? Sometimes they are long. At other times they are very short. Shadows change as the position of the Sun changes.

At midday the Sun is high overhead. The angle at which sunlight strikes Earth is greater than in the morning or evening. The Sun's light is more direct and shadows are very short. At sunrise and sunset, the angle at which sunlight strikes Earth is smaller. The Sun's light is less direct and shadows are very long.

 Quick Check

Summarize How does the Sun's position in the sky seem to change during the day?

Critical Thinking If you wanted to avoid direct sunlight, when should you stay indoors? Explain.

What causes night and day?

As you read this book, you are moving through space. You cannot feel Earth's movement. When you walk, the ground is still. Buildings and trees seem to stay still too. But you and all things on the surface of Earth are moving.

Earth rotates (ROH•tayts) like a giant top that is spinning in space. To **rotate** means to turn. It is the rotating of Earth that causes day and night. As Earth rotates, one side faces the Sun. That side of Earth has daytime. At the same time, the other side of Earth faces away from the Sun. That side of Earth has nighttime.

As Earth turns, the Sun's position seems to move in the sky. When you watch the Sun rise and set, what you see is caused by Earth's rotation. Earth rotates from the west to the east.

Every 24 hours, Earth makes one complete rotation. A full day is 24 hours long, or all of the daytime hours plus all of the nighttime hours.

Day and Night in San Francisco

Read a Diagram

Why is it daytime in California in the diagram on the left and nighttime on the right?

Clue: Look at Earth's position.

Sun

north

California

A Model of Earth

① **Make a Model**

⚠ **Be Careful.**
Push a pencil through a foam ball. The pencil represents Earth's axis. Press a paper clip into the side of the ball. The ball represents Earth. The paper clip represents you.

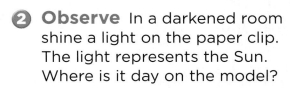

② **Observe** In a darkened room shine a light on the paper clip. The light represents the Sun. Where is it day on the model?

③ **Experiment** Show how Earth rotates by turning the pencil. What happens to the light on the paper clip? Where is it day on the model? Where is it night?

④ **Communicate** How does this model help explain what you know about day and night?

✔ *Quick Check*

Summarize Why does Earth have day and night?

Critical Thinking Compare the two pictures of San Francisco. How does day change into night?

What is an axis?

Have you ever seen a ball spinning on a fingertip? Think of a line drawn from the fingertip to the top of the ball. The line would be straight up and down. The ball spins around this line. This line is called an **axis** (AX•is). An axis is a real or imaginary line through the center of a spinning object.

Earth is shaped like a ball. This shape is called a **sphere** (SFEER). Earth also spins on an imaginary axis. As you can see here, Earth's axis is not straight up and down. It is slightly tilted. The North Pole is at the north end of Earth's axis. The South Pole is at the south end.

 Quick Check

Summarize Describe Earth's axis.

Critical Thinking What if you put a pencil through a ball to model Earth and its axis? How is the model like the real thing? How is it different?

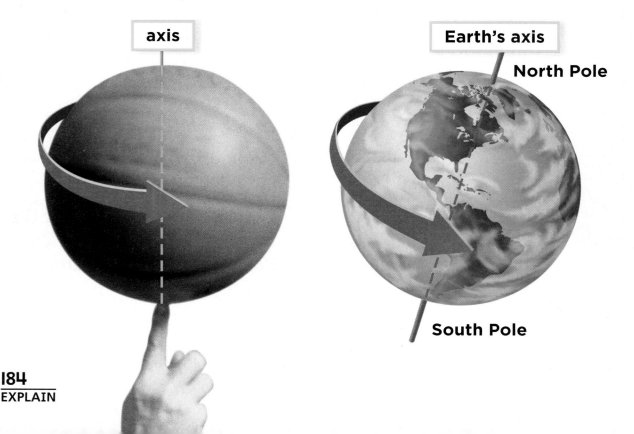

axis

Earth's axis

North Pole

South Pole

Lesson Review

Summarize the Main Idea

Shadows change as the **position of the Sun** in the sky appears to change. (pp. 180–181)

Earth's **rotation** causes day and night. (pp. 182–183)

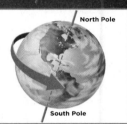
Earth spins on its **axis**, the imaginary line through its center. (p. 184)

Make a FOLDABLES™ Study Guide

Make a three-tab book. Use it to summarize what you learned.

Think, Talk, and Write

1 **Main Idea** Why does the position of the Sun in the sky seem to change?

2 **Vocabulary** What does it mean to *rotate*?

3 **Summarize** How long is a day? Describe the motion of Earth that makes up one day.

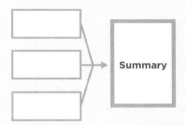

4 **Critical Thinking** If it is 9:00 A.M. in California, is it the same time, later, or earlier in New York? Why? Use a model to explain your answer.

5 **Test Practice** What causes day and night?

   A The Sun rotates on its axis.

   B Earth rotates on its axis.

   C Earth moves around the Sun.

   D The Sun moves around Earth.

Math Link

Solve a Problem
How many times has Earth rotated in your lifetime? Explain how you could solve this problem. Then try to solve it. You can use a calculator to help.

Health Link

Conduct an Interview
Ultraviolet light (UV) from the Sun causes skin to tan or burn. Interview adult family members to find out how they protect their skin from the Sun. Write down what they tell you.

x

Analyze Data

Have you ever noticed that some days seem longer than others? This happens because the Sun rises and sets at different times on different days. Some days seem longer because they have more hours of daylight than others. How did scientists figure this out? One way is to **analyze data** from past years.

① Learn It

When you **analyze data**, you use information that has been gathered to answer questions or solve problems. It is easier to analyze the data if it has been organized and placed on a chart or a graph. That way you can quickly see differences in the data.

② Try It

You learned that scientists **analyze data**. Scientists collect information about sunrise and sunset in certain places. They use the data to figure out the number of daylight hours we have at different times of the year. You can organize and analyze their data to draw conclusions, too.

Average Sunrise and Sunset Data for Los Angeles, California			
Month	Sunrise	Sunset	Approximate Hours of Daylight
January	6:59 A.M.	5:07 P.M.	10
March	6:04 A.M.	6:01 P.M.	12
May	5:52 A.M.	7:48 P.M.	14
July	5:53 A.M.	8:05 P.M.	14
September	6:37 A.M.	7:00 P.M.	$12\frac{1}{2}$
November	6:27 A.M.	4:50 P.M.	$10\frac{1}{2}$

3 IE 5.e. Collect data in an investigation and analyze those data to develop a logical conclusion.

First, organize the data by making a bar graph. Use the graph to show the number of daylight hours there are in each month. Follow these steps to make your bar graph.

▶ List the months along the bottom of the graph. Write the numbers along the left side of the graph.

▶ Draw a bar to match each of the numbers from the data.

▶ Write a title for the graph and label the sides. Use the column headings of the chart to help you.

Now you can use the bar graph to analyze the data. About how many hours of daylight will there be tomorrow? Explain.

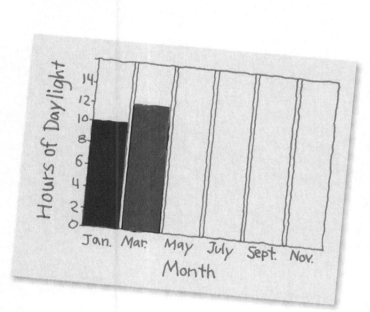

❸ Apply It

It is your turn to **analyze data**. Measure the air temperature every hour for one day. Begin at 8 A.M. and end at 6 P.M. Record your data in a chart. Use the data chart to make a bar graph.

Now you can use your bar graph to analyze your data. When during the day is the air temperature the warmest? When is the air temperature the coolest?

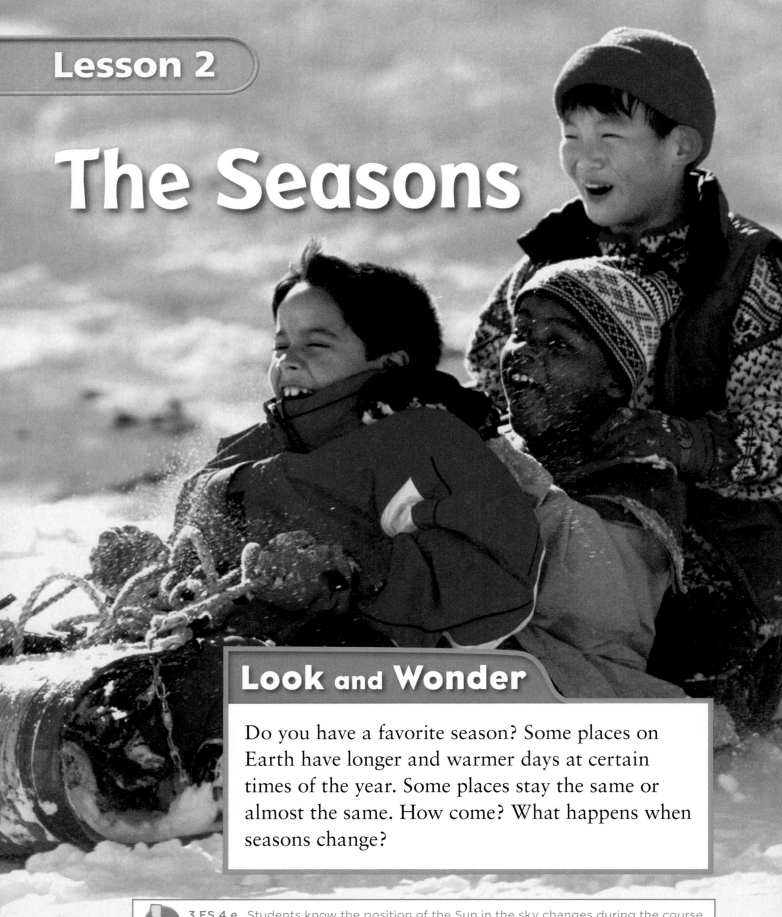

The Seasons

Look and Wonder

Do you have a favorite season? Some places on Earth have longer and warmer days at certain times of the year. Some places stay the same or almost the same. How come? What happens when seasons change?

 3 ES 4.e. Students know the position of the Sun in the sky changes during the course of the day and from season to season.

What happens when seasons change?

Make a Prediction

What happens to the length of shadows as the seasons change? Write a prediction.

Test Your Prediction

Materials

globe

small lump of clay

drinking straw

lamp

1 Make a Model Stick the clay on the globe over California. Stand the straw up in the clay.

Step 1

2 Your teacher will place the lamp in the center of a darkened room so the light hits the middle of the globe. The lamp represents the Sun.

3 Experiment The globe represents Earth. Hold Earth and walk around the Sun. Tip Earth to show its tilted axis. Keep the tilt pointed in the same direction. Keep the straw pointed at the Sun as Earth moves around the Sun.

4 Observe How does the amount of light hitting your part of Earth change? What happens to the length of the straw's shadow as the globe moves?

Draw Conclusions

5 Analyze Data Where was the shadow shortest? Where was it longest?

6 Infer Where was the light most direct?

Step 3

Explore More

How do you think this model might help explain the changing seasons?

 3 IE 5.d. Predict the outcome of a simple investigation and compare the result with the prediction.

Read and Learn

> **Main Idea** 3 ES 4.e
>
> Earth's tilted axis and orbit around the Sun causes the seasons. The position of the Sun in the sky seems to change from season to season.

> **Vocabulary**
>
> **revolve**, p. 190
>
> **orbit**, p. 190
>
> **equator**, p. 194

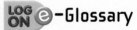
LOG ON e-Glossary
@ www.macmillanmh.com

> **Reading Skill**
>
> **Cause and Effect**

Cause → Effect

Why do seasons change?

You learned that Earth rotates around its axis. This is not the only way Earth moves in space. It also revolves (ri•VOLVZ). An object that moves around another object **revolves**. Earth travels, or revolves, in a regular path around the Sun. This path is called Earth's **orbit** (AWR•bit). It takes Earth one year, or about 365 days, to complete one orbit around the Sun.

Seasons change as Earth rotates and revolves around the Sun because of Earth's tilted axis. Look at the diagram. No matter where Earth is in its orbit, its axis is always tilted in the same direction.

Earth Revolves Around the Sun

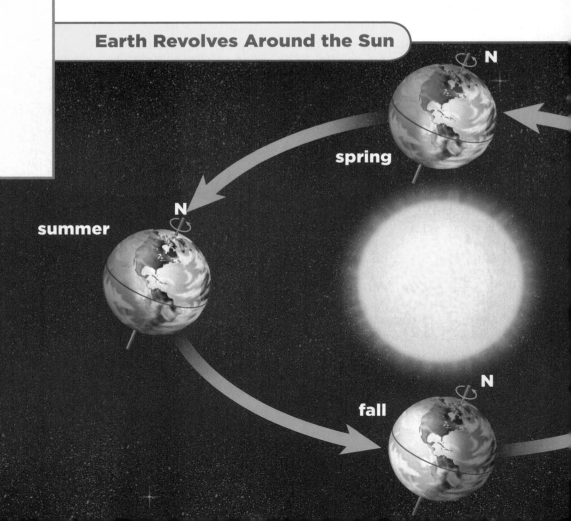

spring

summer

fall

In June, the North Pole is tilted toward the Sun. This means sunlight is more direct. More of the Sun's energy reaches the North Pole. Days are longer. Temperatures are warmer. It is summer there.

By December, Earth has moved to a different position in its orbit. Now the North Pole is tilted away from the Sun. Less direct sunlight and less energy reach the North Pole. Days are shorter and temperatures are cooler. It is winter there. The South Pole is now tilted toward the Sun. It is summer there.

✅ **Quick Check**

Cause and Effect Why do seasons change?

Critical Thinking How would seasons change if Earth took longer to revolve around the Sun?

spring (begins March 20–21)

summer (begins June 21–22)

fall (begins September 22–23)

winter (begins December 21–22)

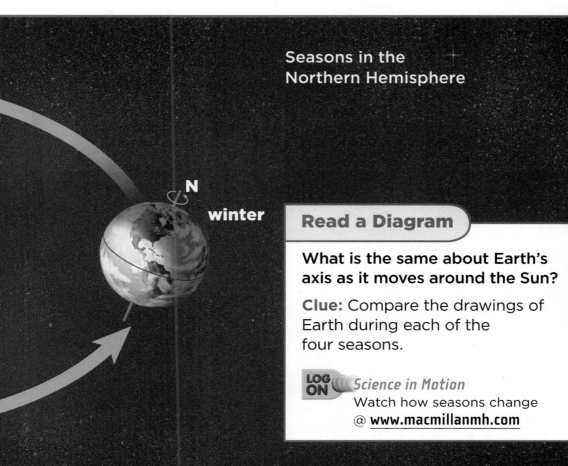

Seasons in the Northern Hemisphere

N winter

Read a Diagram

What is the same about Earth's axis as it moves around the Sun?

Clue: Compare the drawings of Earth during each of the four seasons.

LOG ON *Science in Motion*
Watch how seasons change @ **www.macmillanmh.com**

How does the Sun's path change from season to season?

You learned that on a single day, the Sun appears to rise and follow a path across the horizon. Day, night, and changing shadows are caused by Earth's rotation.

The Sun's position also seems to change from season to season. When it is summer in California, the Sun is high overhead at noon. That is because the northern half of Earth is tilted toward the Sun. This tilt makes the Sun's path seem higher in the sky.

When it is winter in California, the path of the Sun appears low in the sky. California is tilted away from the Sun. The Sun at noon is lower. The southern half of Earth is tilted toward the Sun.

Path of the Sun in Summer and Winter

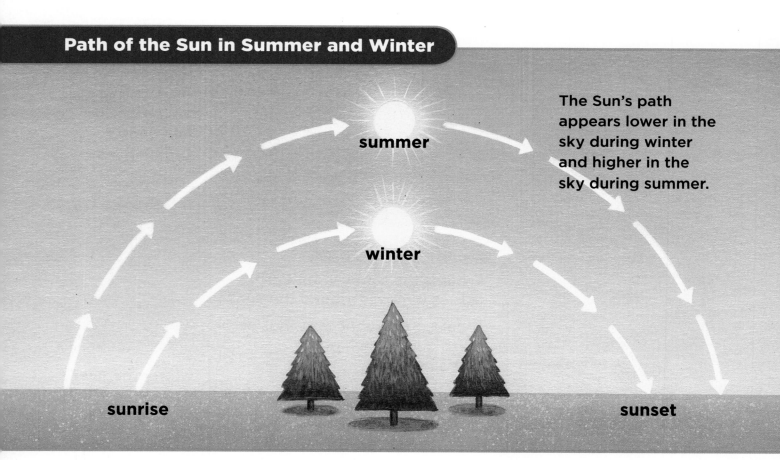

summer

winter

The Sun's path appears lower in the sky during winter and higher in the sky during summer.

sunrise

sunset

In the spring and fall, the path of the Sun is in between high and low. In the spring days are growing longer, and temperatures are higher in California. In the fall days are growing shorter and temperatures are lower in California.

✓ Quick Check

Cause and Effect What causes the Sun to appear higher in the sky during the summer?

Critical Thinking When it is winter in the Southern Hemisphere, does the Sun's path appear high or low? Explain.

≡ Quick Lab

Sunset Times

1 Use research materials to find the average time of sunset for each month where you live.

2 Record this information in a chart.

3 **Draw Conclusions** During which month is sunset the latest? The earliest?

Month	Time of Sunset
January	
February	
March	
April	
May	

El Capitan, Yosemite National Park, California

▲ During the summer, temperatures are warmer, and there are more hours of daylight. It is still daytime at 4 P.M. in California.

▲ During the winter, temperatures are cooler, and there are fewer hours of daylight. At 4 P.M. in California, the Sun is already setting.

What are the seasons like in other places?

The **equator** (ee•KWAY•tuhr) is an imaginary line around the middle of Earth. It separates Earth into two parts. The top part is the Northern Hemisphere. The bottom part is the Southern Hemisphere.

Places near the equator have about the same temperature most of the year. That is because the Sun stays high in the sky all year. Here the Sun's rays are stronger and the temperature is higher. Places farther away from the equator have different seasons. Places closest to the poles have cold weather for most of the year.

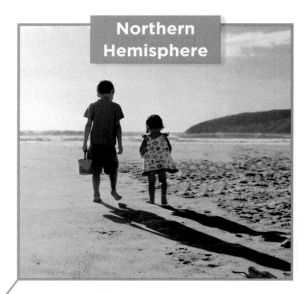

▲ June in California

▲ June near the equator

▲ June in Argentina

✓ Quick Check

Cause and Effect What causes places near the equator to have the same temperature most of the year?

Critical Thinking Why are the seasons in places further from the equator different from the seasons at the equator?

Lesson Review

Summarize the Main Idea

Seasons change because Earth has a tilted axis and it **revolves** around the Sun. (pp. 190–191)

The **Sun's path** in the sky seems to change from season to season. (pp. 192–193)

The **seasons** are different in different places on Earth. (p. 194)

Make a FOLDABLES™ Study Guide

Make a two-tab book. Use it to summarize what you learned.

Think, Talk, and Write

1 **Main Idea** Describe how the seasons change.

2 **Vocabulary** How are rotating and revolving different?

3 **Cause and Effect** What causes the long cold winters at the poles?

Cause	→	Effect

4 **Critical Thinking** How would the seasons be different if Earth were not tilted on its axis?

5 **Test Practice** What season is it in California when the northern half of Earth is tilted toward the Sun?
  A fall
  B spring
  C summer
  D winter

 Writing Link

Write a Report
Some children live where there is almost 24 hours of daylight in the summer, and almost 24 hours of darkness in the winter. Where on Earth would this be? Write a list of questions you would ask if you could interview one of these children. Do research to find the answers.

 Math Link

Solve a Problem
You learned that Earth's tilted axis, as it orbits around the Sun, causes the four seasons. If each season is about the same number of months, about how many months long is each season? How can you tell?

Seasons Where You Live

You have learned about the seasons. Now think about what the seasons are like in California. Do the seasons have different kinds of weather? Does it snow in the winter? Is it hot in the summer? Think about the things you do during the different seasons.

A good personal narrative

▶ tells a story from the writer's personal experience

▶ expresses the writer's feelings

▶ tells events in an order that makes sense

 Write About It

Personal Narrative Choose a season. Tell a true story about something you did during that season. Explain why you still remember the event. How did it make you feel? Describe what the weather was like. Remember to tell the events in an order that makes sense.

 **e-Journal** Write about it online @ **www.macmillanmh.com**

ELA W 3.2.1. Write narratives:
a. Provide a context within which an action takes place.
b. Include well-chosen details to develop the plot.
c. Provide insight into why the selected incident is memorable.

Converting Hours of Daylight

Days are longer in the summer in the Northern Hemisphere. They are shorter in the winter. Look at the chart below. It shows how long the longest day is in San Francisco. It tells how short the shortest day is.

How to convert hours

▶ First decide if you are converting hours into minutes or seconds.

▶ Then, multiply the hours by the number of minutes or seconds there are in one hour. Remember there are 60 minutes in one hour. There are 3,600 seconds in one hour.

▶ Here's an example: 5 hours x 60 minutes/hour = 300 minutes

Longest and Shortest Day in San Francisco	
Date	Approximate hours of daylight
June 21st	15
December 21st	10

Solve It

How long is the longest day in San Francisco in minutes? How long is the shortest day in minutes? What is the difference in minutes between the longest day and the shortest day?

MA MG 3.1.4. Carry out simple unit conversions within a system of measurement (e.g., centimeters and meters, hours and minutes).

197
EXTEND

Lesson 3

The Moon

San Francisco, California

Look and Wonder

Sometimes the Moon looks like a glowing ball. A few weeks later, all you see is a thin sliver. What happened? How does the shape of the Moon appear to change during one week?

 3 ES 4.b. Students know the way in which the Moon's appearance changes during the four-week lunar cycle. •**3 ES 4.d.** Students know Earth is one of several planets that orbit the Sun and that the Moon orbits Earth.

How does the Moon's shape seem to change?

Make a Prediction

How will the Moon's appearance change during a week? Write a prediction.

 Step 1

Test Your Prediction

1 Observe Look at the Moon just after sunset each night for one week.

2 Record Draw the Moon as you see it each night. Also draw where it is in the sky. Label the picture with the day of the week.

Draw Conclusions

3 Analyze Data How does the Moon's shape seem to change each night? How does its location seem to change?

4 Predict What will the Moon's shape be like for the next few nights?

Step 2

Day	Observation
Monday	
Tuesday	
Wednesday	
Thursday	
Friday	

Explore More

Does the Moon rise and set at the same time each night? Make a plan to test your ideas.

 3 IE 5.d. Predict the outcome of a simple investigation and compare the result with the prediction.

What are the phases of the Moon?

Each day the Moon seems to change shape. Sometimes you can only see a small part of the Moon. At other times it is a big bright circle. Still other times you cannot see it at all. Each shape that we see is called a **phase** (FAYZ). Scientists have names for each phase of the Moon. The photos on this page show the eight main phases of the Moon. Have you seen the Moon in each of these phases? In which phase was the Moon last night?

As we see more of the Moon's lit surface, we say the Moon is a waxing (WAKS•ing) moon. **Waxing** means that something is getting bigger. As we see less of the lit surface of the Moon, we say the Moon is a waning (WAYN•ing) moon. **Waning** means that something is getting smaller. A waxing or waning *gibbous* moon is almost full.

Phases of the Moon

new Moon	crescent Moon	first quarter Moon	waxing gibbous Moon

You cannot see the Moon during this phase.	The lighted side of the Moon begins to show.	This is sometimes called a half Moon.	A gibbous Moon is almost full.

▲ This is how you see the Moon with your eyes.

▲ You can see many more details of the Moon through binoculars.

 Quick Check

Sequence What phase of the Moon comes before the new Moon?

Critical Thinking Compare waxing and waning. How are they alike? How are they different?

full Moon

You can see all of the Moon's lighted side.

waning gibbous Moon

This gibbous Moon is getting smaller.

last quarter Moon

The Moon continues to get smaller.

crescent Moon

The lighted side has almost disappeared.

Make a Moon Phase Flip Book

1. Write the name of one of the eight Moon phases on the left side of each index card. See example below.

2. Draw what each phase looks like on the right side of each card.

3. Put the cards in order and staple the book together on the left side.

4. Flip the pages with your thumb to see the Moon's shape change.

5. How is this model of the Moon's phases like the real thing?

First quarter D

Why does the Moon's shape seem to change?

Like Earth, the Moon is shaped like a ball, or sphere. The Moon's shape does not change. It is always a sphere. Why then does the Moon look different each night?

The Moon, like Earth, moves through space. The Moon orbits Earth, much like Earth orbits the Sun. The Moon's shape seems to change because of this orbit. Look at the diagram. One half of the Moon faces the Sun. This half is lighted by the Sun. The other half faces away from the Sun and is in darkness. The Moon does not make its own light. As the Moon orbits Earth, we see different parts of its lighted half. These lighted parts are the different shapes, or phases, we see.

It takes the Moon about four weeks to orbit Earth. During this time it passes through all of its phases. The four-week cycle of changing phases is called the **lunar cycle** (LEW•nuhr SIGH•kuhl).

Like the Sun, the Moon seems to rise, move across the sky, and set. This happens because of Earth's rotation around its axis.

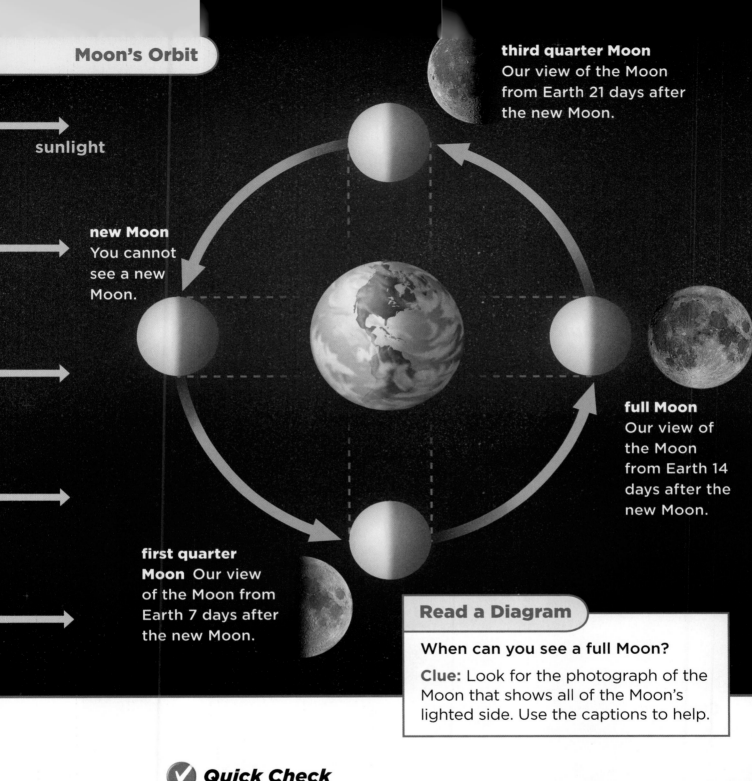

third quarter Moon
Our view of the Moon from Earth 21 days after the new Moon.

sunlight

new Moon
You cannot see a new Moon.

full Moon
Our view of the Moon from Earth 14 days after the new Moon.

first quarter Moon Our view of the Moon from Earth 7 days after the new Moon.

Read a Diagram

When can you see a full Moon?

Clue: Look for the photograph of the Moon that shows all of the Moon's lighted side. Use the captions to help.

✔ **Quick Check**

Sequence Identify the four main phases the Moon passes through during a lunar cycle.

Critical Thinking How can you predict what the shape of the Moon will be tomorrow? Next week?

What is a lunar eclipse?

Have you ever tried to watch television when someone is standing between you and the screen? Sometimes Earth can be like that person. It gets between the Sun and the Moon. It blocks sunlight from reaching the Moon. Look at the diagram below. Earth's shadow is falling on the Moon. When this happens there is a **lunar eclipse** (LEW•nuhr ee•KLIPS). During a lunar eclipse, the Moon moves into Earth's shadow.

 Quick Check

Sequence What happens during a lunar eclipse?

Critical Thinking Can the Sun ever move between Earth and the Moon? Why or why not?

Moon During a Lunar Eclipse

Sun

Earth's shadow

Earth   Moon

◀ When Earth is between the Moon and the Sun, a lunar eclipse occurs.

Lesson Review

Summarize the Main Idea

The changing shapes we see of the Moon are called **phases**. (pp. 200–201)

The Moon's **shape** seems to change because we see different amounts of its lit side. (pp. 202–203)

A lunar **eclipse** occurs when the Moon moves into Earth's shadow. (p. 204)

Make a FOLDABLES™ Study Guide

Make a two-tab book. Use it to summarize what you learned about the Moon.

Phases and the Moon's orbit

Lunar Eclipse

Think, Talk, and Write

1 **Main Idea** Why does the Moon appear to change shape?

2 **Vocabulary** What is a phase of the Moon?

3 **Sequence** List the eight main phases that the Moon passes through during a lunar cycle.

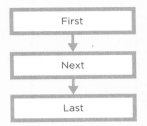

First
↓
Next
↓
Last

4 **Critical Thinking** The Moon is like a ball. Can a ball look like a different shape without actually changing its shape? Explain your answer.

5 **Test Practice** What do we call the phase of the Moon when the Moon's lit side faces away from Earth?

A a full Moon

B a new Moon

C a month

D a crescent Moon

 Writing Link

Write a Story
Write a science-fiction story about what it would be like to live on the Moon. Include characters, a setting, and a sequence of events with a problem that is solved at the end. Share your story with an audience.

 Social Studies Link

Conduct Research
Twenty-seven astronauts have been on, or near, the Moon. Twelve of them have landed and actually walked on the Moon. Do research to find out more about one of these astronauts. Share your findings with the class.

Be a Scientist

Materials

lamp

ball

Why does the Moon's shape appear to change?

Form a Hypothesis

The Moon completes one orbit around Earth every 28 days. How does the Moon's position in space affect how we see the Moon? When do we see a full Moon? When do we see a third-quarter Moon? Write a hypothesis.

Test Your Hypothesis

1 Make a Model Hold the ball and stretch out your arm in front of you. Position your arm so that the ball is a little higher than your head. The ball is the Moon, and your head is Earth.

2 Observe Your teacher will turn on a lamp. The lamp represents the Sun. Turn your back to the light so that the light is shining on the ball. What part of the ball is lit up?

3 Experiment Turn in place while holding the ball. Keep the ball in front of you. Notice the change in light and shadow on the ball.

4 Record Data Record your observations by drawing or describing what you see as you turn.

5 Repeat the experiment several times. Are your observations the same with each trial?

Step 2

Draw Conclusions

6 Analyze Data Where is the ball when it is lit up like a full Moon? Where is the ball when it looks like a half Moon?

7 Infer Why does the Moon's shape appear to change? How do you know?

Inquiry Guided

How does the Moon's position change?

Form a Hypothesis

How does the Moon's position change in the night sky? Write a hypothesis.

Test Your Hypothesis

Design a plan to test your hypothesis. Remember your plan should test only one variable—the Moon's position in the sky. Decide on the materials you will need. Then write the steps you plan to follow.

Draw Conclusions

Did your results support your hypothesis? Why or why not? Share your results with your classmates.

Inquiry Open

What other questions do you have about the Moon? Talk with your classmates about questions you have. How might you find the answers to your questions?

Remember to follow the steps of the scientific process.

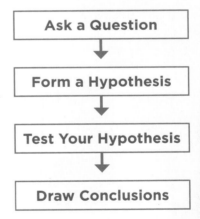

Ask a Question
↓
Form a Hypothesis
↓
Test Your Hypothesis
↓
Draw Conclusions

 3 IE 5.a. Repeat observations to improve accuracy and know that the results of similar scientific investigations seldom turn out exactly the same because of differences in the things being investigated, methods being used, or uncertainty in the observation.

TO THE MOON!

Do you ever wonder about the Moon? How do we learn what the Moon is actually like? First, people used their eyes to observe the Moon. Then they developed tools like telescopes. Then astronauts (and robots) went up to the Moon to study it up close.

1957 *Sputnik I* is the first spacecraft to travel into space.

1959 *Luna 1* is the first spacecraft to land on the Moon. It sends pictures back to Earth. This is the first time anyone can see what the far side of the Moon looks like.

 ELA R 3.2.6. Extract appropriate and significant information from the text, including problems and solutions.

NASA plans to send expeditions back to the Moon to learn more about it and what it takes to live in its extreme environment. ▼

A sequence

▶ gives events in order

▶ tells what happens first, next, and last

▶ uses time-order words, such as *first*, *next*, and *last*, to tell the order of events

1972 *Apollo 17* is the last manned mission to the Moon. The crew spent 75 hours there. Astronauts Gene Cernan and Harrison Schmitt drove a lunar roving vehicle around the surface of the Moon to collect samples.

1969 *Apollo 11* mission is the first to land a man on the Moon. Neil Armstrong and Buzz Aldrin are the first astronauts to walk on the Moon and collect Moon samples.

Write About It

Sequence of Events Use the time line to fill in a sequence-of-events chart. List how scientists gathered information about the Moon. Tell what happened first, next, and last. Then use your chart to write a summary about exploring the Moon.

 e-Journal Write about it online @ **www.macmillanmh.com**

Summarize the Main Ideas

Shadows change as the position of the Sun in the sky appears to change. Earth's rotation causes day and night. (pp. 178–185)

Seasons change because Earth has a tilted axis and it revolves around the Sun. (pp. 188–195)

The Moon appears to change shape because we see different amounts of its lighted side. The changing shapes are phases. (pp. 198–205)

Make a **FOLDABLES**™
Study Guide

Tape your lesson study guides on a piece of paper as shown. Use your study guide to review what you have learned in this chapter.

Fill each blank with the best word from the list.

axis, p. 184

equator, p. 194

lunar cycle, p. 202

lunar eclipse, p. 204

orbit, p. 190

phase, p. 200

revolves, p. 190

waning, p. 200

1. The _____ separates Earth into the Northern Hemisphere and the Southern Hemisphere. 3 ES 4.e

2. A _____ occurs when the Moon moves into Earth's shadow. 3 ES 4.b

3. A shape formed by the lit surface of the Moon that can be seen from Earth is called a _____. 3 ES 4.b

4. An object that _____ moves around another object. 3 ES 4.d

5. The Moon's four-week cycle of changing phases is called the _____. 3 ES 4.b

6. The Moon is _____ when we see less of its lit surface. 3 ES 4.b

7. A real or imaginary line through the center of a spinning object is an _____. 3 ES 4.e

8. Earth's _____ is the path it takes as it moves around the Sun. 3 ES 4.e

Discuss or write about each of the following.

9. Sequence What happens during a lunar eclipse? 3 ES 4.b

10. Explanatory Writing What causes day and night? 3 ES 4.e

11. Analyze Data The bar graph shows average monthly hours of daylight for six months in California. Which month has the fewest daylight hours? Which months have the most? 3 ES 4.e

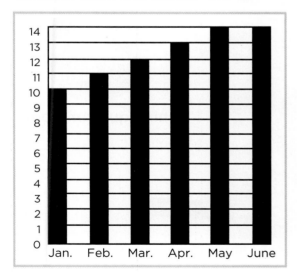

12. Critical Thinking If half of the Moon is always lit by the Sun, why don't we always see a full Moon? 3 ES 4.d

Answer each of the following in a complete sentence.

13. Why do the North and South Poles have different seasons on any given day? 3 ES 4.e

14. At what time of day is the Sun likely to be in this position? Give reasons for your answer. 3 ES 4.e

15. Why are temperatures in the Northern Hemisphere warmer in summer and cooler in winter? 3 ES 4.e

16. Which area of Earth most likely has the least change in summer and winter temperatures? Give reasons for your answer. 3 ES 4.e

 How do Earth and the Moon move through space? 3 ES 4

CHAPTER 4

Draw a Diagram

- Draw a diagram that shows how the orbit of the Moon around Earth causes the phases of the Moon.

- Include each of the four phases shown in the photos. Be sure to include Earth and the Sun.

- Label each phase of the Moon. Draw and label arrows to show when the Moon is waxing and when it is waning.

- Underneath your diagram, write the date when each phase would likely occur. Begin with the new Moon phase occurring on July 1.

Items to Include

first-quarter Moon

full Moon

new Moon

third-quarter Moon

1 Why is the weather warmer in California during the summer than in the winter? 3 ES 4.e

A Earth is closer to the Sun in summer.

B The Northern Hemisphere is tilted toward the Sun in summer.

C The Northern Hemisphere is tilted away from the Sun in summer.

D The Sun is hotter in the summer.

2 Why does the Moon appear to rise and set in the sky? 3 ES 4.b

A Earth moves around the Moon.

B The Moon moves around the Sun.

C The Moon moves across the sky.

D Earth rotates on its axis.

3 Which of the following best explains why the Sun appears to move across the sky each day? 3 ES 4.e

A Earth's rotation

B Earth's tilt on its axis

C Earth's distance from the Sun

D Earth's revolution

4 What would happen if Earth's axis were not tilted? 3 ES 4.e

A There would be only one season.

B There would be only two seasons.

C There would be seasons every other year.

D There would be four seasons.

5 The shape of the Moon looks like it is changing because 3 ES 4.b

A it is rotating around the Sun.

B it reflects light from the Sun in different positions around Earth.

C it is closer to Earth in summer and further away in winter.

D the rotation of Earth changes its size.

6 Look at the calendar showing the Moon's phases.

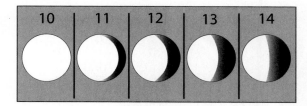

By observing, a student could predict 3 IE 5.e

A the time the Moon will rise the next day.

B what the clouds will look like the next day.

C the time the Sun will rise the next day.

D what the Moon will look like the next day.

7 Which of the following is a lunar-cycle sequence? 3 ES 4.b

A new Moon, full Moon, half Moon

B crescent Moon, half Moon, new Moon

C full Moon, new Moon, crescent Moon

D new Moon, half Moon, full Moon

CHAPTER 5

Our Solar System

What objects do we see in the night sky?

214

Lesson 1

The Sun and Its Planets

PAGE 218

Lesson 2

Telescopes: Discovering the Solar System

PAGE 228

Lesson 3

The Stars

PAGE 236

 3 ES 4. Objects in the sky move in regular and predictable patterns

215

Literature
Personal Narrative

ELA R 3.3.6. Identify the speaker or narrator in a selection. ELA W 3.2.1. Write narratives: **a.** Provide a context within which an action takes place. **b.** Include well-chosen details to develop the plot. **c.** Provide insight into why the selected incident is memorable.

space shuttle launch

To Space & Back

by Sally Ride with Susan Okie

3 . . . 2 . . . 1 . . .

The rockets light! The shuttle leaps off the launch pad in a cloud of steam and a trail of fire. Inside, the ride is rough and loud. . . . In only a few seconds we zoom past the clouds. Two minutes later the rockets burn out, and with a brilliant whitish-orange flash, they fall away from the shuttle as it streaks on toward space. Suddenly the ride becomes very, very smooth and quiet. . . .

Sally Ride

Launch plus eight and one-half minutes. The launch engines cut off. Suddenly the force is gone, and we lurch forward in our seats. During the next few minutes the empty fuel tank drops away and falls to Earth, and we are very busy getting the shuttle ready to enter orbit. But we are not too busy to notice that our books and pencils are floating in midair. We're in space!

Write About It

Response to Literature Sally Ride tells about her experiences when the shuttle blasted off. How would such a trip make you feel? Write a story about a trip in space. Create a character and tell what things this character sees and does in space.

 e-Journal Write about it online @ **www.macmillanmh.com**

The Sun and Its Planets

Look and Wonder

What is that bright point of light near the Moon? It is not a star. It is the planet Venus! What are the planets? How do they move through space?

 3 ES 4.d. Students know that Earth is one of several planets that orbit the Sun and that the Moon orbits Earth.

How do the planets move through space?

Purpose

To explore how the position of the planets changes.

Procedure

1 Put a chair in the center of the room. Label the chair *Sun*. Tape a line from the chair to a wall.

2 Form two groups. Each student in the first group will take a sign and line up in order along the tape.

3 **Make a Model** Model how the planets move by walking in a circle around the Sun. Take the same-size steps. Count your steps together.

4 **Observe** Students in the second group should observe how the planets move. Do all the planets complete one circle around the Sun in the same number of steps?

5 Trade roles and repeat the experiment.

Draw Conclusions

6 **Compare** How are the orbits similar? How are they different?

7 **Infer** How do the planets move through space?

Explore More

What planets are visible in the night sky in the area where you live?

3 IE 5.e. Collect data in an investigation and analyze those data to develop a logical conclusion.

Materials

masking tape

8 planets cards and 1 Sun card

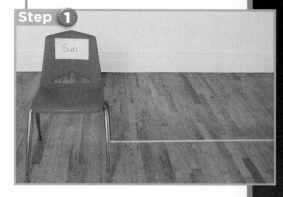
Step **1**

Step **2**

Read and Learn

▶ **Main Idea** 3 ES 4.d

Earth is one of several planets that orbit the Sun.

▶ **Vocabulary**

planet, p. 220

solar system, p. 220

star, p. 220

asteroid, p. 224

comet, p. 224

meteor, p. 224

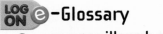 LOG ON ℮–Glossary
@ www.macmillanmh.com

▶ **Reading Skill**

Draw Conclusions

Text Clues	Conclusions

▶ **Technology**

 SCIENCE QUEST — Explore planet Earth with the Secret Agents.

What is the solar system?

Did you know that Earth is not the only planet? A **planet** is a large sphere, or ball, in space that orbits a star, such as our Sun. Some planets are smaller than Earth. Some are larger. Each planet in our solar system rotates on its axis and revolves around the Sun. The **solar system** is made up of the Sun and the planets and other objects that orbit around it. The planets are Mercury, Venus, Earth, Mars, Jupiter, Saturn, Uranus, and Neptune. The diagram shows how the planets and Sun are arranged in our solar system.

The Sun is a star. A **star** is a hot, glowing ball of gases. The Sun is only a medium-sized star. It looks larger than any other star because it is the closest star to Earth.

The Solar System

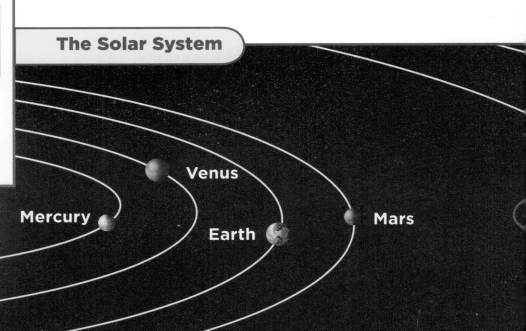

Sun

Mercury

Venus

Earth

Mars

Planets often look like stars in the sky. Like the Moon, planets do not make their own light. They appear to shine because they reflect sunlight. The Moon looks large because it is close to Earth. The planets are much farther away. Many planets have one or more moons that orbit them.

 Quick Check

Draw Conclusions Why can we see some planets in the night sky?

Critical Thinking How does the distance of a planet from the Sun affect the time it takes it to orbit the Sun?

Quick Lab

Why do planets shine?

1 Wrap a small ball in foil. This ball represents a planet. Use a flashlight to represent the Sun.

foil

ball

2 **Observe** In a darkened room, move the planet in a circle around the Sun.

3 **Infer** What makes the planet shine? What else did you observe?

Read a Diagram

Which planets are closest to Earth?

Clue: Find Earth on the diagram. Which planets are next to Earth?

LOG ON *Science in Motion* Watch the planets @ www.macmillanmh.com

Jupiter

Neptune

Uranus

Saturn

What are the planets like?

The four planets that are closest to the Sun are Mercury, Venus, Earth, and Mars. We call these the *inner planets*. The inner planets are all small. They are made up of solid, rock-like material. They are also warmer than the other planets because they are closer to the Sun. The four planets farthest from the Sun are Jupiter, Saturn, Uranus, and Neptune. These are the *outer planets*.

Inner Planets

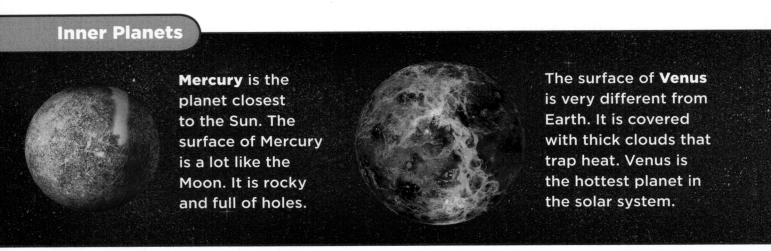

Mercury is the planet closest to the Sun. The surface of Mercury is a lot like the Moon. It is rocky and full of holes.

The surface of **Venus** is very different from Earth. It is covered with thick clouds that trap heat. Venus is the hottest planet in the solar system.

Outer Planets

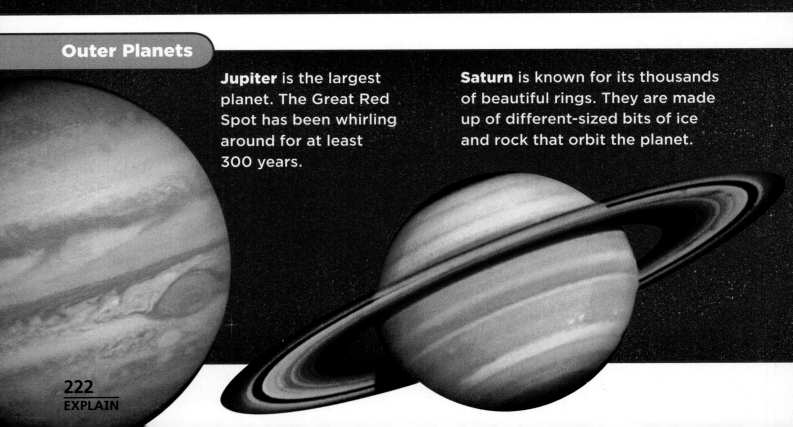

Jupiter is the largest planet. The Great Red Spot has been whirling around for at least 300 years.

Saturn is known for its thousands of beautiful rings. They are made up of different-sized bits of ice and rock that orbit the planet.

The solar system also contains several *dwarf planets*. One of these dwarf planets is Pluto, which was once the ninth planet. Another (2003 UB313) has been named Eris. Ceres, the largest *asteroid*, is also a dwarf planet.

 Quick Check

Draw Conclusions How is Earth different from the other planets?

Critical Thinking Which planet is the hottest planet? Explain why.

 **Earth** is our home. It is the only planet known to produce oxygen and to have liquid water and living things.

 **Mars** is known as the Red Planet because it has reddish-brown soil. Mars has polar ice caps that contain frozen water.

Uranus is called the "sideways" planet because it rotates on its side.

Neptune is more than two billion miles from Earth. It has a Great Dark Spot similar to Jupiter's Great Red Spot.

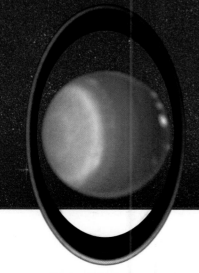 

What else is in our solar system?

Asteroids (AS•tuh•roydz), comets (KAH•muhts), and meteors (MEE•tee•uhrz) also orbit the Sun. **Asteroids** are chunks of rock or metal. Thousands orbit in the asteroid belt between the inner and outer planets. **Comets** are mostly ice mixed with bits of rocks and dust. Comets have long, narrow orbits. **Meteors** are small pieces of rock or metal that have broken off from comets or asteroids.

▲ This object is called Eris. It is classified as a dwarf planet.

◀ Comet Hyakutake was a very bright comet that passed Earth in 1996.

 Quick Check

Draw Conclusions How are meteors related to asteroids and comets?

Critical Thinking Why might it be difficult for scientists to decide if an object is a planet?

▲ Asteroids may be pieces of planets that broke apart.

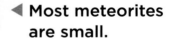

◀ Most meteorites are small.

A meteor that hits Earth is called a *meteorite.* This crater was made when a huge meteorite crashed into Earth thousands of years ago.

Summarize the Main Idea

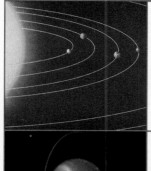

The **solar system** is made up of the Sun and the planets, and other objects that orbit around it. (pp. 220–221)

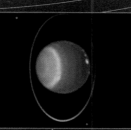

There are four **inner planets** and four **outer planets**. (pp. 222–223)

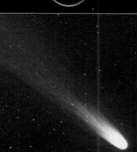

Asteroids, **comets**, and **meteors** are other objects in our solar system. There are also at least three dwarf planets. (p. 224)

Make a FOLDABLES™ Study Guide

Make a layered-look book. Use it to summarize what you read about the solar system.

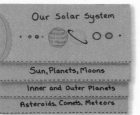

Our Solar System

Sun, Planets, Moons
Inner and Outer Planets
Asteroids, Comets, Meteors

Think, Talk, and Write

1 **Main Idea** Describe our solar system.

2 **Vocabulary** What is a star?

3 **Draw Conclusions** Why do we see the planets in different places at different times?

Text Clues	Conclusions

4 **Critical Thinking** What if the outer planets were farther away from the Sun? How would this affect their orbits around the Sun?

5 **Test Practice** What are the four planets that are made up mostly of rock?
A Jupiter, Mars, Saturn, Earth
B Saturn, Venus, Uranus, Earth
C Mercury, Mars, Venus, Uranus
D Mercury, Venus, Earth, Mars

 **Writing Link**

Write a Report
Suppose you could visit another planet in our solar system. Research its conditions. Write a report about what you would need to live there.

 **Math Link**

Make a Chart
Use research materials to find out how far each planet in the solar system is from the Sun. Use this information to make a chart.

Observe

You know that Earth is only one of the planets in our solar system. How do scientists learn about the other planets? How do they learn about meteors, comets, and asteroids? They **observe** the Sun, planets, moons, and other objects in our solar system to learn about them.

① Learn It

When you **observe**, you use one or more of your senses to learn about an object or event. Remember, your senses are sight, hearing, smell, taste, and touch. Scientists use their senses to observe things. They often use tools to help them make observations. Scientists use observations to draw conclusions about objects and events.

⚠ **Be Careful.** It can be dangerous to taste things in science. You should not taste things unless your teacher tells you to.

② Try It

You can **observe** things, too. Look at the detail of the comet below. Observe its color and shape. Look for unique features that help you identify what it is. What observations can you make that help you know this is a detail of a comet?

❸ Apply It

The photos below show details of planets and other objects in our solar system. **Observe** each photo carefully. Use your observations to identify what each is a detail of. What evidence in the photos supports how you have identified them?

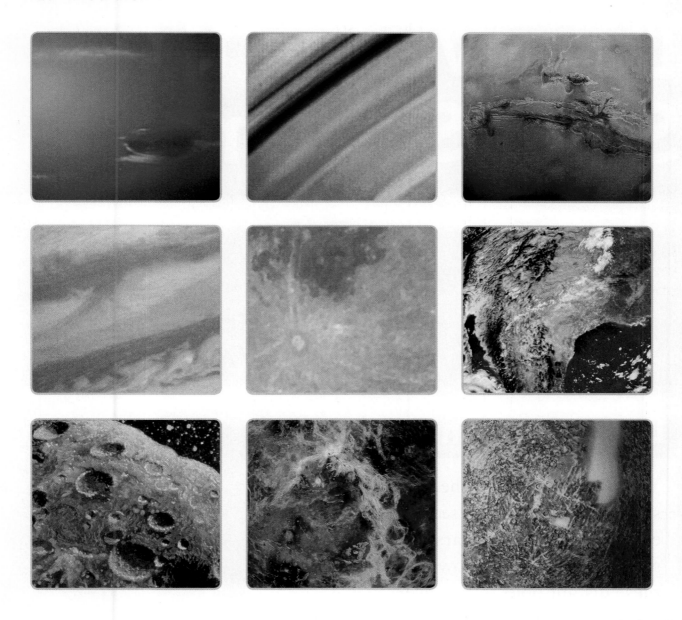

3 IE 5.b. Differentiate evidence from opinion and know that scientists do not rely on claims or conclusions unless they are backed by observations that can be confirmed.

227
EXTEND

Telescopes: Discovering the Solar System

Look and Wonder

When you look up at the Moon in the night sky, what else can you see? If the sky is dark enough, you can see stars. You might also see a planet or two. How do we learn about these distant objects in space?

3 ES 4.c. Students know telescopes magnify the appearance of some distant objects in the sky, including the Moon and the planets. The number of stars that can be seen through telescopes is dramatically greater than the number that can be seen by the unaided eye.

How do telescopes help us learn about distant objects?

Purpose

To learn what telescopes do.

⚠️ **Be Careful.** Never look at the Sun with your eyes or a telescope.

Procedure

1. Put the thick lens at one end of the small tube. Use the clay to hold the lens in place.

2. Do the same for the thin lens and the large tube.

3. Slide the open end of the small tube into the open end of the large tube.

4. **Observe** Look at a distant object. Now look at it through the thick lens of your telescope.

Draw Conclusions

5. **Compare** Describe the difference in what you see with and without your telescope.

6. **Infer** How do telescopes help us learn about distant objects?

Explore More

Experiment How will the Moon look through binoculars? How will it look through your telescope?

 3 IE 5.a. Repeat observations to improve accuracy and know that the results of similar scientific investigations seldom turn out exactly the same because of differences in the things being investigated, methods being used, or uncertainty in the observation.

Materials

modeling clay

1 thick lens

1 small cardboard tube

1 thin lens

1 large cardboard tube

Step 1

Step 3

Main Idea 3 ES 4.c

Telescopes are tools that make objects in space look larger, closer, and clearer.

Vocabulary

telescope, p. 230

lens, p. 230

LOG ON e-Glossary
@ www.macmillanmh.com

Reading Skill

Summarize

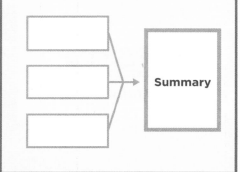

Summary

You can see many more stars with a telescope than you can with just your eyes. ▶

What is a telescope?

The stars, planets, and the Moon are very far away. How do scientists learn about them? Scientists use telescopes (TEL•uh•skohps) to study distant objects in space. A **telescope** is a tool that gathers light to make faraway objects appear larger, closer, and clearer. Telescopes gather light with lenses (LENZ•uhz). A **lens** is a clear material that changes the path of light rays. Lenses are often made from curved pieces of glass. Lenses help us see objects in more detail.

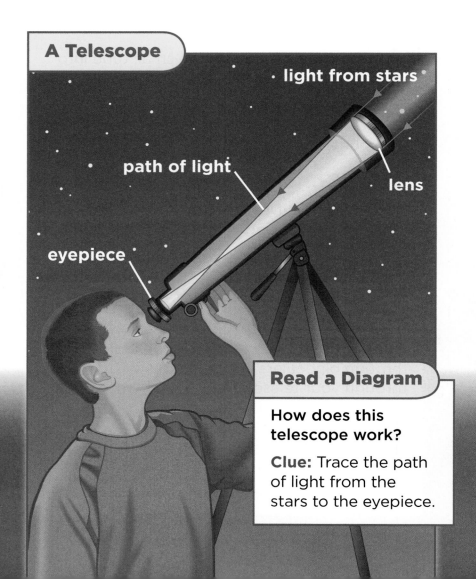

A Telescope

light from stars

path of light

lens

eyepiece

Read a Diagram

How does this telescope work?

Clue: Trace the path of light from the stars to the eyepiece.

One of the best places for a telescope is in space. The Hubble Space Telescope travels around Earth. It takes pictures and sends them back to Earth. It can see objects in space more clearly than telescopes on Earth.

Scientists also study space with other kinds of telescopes. For example, radio telescopes collect radio waves. We cannot see radio waves. Scientists use computers to turn radio waves into pictures. That is how they learn about objects in space that we cannot see.

 Quick Check

Summarize What can you see with the help of a telescope?

Critical Thinking Why is space a good place for a telescope?

Quick Lab

A Water Lens

1. Cover a piece of newspaper with some wax paper.

2. **Observe** Put a small drop of water over a letter. How does the letter look?

3. **Experiment** How does the size of the drop affect the way the print looks?

4. **Infer** How is the lens in a telescope like the drop of water?

Hubble Space Telescope

◄ **radio telescope**

How did we learn about space?

At first, people believed that Earth was at the center of the solar system. They thought that the Sun traveled around Earth. Then, in 1543, a scientist named Copernicus said that the Sun, not Earth, was at the center of the solar system. In 1609, Galileo used his telescope to discover evidence that Earth orbits the Sun.

Since then, scientists have learned much more about our solar system by using telescopes. Scientists saw Uranus, Neptune, and Pluto for the first time. Scientists also learned that there are billions of stars.

We have learned a lot about space by using telescopes. There are many more questions left to answer. With the help of tools such as telescopes, we are learning more each day.

▲ Galileo

✔ Quick Check

Summarize What have scientists learned with the help of telescopes?

Critical Thinking Why do you think Galileo did not find Uranus, Neptune, and Pluto with his telescope?

▲ This telescope helped Galileo discover our Moon's craters and four of Jupiter's moons.

Lesson Review

Summarize the Main Idea

Telescopes are tools that make distant objects appear larger, closer, and clearer. (pp. 230–231)

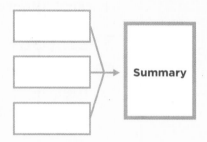

Telescopes such as the Hubble Space Telescope help us to see and learn about objects in space. (pp. 230–231)

Scientists such as Galileo first learned about space by **using telescopes**. (p. 232)

Make a FOLDABLES Study Guide

Make a two-tab book. Use it to summarize what you learned about telescopes.

Think, Talk, and Write

1. **Main Idea** How do telescopes help people learn about our solar system?

2. **Vocabulary** What is a telescope?

3. **Summarize** What are some things scientists have learned with the help of telescopes?

Summary

4. **Critical Thinking** Why did it take a long time to figure out how our solar system works?

5. **Test Practice** What did Galileo find out with the help of a telescope?
   A that Earth is round
   B that the Moon orbits Earth
   C that Earth orbits the Sun
   D that the Sun orbits Earth

 Writing Link

Writing That Compares
Compare the Hubble Space Telescope with a radio telescope. Use research materials to find out how they obtain pictures. Write about how the telescopes are alike and how they are different.

 Art Link

Make a Poster
Use research materials to find a picture taken by the Hubble Space Telescope. Then find a picture that was made using a radio telescope. Draw or paste these pictures on your poster. Label them. Explain what each picture shows.

Be a Scientist

Materials

index cards

masking tape

tape measure

telescope

How can you make distant objects appear closer and clearer?

Form a Hypothesis

If an object is close to you, you can see it clearly. You can observe its details. Can a telescope help you observe distant objects clearly? Write a hypothesis.

Test Your Hypothesis

1 Ask a partner to write a secret message on an index card. Use the photograph as a guide for how big the letters should be. Keep the message hidden.

write about this size.

Step 1

2 **Measure** Put a piece of tape on the floor. Measure 3 m from the edge of the tape. Mark this distance with tape. Label it *Three Meters*. Continue to measure and label 3-m distances four more times. Your last piece of tape should be 15 m from your first piece.

Step 2

3 **Experiment** Stand on the last piece of tape while your partner stands on the first with the secret message. Can you read the message? If not, move forward 3 m and try again. Keep moving forward 3 m at a time until you are able to correctly read the secret message.

4 **Record Data** How close did you need to be to read the message?

5 **Use Variables** Ask your partner to write a new message on an index card. Repeat steps 3 and 4 using a telescope. Then trade roles and do the experiment again.

Draw Conclusions

6 Analyze Data Describe the differences in how you saw the secret message with and without the telescope.

7 Infer How might telescopes help you learn more about faraway objects in space?

Inquiry Guided

How do stars appear to change position?

Form a Hypothesis

The stars appear to change position in the night sky. How do they change? Write a hypothesis.

Test Your Hypothesis

Design a plan to test your hypothesis. What materials will you use? Write the steps you plan to follow.

Draw Conclusions

Did your results support your hypothesis? Why or why not? Share your results with your classmates.

Inquiry Open

What other questions do you have about telescopes and our solar system? Talk with your classmates about questions you have. How might you find the answers to your questions?

Remember to follow the steps of the scientific process.

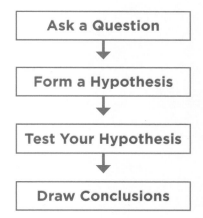

Ask a Question
↓
| Form a Hypothesis |
↓
| Test Your Hypothesis |
↓
| Draw Conclusions |

 3 IE 5.e. Collect data in an investigation and analyze those data to develop a logical conclusion.

The Stars

Look and Wonder

Why do the stars appear to move across the night sky? Why do we not see stars during the day?

3 ES 4.a. Students know the patterns of stars stay the same, although they appear to move across the sky nightly, and different stars can be seen in different seasons.

Why do we only see the stars at night?

Make a Prediction

Why do we not see stars in the daytime sky? Write a prediction.

Test Your Prediction

1. Draw a 3 cm dot with chalk on black paper.

2. Draw a 3 cm dot with chalk on white paper.

3. Have your partner hold both papers 3 m away from you.

4. **Observe** Describe what you see.

Draw Conclusions

5. Why was it easy to see one dot and not the other?

6. **Infer** Suppose the dots on the papers were stars. Why do you think you can only see the stars at night?

Explore More

Can we ever see the Moon during the day? Why or why not?

 3 IE 5.e. Collect data in an investigation and analyze those data to develop a logical conclusion.

Materials

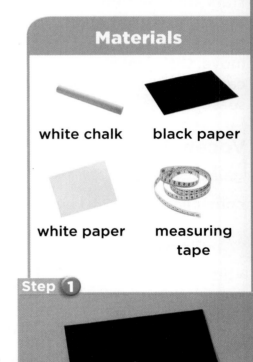

white chalk   black paper

white paper   measuring tape

Step 1

Step 3

Main Idea 3 ES 4.a

The patterns of the stars stay the same in the night sky although the stars appear to move. Different stars can be seen in different seasons.

Vocabulary

galaxy, p. 238

constellation, p. 240

LOG ON **e**-Glossary
@ www.macmillanmh.com

Reading Skill

Main Idea

The Sun looks larger and brighter than any other star because it is the closest star to Earth.

What are stars?

A star is a hot, glowing ball of gases. The Sun is a medium-sized star. It is much smaller and younger than many other stars in our galaxy (GAL• ahk•see). A **galaxy** is a very large group of stars. Our solar system is in a galaxy we call the *Milky Way*.

We see other stars as tiny points of light in the night sky. Even stars that are larger than the Sun appear very small. This is because these stars are very far away.

The stars are always in the sky. We just cannot see them during the day. The Sun is so close that its light is the only light we can see.

Look at the night sky on a clear evening. Choose a group of stars. Make a drawing to help you remember what they look like and where they are. Check the sky again after one hour. Why are the stars not in the same place? Remember that Earth rotates on its axis. The stars did not move. They only appeared to move because of Earth's rotation.

Some star-like objects do move in the night sky. These "stars" are planets. As Earth and the other planets revolve, their positions change.

Quick Check

Main Idea How does our Sun compare to other stars?

Critical Thinking Why do some stars look brighter than others?

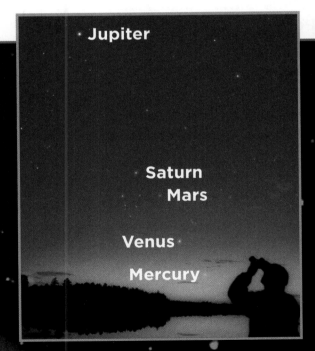

On March 22, 2004, five planets were seen together in the night sky. They will not be seen together again

This photo taken by the Hubble Space Telescope shows a very large star in the Pistol Nebula.

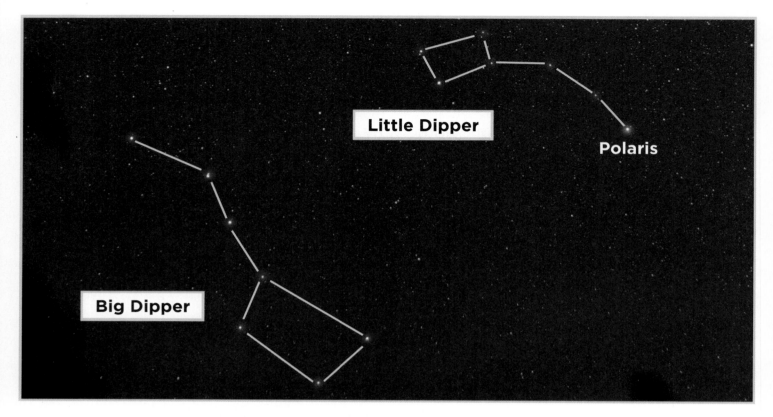

Little Dipper

Polaris

Big Dipper

▲ The two stars on the pouring side of the Big Dipper point to Polaris. Polaris is the bright star at the end of the Little Dipper's handle. Polaris is the North Star. It always points to the North Pole.

What is a constellation?

Have you ever noticed clouds shaped like animals, people, or things? Long ago, people thought stars also formed pictures in the night sky. We can see them, too. These star groups are called constellations (kahn•stuh•LAY•shuhnz).

A **constellation** is a group of stars that form a picture. People named constellations after the pictures they saw. For example, the Big Dipper and the Little Dipper got their names because they are shaped like tools that hold water. People from different places saw different pictures in the night sky. They made up different stories about the constellations. Constellations helped people to make sense of the night sky.

As Earth rotates and revolves, you see different constellations. Thousands of years ago people also noticed that constellations seemed to move. They used constellations to tell time. Farmers studied them to tell the seasons. Sailors looked at them to tell direction at night. They knew the North Star always points North.

Today scientists use 88 constellations to group the stars. Many of them are the same patterns people used long ago.

 Quick Check

Main Idea How did people use constellations?

Critical Thinking Why do the constellations appear to move in the night sky?

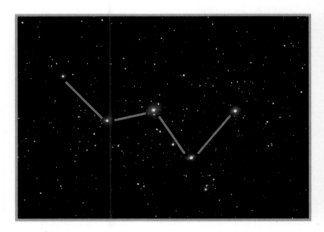

▲ Cassiopeia is named after a queen from a Greek story.

▲ Scorpius looks like a scorpion to some people.

Why do we see different stars during different seasons?

As Earth revolves around the Sun, we see different constellations. Each month new stars appear.

In the winter, you cannot see all the stars that were in the summer sky. These stars are now on the opposite side of our orbit. Find Orion in the diagram. In winter, you look out into space at night away from the Sun. You see Orion in winter.

In summer, you have moved to the other side of the Sun. Orion is in the direction of the Sun. That means Orion is in the sky during the day. Some stars, like Polaris, can be seen all year.

 Quick Check

Main Idea Why do we see different constellations during the different seasons?

Critical Thinking Could you see Earth from Orion in summer? Explain.

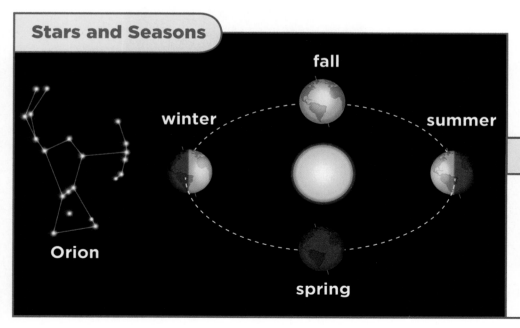

Stars and Seasons

fall

winter

summer

Orion

spring

Read a Diagram

Can you see Orion in the summer?

Clue: Compare the view of Orion from the winter sky and the summer sky.

Lesson Review

Summarize the Main Idea

 **Stars** are large glowing balls of gases. Our Sun is a medium-sized star. (pp. 238–239)

A **constellation** is a pattern or picture outlined by stars. (pp. 240–241)

Different constellations can be seen during different seasons. (p. 242)

Make a FOLDABLES™ Study Guide

Make a shutter fold. Use it to summarize what you read.

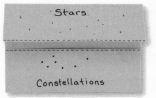

Think, Talk, and Write

1 **Main Idea** In July, you see a constellation that you can find easily. In December, you cannot find it. Explain why.

2 **Vocabulary** What is a constellation?

3 **Main Idea** Why did people group the stars into constellations?

4 **Critical Thinking** If we lived on another planet, would we see the same constellations? Why?

5 **Test Practice** Why can we only see some constellations during the spring and summer months?
   A Earth revolves around the Sun.
   B Orion, the hunter, is chasing them.
   C The Sun is shining on them.
   D The stars revolve around the Sun.

Math Link

Using Data
The smallest stars are called neutron stars. Some measure only ten miles across. If a line of neutron stars measures a total of 30 miles across, how many neutron stars are there?

Art Link

Draw Constellations
Ask a parent or guardian to help you observe the night sky in an area without lights. Draw different pictures that the stars make. Use a local star map to compare your drawings to the constellations.

MEET ORSOLA DE MARCO

Do you ever wonder about the stars? Orsola de Marco does. She is a scientist at the American Museum of Natural History in New York. Orsola studies stars that are found together in pairs. As far as we know, our Sun is a star that stands alone. But most stars in the universe have a partner. They are called binary stars.

Orsola de Marco is an astrophysicist. She studies stars.

AMERICAN
MUSEUM of
NATURAL
HISTORY

ELA R 3.2.6. Extract appropriate and significant information from the text, including problems and solutions.

These binary stars orbit each other at a very close distance. Scientists think that one star is being absorbed by the other. The "butterfly" shaped "wings" are probably caused by gases from the surface of the central star.

A summary

▶ states the main idea

▶ gives the most important details

▶ is brief

▶ is told in your own words

Of course Orsola cannot go to the stars to learn about them. Instead, she travels to Arizona, Hawaii, and Chile to use large telescopes. She gazes billions of miles into space to get a good look at binary stars. She watches how the stars affect each other. When a star gets old it becomes larger. If there is another star nearby, it might get eaten up, or absorbed, by the expanding old star. No one is sure what will happen after that. Will the smaller star just disappear? Orsola is working to find out.

Write About It

Summarize Read the article with a partner. List the most important information in a chart. Then use the chart to summarize the article. Remember to start with a main-idea sentence and to keep your summary brief.

Stars to Freedom

Before the Civil War, many African Americans were enslaved in the South. They used the Big Dipper to find their way to freedom in the North. The Big Dipper showed them the direction in which they had to travel. They used the Big Dipper because it points to the North Star. African Americans used a folk song called "Follow the Drinking Gourd" as a code that would help them follow the route to the North. They called the Big Dipper the "drinking gourd" because it looked like a big spoon used for drinking water.

A good expository paragraph

▶ **has a topic sentence that tells the main idea**

▶ **supports the main idea with facts and details**

▶ **draws a conclusion based on the facts**

▲ **the Big Dipper and the Little Dipper**

 Write About It

Expository Writing Write a paragraph that summarizes "Stars to Freedom." Include a topic sentence. Then tell the most important facts and details. Explain how people used the Big Dipper to travel to freedom. Leave out details that are not important to the main idea.

LOG ON **e-Journal** Write about it online @ **www.macmillanmh.com**

▲ **a drinking gourd**

 ELA W 3.1.1. Create a single paragraph:
a. Develop a topic sentence.
b. Include simple supporting facts and details.

Finding the Distance Between Stars

Have you ever wondered how far away from Earth some of the stars are? Scientists use light years to measure distances. A light year is the distance light travels in one year. Light travels about 6 trillion miles in one year!

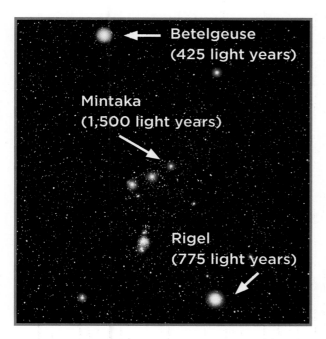

▲ Betelgeuse, Mintaka, and Rigel are some of the stars in the Orion constellation.

How to Subtract 3-Digit Numbers

► First subtract the ones. Regroup if necessary.

$$\begin{array}{r} \overset{3\ 12}{6\cancel{4}\cancel{2}} \\ -467 \\ \hline 5 \end{array}$$

► Then subtract the tens. Regroup if necessary.

$$\begin{array}{r} \overset{5\ 13\ 12}{\cancel{6}\cancel{4}\cancel{2}} \\ -467 \\ \hline 75 \end{array}$$

► Subtract the hundreds. Regroup if necessary.

$$\begin{array}{r} \overset{5\ 13\ 12}{\cancel{6}\cancel{4}\cancel{2}} \\ -467 \\ \hline 175 \end{array}$$

 ## Solve It

The picture above tells you how far some stars are from Earth. Which of these stars is closest to Earth? Which one is farthest away from Earth? How far apart are they? Use subtraction to find the distance.

 MA NS 3.1.2. Compare and order whole numbers to 10,000.
MA NS 3.2.1. Find the sum or difference of two whole numbers between 0 and 10,000.

Summarize the Main Idea

Earth is one of several planets that orbit the Sun. (pp. 218–225)

Telescopes make objects in space look larger, closer, and clearer. (pp. 228–233)

The pattern of the stars stays the same. We see different stars in different seasons. (pp. 236–243)

Make a FOLDABLES™ Study Guide

Tape your lesson study guides on a piece of paper as shown. Use your study guide to review what you have learned in this chapter.

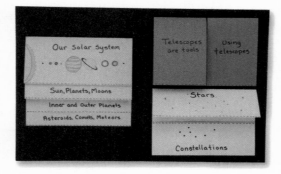

Fill each blank with the best word from the list.

asteroid, p. 224   **planet**, p. 220

constellation, p. 240   **solar system**, p. 220

galaxy, p. 238   **star**, p. 220

lens, p. 230   **telescope**, p. 230

1. Faraway objects appear larger, closer, and clearer when viewed through a _____. 3 ES 4.c

2. A group of stars that seem to form a picture in the sky is called a _____. 3 ES 4.a

3. A large sphere in space that orbits a star, such as our Sun, is called a _____. 3 ES 4.d

4. A chunk of rock or metal that orbits the Sun is an _____. 3 ES 4.d

5. The Sun and the objects that orbit around it make up a _____. 3 ES 4.d

6. A hot ball of glowing gases is called a _____. 3 ES 4.a

7. Most telescopes contain a curved piece of glass called a _____. 3 ES 4.c

8. A _____ is a very large group of stars. 3 ES 4.a

LOG ON **e-Review** Summaries and quizzes online @ **www.macmillanmh.com**

Discuss or write about each of the following.

9. Summarize Earth revolves. How does this movement affect our view of space? 3 ES 4.a

10. Writing That Compares How are the inner and outer planets alike? Different? 3 ES 4.d

11. Observe Why are the constellations shown in the photo called the Big Dipper and Little Dipper? 3 ES 4.a

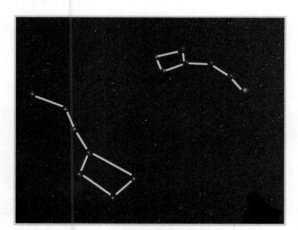

Big and Little Dipper

12. Critical Thinking Which of these planets has a longer orbit? Why? 3 ES 4.d

Venus   **Pluto**

Answer each of the following in a complete sentence.

13. If planets do not give off light, how can they be seen in the night sky? 3 ES 4.d

14. How are asteroids like planets? 3 ES 4.d

15. How has our understanding of the solar system changed over time? 3 ES 4.c

16. If stars are always in the sky, why can we not see them during the day? 3 ES 4.a

17. How does a telescope make distant objects appear larger, closer, and clearer? 3 ES 4.c

★ What objects do we see in the night sky? 3 ES 4

CHAPTER 5

Design a Matching Game

- Design a card matching game that shows the parts of the solar system.

- Make a two-card set for each item. Draw a picture on one card and label it. Write one or more facts for your picture on the other card.

- Make as many card pairs as you like, but be sure to include the Sun, Moon, and each of the items shown.

- Play the game with a partner. Whoever matches the most pairs wins.

four inner planets

four outer planets

asteroids

250

1 **Why do the constellations look like they are moving in the night sky?** 3 ES 4.a

A As Earth revolves, the stars look like they are getting brighter.

B As Earth rotates, the stars look like they are moving.

C The stars are moving across the Moon.

D The stars are moving around the Sun.

2 **Which has more stars?** 3 ES 4.a

A solar system

B Earth

C galaxy

D constellation

3 **How are planets and stars different?** 3 ES 4.a

A Planets have their own light; stars reflect light from the Sun.

B Planets seem to travel; stars stay in patterns.

C Planets move in a pattern; stars move in all directions.

D Planets are far away; stars are closer to Earth.

4 **Which of the following lists the correct order of the four planets closest to the Sun?** 3 ES 4.d

A Mercury, Venus, Earth, Mars

B Earth, Mercury, Venus, Mars

C Mars, Venus, Earth, Mercury

D Mercury, Venus, Mars, Jupiter

5 **By using a telescope to observe objects in the night sky, a student could see more details of the Moon because a telescope** 3 IE 5.b

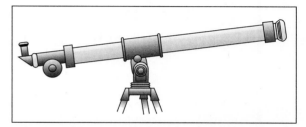

A makes objects that are far away look closer.

B makes objects that are far away look darker.

C makes objects that are far away look smaller.

D makes objects that are far away look brighter.

6 **Which of the following explains why the Moon looks larger than the planets?** 3 ES 4.d

A It is big and bright.

B It is closer to Earth.

C It is closer to the Sun.

D It has its own light.

What a Difference Day Length Makes

How do you know when spring is coming? Maybe you hear birds singing and see leaves growing on trees. How do you know it will soon be winter? Maybe you see birds flying south and trees changing color. Have you ever wondered how the birds and trees know it's time to do these things?

Summer

▲ In summer, rabbits have thinner and lighter fur. Their skin releases heat to keep them cool.

Winter

▲ In winter, rabbits grow thicker and heavier fur to keep warm.

Plants and animals don't have calendars or wear wristwatches, of course. Yet they do notice something important. Their bodies keep track of the changing length of the days. The change is small and slow, but it has a big effect.

In the fall, the Sun rises a little later and sets a little earlier each day. These shorter days tell plants and animals to start getting ready for winter. Trees lose their leaves. Some birds fly south. Rabbits, deer, and bears grow warm winter coats. Squirrels gather nuts and line their nests with leaves.

When spring is on the way, the Sun begins to rise earlier and set later. The longer days tell birds to migrate north, sing songs to attract mates, and begin building nests. Plants and trees wake up and begin growing leaves and flowers.

How does the changing length of day make you feel? Do you do different things at different times of the year? For many living things, how long a day is makes a big difference!

Fall

▲ When days get shorter and leaves start to fall, chipmunks gather nuts. They stuff them in their cheeks and carry them back to their nests.

Spring

▲ In spring, the Sun rises earlier. Animals come out of their shelters to feast on the growing plants.

3 ES 4. Objects in the sky move in regular and predictable patterns.
ELA R 3.2.3. Demonstrate comprehension by identifying answers in the text.

Map Maker

Do you like working on puzzles with small pieces? Are you good at giving directions or describing places? You might think about becoming a map maker.

Scientists who make maps have many different skills. Some gather data about the geography of an area. Others make three-dimensional models of landforms. Still others use data and models to draw the maps with computerized mapping programs.

▲ This scientist is gathering data about landforms.

There are things you can do right now to prepare for this job. Learn about Earth's land and water. Play games that require you to solve a problem. In high school, take math, science, and computer classes. Then, get a college degree.

Here are some other Earth Science careers:

- weather forecaster
- oceanographer
- jewelry designer
- astronomer

This surveyor is using a *transit*. The information he records will help him map an area.

LOG ON e-Careers @ www.macmillanmh.com

Chapter 6

Chapter 7

Chapter 8

Physical Science

Most of an iceberg is under water.

Matter

 What are some forms of matter and how can they change?

Merced River, Yosemite National Park, California

Lesson 1

Solids, Liquids, and Gases

PAGE 260

Lesson 2

Building Blocks of Matter

PAGE 272

Lesson 3

Changing Matter

PAGE 284

3 PS 1. Energy and matter have multiple forms and can be changed from one form to another.

Literature
Poem

ELA R 3.3.1. Distinguish common forms of literature (e.g., poetry, drama, fiction, non-fiction). **ELA W 3.2.2.** Write descriptions that use concrete sensory details to present and support unified impressions of people, places, things, or experiences.

cold air, water, and ice

Freezing Rain

by John Frank

A soft rain falls
Through the winter air
That chills the mountain pass,
And clings to the trees
That crown the hills
And turns them into glass.

Write About It

Response to Literature During the winter, rain freezes into ice. What word does the author use in the poem to describe ice? What are some words that describe things around you? Choose an object to write about. Use as many words as you can to describe the object.

LOG ON **e-Journal** Research and write about it online @ **www.macmillanmh.com**

Solids, Liquids, and Gases

Look and Wonder

Have you ever watched a hang glider soar through the air? What can you see from high in the sky? How does the ground look? How can you describe the objects and places below?

 3 PS 1.e. Students know matter has three forms: solid, liquid, and gas.
3 PS 1.f. Students know evaporation and melting are changes that occur when the objects are heated.

How do you describe objects?

Purpose

In this activity you will explore ways to describe objects.

Procedure

1 Observe Select a "mystery object" in your classroom. Observe the object. What color is it? How does it feel? What is the object's shape and size?

2 Communicate Record your observations in a concept web like the one shown. Label each line with a word that describes your "mystery object." Leave the circle blank.

3 Infer Trade concept webs with a partner. Think about the descriptive words. What classroom object do the words describe? Label the circle with the name of your partner's "mystery object."

Draw Conclusions

4 Were you able to guess your partner's "mystery object"? Was your classmate able to guess your mystery object?

5 What helped you most in guessing your partner's object?

Explore More

Experiment How might your concept web be different if you were blindfolded and could only touch the "mystery object"? Try it again to find out.

 3 IE 5.e. Collect data in an investigation and analyze those data to develop a logical conclusion.

Materials

classroom objects

hand lens

Step 1

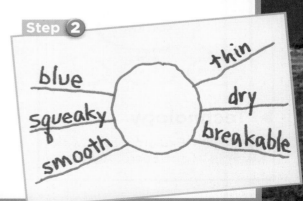
Step 2

Read and Learn

What is matter?

If you look around, you will see many things with different sizes, colors, and shapes. Things differ in the way they look, feel, sound, and smell. All the things around you are alike in one way. All are kinds of matter (MA•tuhr).

Matter is anything that takes up space. You are matter. This book is matter. Even the air you breathe is matter. All of these things take up space. Matter also has mass. **Mass** is a measure of the amount of matter in an object. A brick and a sponge might have the same size and shape. However, the mass of the brick is greater than the mass of the sponge. That is because the brick contains more matter than the sponge.

Properties of Matter

Each kind of matter has its own *properties* (PROP•uhr•teez), or traits. Color and shape are properties that you can see. The way an object tastes, smells, feels, and sounds are other properties that you can observe. Properties can be used to describe and identify matter.

Many properties of matter can be measured. You measure the length and width of an object with a ruler or meterstick. You measure the mass of an object with a pan balance.

▲ Everywhere you go, you are surrounded by matter.

A pan balance is used to measure the mass of objects. Which object has greater mass? Why? ▶

bag of popcorn

bag of marbles

 Quick Check

Main Idea What are two properties of all types of matter?

Critical Thinking Why is the *idea* of the number 3 not matter, but 3 bricks are matter?

How do we classify matter?

One way scientists classify matter is in groups called *states*. Three states of matter are solids, liquids, and gases. Each of these states of matter has certain properties.

Most of the things you see around you are solids (SAHL•idz). Pencils, desks, pillows, and chairs are all examples of solids. A **solid** is matter that has a definite shape and volume (VAHL•yewm). **Volume** is the amount of space that an object takes up. This book is a solid. It has a definite shape. It takes up a definite amount of space.

A **liquid** (LIK•wid) is matter that has a definite volume but does not have a definite shape. A liquid takes the shape of its container. Water, oil, juice, and shampoo are liquids. Milk is a liquid, too. When it is inside a carton, milk takes the shape of the carton. When you pour milk into a glass, it takes the shape of the glass. Whatever the shape or size of its container, milk's volume does not change. It takes up the same amount of space regardless of what it is in.

▲ The glass is a solid. It has a definite shape and volume. Does the liquid have a definite shape and volume?

▲ Liquids take the shape of their containers. Liquids also take up a definite amount of space inside their containers.

Gases are the third state of matter. Most gases are invisible. You cannot see them, but they are all around you. Air is made of gases that you need to survive. A **gas** is matter that does not have a definite shape or volume. What happens when you blow into a balloon? The gas takes the shape of its container—the balloon. Because the gas does not have a definite volume, it spreads out and fills the balloon.

✅ Quick Check

Main Idea What are the states of matter?

Critical Thinking Compare solids, liquids, and gases. How are they alike? How do they differ?

◄ The gas used to fill all these balloons came from this one small tank. Gases do not have a definite volume. They spread out and fill whatever they are in.

Helium

≡ Quick Lab

Solids, Liquids, and Gases

gas

1. Blow into an empty bag. Then quickly seal the bag.

2. Fill a second small bag with some water and quickly seal this bag. Put a rock in a third small bag and seal the bag.

liquid

3. **Observe** Each bag contains matter in a different state. How does each bag look and feel? Record your observations in a chart.

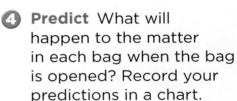

solid

4. **Predict** What will happen to the matter in each bag when the bag is opened? Record your predictions in a chart.

5. **Observe** Open each bag. What happens?

   ⚠ **Be Careful.** Hold the bag filled with water over a container.

6. **Communicate** Describe the properties of a solid, liquid, and gas. Tell how the three states of matter are different from one another.

When solid steel gains enough heat energy, it will melt or turn into a liquid.

What happens when heat is added to matter?

When matter is heated, it gains heat energy. Its temperature rises. If enough heat energy is added to matter, its state can change.

Adding Heat to Solids

The amount of heat energy needed to cause matter to change state varies. When a solid gains enough heat energy it will **melt**, or turn into a liquid. Chocolate and ice cream melt after gaining a small amount of heat energy. Rocks deep beneath Earth's surface melt after gaining a huge amount of heat energy.

▲ The Golden Gate Bridge is made from tons of solid steel.

The lava flowing from this volcano is rock that melted deep beneath Earth's surface. ▶

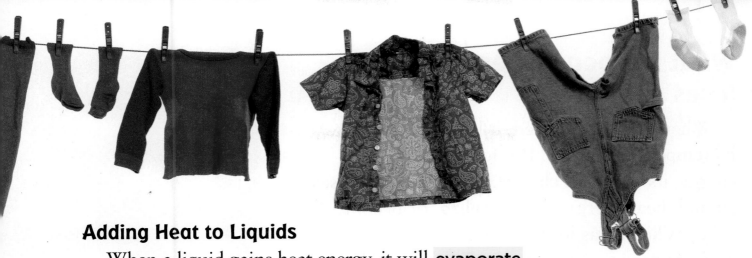

Adding Heat to Liquids

When a liquid gains heat energy, it will **evaporate** (i•VAP•uh•rayt), or turn into a gas. For example, when wet clothes are placed on a clothesline, the water in the clothes evaporates. The liquid water in the clothes gains heat energy and turns into a gas. The gas state of water is called *water vapor*. You cannot see water vapor, but it is part of the air around you. As the liquid water turns into water vapor your clothes get dry.

▲ When the liquid water in these clothes gains enough heat energy, it will evaporate, or turn into a gas.

Gaining Heat Energy

ice cubes　　　water　　　steam

✔ Quick Check

Main Idea What happens to matter when it gains heat energy?

Critical Thinking You wash your hair and blow it dry. What happens to the water in your hair? What causes this to happen?

Read a Diagram

What happens when heat is added to ice cubes?

Clue: Arrows help show a sequence.

 Science in Motion
Watch how matter changes @ www.macmillanmh.com

What happens when matter loses energy?

When matter is cooled, it loses heat energy. Its temperature drops. If it loses enough heat energy, its state can change. When a liquid loses enough heat energy, it will **freeze**, or become a solid. When a gas loses enough heat energy, it will **condense** (kuhn•DENS), or become a liquid. For example, on cool mornings, small droplets of water called *dew* can appear on objects. This happens when water vapor in the air touches cool objects and loses heat energy. The water vapor condenses and forms dew.

▲ The dew on this spider web formed when water vapor cooled and condensed.

 Quick Check

Main Idea How are freezing and condensation alike?

Critical Thinking Why does liquid water turn to ice after being placed in a freezer?

◀ When carbon dioxide gas loses enough heat energy, it will change state and become solid.

When juice is cooled enough, it will change state and become solid. ▶

Lesson Review

Summarize the Main Idea

Matter is anything that has mass and takes up space. (pp. 262–263)

Matter is classified into **three states**—solids, liquids, and gases. (pp. 264–265)

Matter can **change** state by gaining or losing heat energy. (pp. 266–268)

Make a FOLDABLES™ Study Guide

Make a trifold book. Use it to summarize what you learned about matter.

Think, Talk, and Write

① **Main Idea** What is matter?

② **Vocabulary** What are the three states of matter?

③ **Main Idea** What are some properties of a solid that you can measure?

④ **Critical Thinking** After taking a hot shower, Luis noticed drops of water on the bathroom mirror. What caused the water drops to form?

⑤ **Test Practice** Air is an example of this state of matter.

   A liquid

   B solid

   C shape

   D gas

Writing Link

Write an Article
What happens when oil and water mix? In 1989 a ship spilled oil into the water off the coast of Alaska. Research the *Exxon Valdez* oil spill. Write a short news article describing what happened.

Math Link

Solve a Problem
It takes 80 calories of heat energy to melt one gram of solid water (ice) to liquid water. It takes 539 calories of heat energy to change one gram of water from the liquid state to the gas state. How many more calories are needed for evaporation than for melting?

Focus on Inquiry Skills

Measure

You learned that matter is anything that takes up space and has mass. Water is matter that comes in three forms: solid, liquid, and gas. Does the solid form of water have the same mass as the liquid form? To answer questions like this, scientists **measure** things.

measuring cup

① Learn It

When you **measure**, you find the size, distance, time, volume, area, mass, or temperature of an object. Scientists use many tools to measure things. Some of these tools are shown on this page. Scientists use measurements to describe and compare objects.

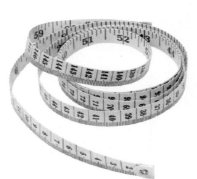

tape measure

② Try It

You know that scientists **measure** things to answer questions. You can measure too, to answer this question. Do solid ice cubes have the same mass after they melt?

balance

thermometer

3 IE 5.c. Use numerical data in describing and comparing objects, events, and measurements.

▶ To start, place several ice cubes in a cup. Then, cover the cup with plastic wrap so the water cannot evaporate.

▶ Measure mass by placing the cup on one end of a pan balance. Add masses to the other side of the balance until both sides are even. Record the mass on a chart.

Beginning Mass	Mass Every Half Hour	Ending Mass

▶ Measure the mass every $\frac{1}{2}$ hour until the ice is completely melted.

▶ Now use your measurements to answer the question. Do solid ice cubes have the same mass after they melt?

❸ Apply It

Now **measure** to answer this question: Does ice cream have the same mass after it melts? How does mass change when matter changes state?

Building Blocks of Matter

Look and Wonder

Suppose you had a bead collection. How would you organize your collection? How do you think scientists classify matter?

3 PS 1.h. Students know all matter is made of small particles called atoms, too small to see with the naked eye. **•3 PS 1.i.** Students know people once thought that earth, wind, fire, and water were the basic elements that made up all matter. Science experiments show that there are more than 100 different types of atoms, which are presented on the periodic table of the elements.

How can you classify matter?

Purpose

Find out ways matter can be classified.

Procedure

1 Observe Observe the properties of each object. Record your observations on a chart.

2 Classify Divide the objects into groups that have similar properties.

3 Communicate Write a name for each group that describes how its items are alike.

Draw Conclusions

4 Analyze Data Did some objects in one group have the same properties as objects in another group? How did you decide how to classify each object?

5 Infer Why are scientists careful about classifying matter?

Materials

everyday objects

| Step 1 | |
Object	Properties

Explore More

Experiment What if you have a can of peanuts and a can of stewed tomatoes? The cans look the same except for the labels. How could you tell the cans apart if someone takes off the labels? What experiments can you do to find out what is in the cans without opening them?

 3 IE 5.e. Collect data in an investigation and analyze those data to develop a logical conclusion.

What are elements?

You know that everything around you is made up of matter. But do you know what makes up matter? Ancient people wondered what made up the things in their world, too. They made observations and performed investigations. They decided that all matter was made up of earth, air, fire, and water.

Today scientists use experiments and modern tools, such as high-powered microscopes, to observe matter. These tools let scientists observe things that ancient people could not observe. Today we know that all matter is made up of elements (EL•uh•munts). **Elements** are the building blocks of matter. More than 100 different elements have been named. Everything is made up of one or more of these elements.

fire

water

air

earth

People once thought that earth, air, fire, and water were the basic elements that made up all matter. ▶

Some elements, such as gold or copper, have names that you may have heard. Others are named for famous scientists or even for places. *Einsteinium* is named for Albert Einstein. *Californium* is named for California.

One or More Elements

Some matter is made up of mostly one element. An iron nail contains mostly the element iron. Aluminum (a•LEW•muh•nuhm) foil contains mostly the element aluminum.

Most matter is made up of more than one element. Water is made up of the elements hydrogen and oxygen. These same two elements are also found in sugar. Sugar also contains a third element called *carbon*. Elements join in different ways and in different amounts to form everything in our world.

Elements

A few elements are shown here.

iron

silver

gold

aluminum

neon

✔ Quick Check

Draw Conclusions Why are elements called the building blocks of matter?

Critical Thinking Why are the properties of water and sugar different?

graphite   diamond   sugar

▲ These three kinds of matter all contain the element carbon.

What are atoms?

Elements are made up of tiny particles called atoms (AT•uhmz). An **atom** is the smallest unit of an element that has the properties of that element. All atoms of a specific element are identical to each other.

Think about dividing an object into smaller and smaller pieces. Eventually you would get to the smallest piece of the object that still has the same properties—an atom.

Atoms are everywhere, but you cannot see them. An atom is tinier than a speck of dust. It is too small to be seen with your eyes. Atoms cannot even be seen through most microscopes. Scientists study atoms with special instruments called *electron microscopes*. These high-powered tools help scientists learn about these tiny bits of matter.

This is how carbon looks under a scanning tunneling microscope. ▼

Carbon Atoms

Read a Photo

How do scientists study atoms?

Clue: Look at the tools the scientist is using.

◀ Scientists study atoms with a scanning tunneling microscope.

How can objects be made up of anything that tiny? Look at a magazine cover. The colors you see look solid. But if you look at a magazine cover with a microscope, you will see a pattern of colored dots.

✓ Quick Check

Draw Conclusions Water is made up of the elements hydrogen and oxygen. What kinds of atoms does water contain?

Critical Thinking Why do scientists study things that are too small to see with your eyes?

Atoms are very small. If you could compare the size of an atom to the size of an apple, this would be the same as comparing the size of an apple to the size of Earth. ▼

Model of an Atom

1. **Observe** Look carefully at a piece of aluminum foil. Make a list of its properties.

2. **Tear** the foil in half. Then tear each half in two. Continue tearing the pieces until you have tiny bits of foil.

3. **Compare** What are the properties of the foil bits? Read the properties you listed for the whole sheet of foil. Are the properties the same?

4. **Draw Conclusions** Did the properties of the foil change as its size changed? Are the bits of aluminum foil still aluminum? How are the bits of foil similar to atoms of an element?

How do we arrange elements?

The **periodic table** (peer•ee•AH•dik TAY•buhl) is a chart that lists all the known elements. The letter or letters in each box are symbols for the elements.

Each column in the periodic table lists a group of elements. All the elements in a group have similar properties. The table also classifies elements as metals (MET•uhlz) or nonmetals. Iron (Fe) is a metal. So are the other elements listed on the left side of the table. Carbon (C), is a nonmetal. It is listed on the right side of the table with other nonmetals.

Iron is an element used to make many things such as nails, horseshoes, and machines. What is the symbol for this important element?

 Quick Check

Draw Conclusions What is the periodic table?

Critical Thinking Why are the elements helium (He), neon (Ne), and argon (Ar) located in the same column of the periodic table?

The Periodic Table of the Elements

Key

11	— Atomic number
Na	— Element symbol
Sodium	— Element name

☐ Metals
☐ Metalloids (semimetals)
☐ Nonmetals

1																	18
1 **H** Hydrogen	2											13	14	15	16	17	2 **He** Helium
3 **Li** Lithium	4 **Be** Beryllium											5 **B** Boron	6 **C** Carbon	7 **N** Nitrogen	8 **O** Oxygen	9 **F** Fluorine	10 **Ne** Neon
11 **Na** Sodium	12 **Mg** Magnesium	3	4	5	6	7	8	9	10	11	12	13 **Al** Aluminum	14 **Si** Silicon	15 **P** Phosphorus	16 **S** Sulfur	17 **Cl** Chlorine	18 **Ar** Argon
19 **K** Potassium	20 **Ca** Calcium	21 **Sc** Scandium	22 **Ti** Titanium	23 **V** Vanadium	24 **Cr** Chromium	25 **Mn** Manganese	26 **Fe** Iron	27 **Co** Cobalt	28 **Ni** Nickel	29 **Cu** Copper	30 **Zn** Zinc	31 **Ga** Gallium	32 **Ge** Germanium	33 **As** Arsenic	34 **Se** Selenium	35 **Br** Bromine	36 **Kr** Krypton
37 **Rb** Rubidium	38 **Sr** Strontium	39 **Y** Yttrium	40 **Zr** Zirconium	41 **Nb** Niobium	42 **Mo** Molybdenum	43 **Tc** Technetium	44 **Ru** Ruthenium	45 **Rh** Rhodium	46 **Pd** Palladium	47 **Ag** Silver	48 **Cd** Cadmium	49 **In** Indium	50 **Sn** Tin	51 **Sb** Antimony	52 **Te** Tellurium	53 **I** Iodine	54 **Xe** Xenon
55 **Cs** Cesium	56 **Ba** Barium	57 **La** Lanthanum	72 **Hf** Hafnium	73 **Ta** Tantalum	74 **W** Tungsten	75 **Re** Rhenium	76 **Os** Osmium	77 **Ir** Iridium	78 **Pt** Platinum	79 **Au** Gold	80 **Hg** Mercury	81 **Tl** Thallium	82 **Pb** Lead	83 **Bi** Bismuth	84 **Po** Polonium	85 **At** Astatine	86 **Rn** Radon
87 **Fr** Francium	88 **Ra** Radium	89 **Ac** Actinium	104 **Rf** Rutherfordium	105 **Db** Dubnium	106 **Sg** Seaborgium	107 **Bh** Bohrium	108 **Hs** Hassium	109 **Mt** Meitnerium	110 **Ds** Darmstadtium	111 **Rg** Roentgenium	**Uub** Ununbium						

58 **Ce** Cerium	59 **Pr** Praseodymium	60 **Nd** Neodymium	61 **Pm** Promethium	62 **Sm** Samarium	63 **Eu** Europium	64 **Gd** Gadolinium	65 **Tb** Terbium	66 **Dy** Dysprosium	67 **Ho** Holmium	68 **Er** Erbium	69 **Tm** Thulium	70 **Yb** Ytterbium	71 **Lu** Lutetium
90 **Th** Thorium	91 **Pa** Protactinium	92 **U** Uranium	93 **Np** Neptunium	94 **Pu** Plutonium	95 **Am** Americium	96 **Cm** Curium	97 **Bk** Berkelium	98 **Cf** Californium	99 **Es** Einsteinium	100 **Fm** Fermium	101 **Md** Mendelevium	102 **No** Nobelium	103 **Lr** Lawrencium

Lesson Review

Summarize the Main Idea

Elements are the building blocks of matter. (pp. 274–275)

An **atom** is the smallest unit of an element that has the properties of the element. (pp. 276–277)

11 Na Sodium

The **periodic table** is a chart that displays information about the elements. (p. 278)

Make a FOLDABLES™ Study Guide

Make a three-tab book. Use it to summarize what you learned about elements and atoms.

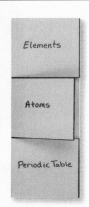

Elements

Atoms

Periodic Table

Think, Talk, and Write

1 Main Idea What are the building blocks of matter?

2 Vocabulary What is an atom?

3 Draw Conclusions What are some questions you could answer by reading the periodic table?

Text Clues	Conclusions

4 Critical Thinking How do high-powered microscopes help us understand matter?

5 Test Practice Which of the following is an element?
- **A** oxygen
- **B** sand
- **C** pebbles
- **D** cells

Writing Link

Write a Report
Research and write a story about Glenn Seaborg and his role in the discovery of elements in the periodic table.

Math Link

Make a Bar Graph
Scientists discovered elements over the years. In 1789 scientists knew only 33 elements. By 1850 they had identified 57. In 1900 the number grew to 81 and in 1950 to 96. Today we know 115 elements. Make a bar graph that shows this information.

Meet Neil deGrasse TYSON

Did you know that you are "stardust"? Neil deGrasse Tyson can tell you what that means. He is a scientist at the American Museum of Natural History in New York. He studies how the universe works.

Your body is full of hydrogen, carbon, calcium and many other atoms. All these atoms were first formed in the stars a long time ago. So were the silicon, iron, and oxygen atoms that form most of Earth's inside. How did these elements make their way from the stars to your body?

Most elements form inside the fiery and dense centers of stars. Hydrogen, the simplest of the elements, combines to form helium, carbon, and all the other elements in these conditions. Throughout their lives, stars scatter elements into space. Over millions of years, these elements combine to form new stars, or planets, or even living things, like you!

▲ Neil deGrasse Tyson is an astrophysicist, a scientist who studies how the universe works.

AMERICAN MUSEUM OF NATURAL HISTORY

ELA R 3.2.5. Distinguish the main idea and supporting details in expository text.

▲ A nebula is a cloud of gas and star dust in space. The Horsehead Nebula, above, gets its name from its horselike shape.

A main idea

▶ tells what the article is mostly about

▶ is supported by details, facts, and examples

 Write About It

Main Idea Read the article with a partner. What is the main idea? What details add to the main idea? Use a main-idea chart. Then write a few sentences to explain the main idea.

 e-Journal Write about it online @ **www.macmillanmh.com**

Matter, Matter Everywhere

In this chapter, you learned that everything is made up of matter. You learned what an atom is. You learned what all matter is made of. Think about how you would help a friend understand what matter is. What would you say to explain what elements are? Are some kinds of matter made up of more than one element? What facts would you give about atoms?

A good expository paragraph

▶ introduces the main idea

▶ supports the main idea with facts and details about the topic

▶ draws a conclusion based on the facts and details

sodium + chlorine = salt

iron + oxygen = rust

carbon + oxygen + hydrogen = wood

 Write About It

Expository Writing Write a paragraph telling about the building blocks of all matter. Begin your paragraph with a topic sentence. This sentence should state the main idea. Then include facts and details that support the main idea or add more information about it. End with a conclusion based on your facts and details.

 e-Journal Write about it online @ **www.macmillanmh.com**

 ELA W 3.1.1. Create a single paragraph:
a. Develop a topic sentence.
b. Include simple supporting facts and details.

Shapes That Matter

Have you ever looked very carefully at salt or sugar? It is hard to tell them apart because they both are white, have small grains, and feel the same. If you look closely, you will see that both are cube-shaped.

A cube is a three-dimensional shape. Look at the three-dimensional shapes below, and describe how they are alike and how they are different.

How to identify a cube or a rectangular solid

▶ A cube has six identical square faces. All sides of a cube are the same size exactly.

▶ A rectangular solid has 4 equal-size rectangular faces and 2 equal-size square faces.

Number of	Cube	Rectangular Solid
faces	6	6
vertices	8	
square faces		2
rectangular faces		4

 Solve It

Copy the chart and fill in the missing information about the cube and rectangular solid. How are the two shapes alike? How are they different?

 MA MG 3.2.5. Identify, describe, and classify common three-dimensional geometric objects (e.g., cube, rectangular solid, sphere, prism, pyramid, cone, cylinder).

Changing Matter

Look and Wonder

Have you ever baked a cake? Why doesn't a cake taste like the ingredients it is made from? Why does mixing things sometimes cause the properties of those things to change?

3 PS 1.g. Students know that when two or more substances are combined, a new substance may be formed with properties that are different from those of the original materials.

How does matter change?

Make a Prediction

Matter can change in many ways. How do flour and baking soda change when each is mixed with vinegar? Write a prediction.

Test Your Prediction

① **Observe** List the properties of each substance. Record your observations in a chart.

② **Experiment** Put 2 tablespoons of flour in one container. Add 50 milliliters of vinegar. Quickly put the balloon over the container's opening. Observe what occurs. Record your observations in your chart.

③ Repeat step 2 using baking soda in place of flour.

④ **Communicate** Draw a picture at the bottom of each column of your chart to show what happened to the balloons.

Draw Conclusions

⑤ Did your results match your prediction? Explain.

⑥ **Infer** What do you think caused the differences in the balloons?

Explore \ More

Experiment What might happen to the balloon if you add 2 tablespoons of baking soda and 50 milliliters of water to a container?

 3 IE 5.d. Predict the outcome of a simple investigation and compare the result with the prediction.

Materials

vinegar, flour, and baking soda

two clear plastic bottles and balloons

goggles

measuring cup and spoons

Step ②

Main Idea 3 PS 1.g

Matter can change. Physical changes cause matter to look different. Chemical changes cause a different kind of matter to form.

Vocabulary

physical change, p. 286

mixture, p. 287

chemical change, p. 288

LOG ON e-Glossary
@ www.macmillanmh.com

Reading Skill

Predict

What I Predict	What Happens

What are physical changes?

Matter can change. A **physical change** (FIZ•i•kuhl CHAYNJ) is a change in the way matter looks. Matter looks different after a physical change, but the makeup of the matter has not changed. It is still the same kind of matter.

Tearing a sheet of paper in half is a physical change. The size of the ripped paper differs from the size of the original sheet, but it is still paper. Stretching a rubber band is also a physical change. The size and shape of the rubber band changes, but it is still a rubber band.

It is also a physical change when matter changes state. When liquid water freezes, its state changes from liquid to solid. The water looks different, but it is still water. Liquid water and solid water are made up of the same elements. They both contain the same hydrogen and oxygen atoms.

When water changes state from a liquid to a solid, it goes through a physical change. ▶

When you mix different kinds of matter, you may get a **mixture** (MIKS•chuhr). In a mixture the properties of each kind of matter do not change. Fruit salad is a mixture of fruit. A mixture can be any combination of solids, liquids, and gases. A mixture can be separated into its original parts.

 Quick Check

Predict What will happen when you mix an egg and flour?

Critical Thinking Make a list of three physical changes you could make to a piece of paper.

▲ How can you separate the fruits in this mixture?

When sand is molded, its shape changes. It is still sand.

When glass changes state from a solid to a liquid, it goes through a physical change. ▼

What are chemical changes?

Some changes cause matter to become different substances. This change is called a chemical change (KEM•i•kuhl CHAYNJ). A **chemical change** is a change that causes different kinds of matter to form. The properties of the new matter are different from those of the original substances.

A burning log goes through a chemical change. The log starts off as solid wood. When you set the log on fire, it changes chemically. Carbon dioxide gas and ash form. The properties of these substances are very different from those of wood. That is because they are made up of different combinations of elements.

Food spoils as a result of chemical changes. Substances in food can break down and form new substances. When this happens, food may change color or have a bad smell.

▲ How do the properties of a wooden log differ from those of ashes?

Days after being picked from a tree, chemical changes make these bananas begin to spoil. ▶

When you bake a cake, the ingredients go through a chemical change. They form new substances. The properties of this new matter are not the same as the original ingredients. That is why the baked cake has a taste that differs from eggs, milk, and flour.

 Quick Check

Predict What will happen if you light a candle?

Critical Thinking When you cook an egg to make scrambled eggs, do you cause a physical change or a chemical change?

≡Quick Lab

Chemical Changes

1 **Observe** Look closely at some pennies. Make a list of their properties.

2 Place 1 teaspoon of salt in a bowl. Add 150 milliliters of vinegar. Stir until the salt dissolves.

3 **Compare** Dip a penny halfway into the liquid. Slowly count to 20 as you hold the coin there. Then remove the penny. Compare the half you held with the half that was in the liquid.

4 **Infer** What caused the change of appearance?

A Chemical Change

ingredients   **dough**   **bread**

Read a Diagram

What caused the bread dough to undergo a chemical change?

Clue: Look at the pictures to see how this happened.

What are the signs of a chemical change?

Certain signs can show that a chemical change has happened. Here are a few.

Light and Heat

As a candle burns, it releases light and heat energy. New kinds of matter form. The light and heat are signs of a chemical change.

▲ Heat and light are signs of a chemical change.

Color Change

Sometimes a color change shows that a chemical change has happened. When fruit spoils, it may turn brown. The color change shows that the fruit is changing to a different kind of matter. Dark reddish-brown spots of rust may appear on objects made of iron, such as cars and bicycles. The properties of rust differ from the properties of iron. This is because rust is a different kind of matter.

▲ A chemical change has caused some of the iron in this car to rust.

Formation of Gas

When baking soda and vinegar mix, a chemical change happens. A new substance, carbon dioxide gas, forms. As the gas forms, you see bubbles. The bubbles tell you that a chemical change is occurring.

 Quick Check

Predict What will happen to milk if you leave it in the sun?

Critical Thinking Is water boiling a physical change or a chemical change? Why?

▲ The formation of a gas is a sign of a chemical change.

Lesson Review

Summarize the Main Idea

Physical changes cause matter to look different. Mixing, tearing, and melting are physical changes. (pp. 286–287)

Chemical changes cause different kinds of matter to form. (pp. 288–289)

Light, heat, color change, and formation of gas are signs of a chemical change. (p. 290)

Make a FOLDABLES Study Guide

Make a shutter fold. Use it to summarize what you learned about how matter changes.

Physical Changes

Chemical Changes

Think, Talk, and Write

① **Main Idea** What are two ways matter can change?

② **Vocabulary** What is a mixture?

③ **Predict** Two clear liquids are mixed together. A green powder forms. What kind of change is this?

What I Predict	What Happens

④ **Critical Thinking** Mrs. Hall noticed a brass pot was discolored. She wiped the pot with a special cleaner. The pot returned to its original color. What kind of change happened?

⑤ **Test Practice** Which of the following is a physical change?
  A baking a cake
  B ice melting
  C metal rusting
  D wood burning

 Writing Link

Write an Essay
What if the ice at Earth's poles changes from ice to water? How would life change for the people and animals on Earth?

 Math Link

Solve a Problem
A log takes one hour to burn down to ash. A banana turns brown and mushy in four days. How many minutes did the longest chemical change take?

Be a Scientist

Materials

chalk

hand lens

black construction paper

vinegar

eyedropper

How can physical and chemical changes affect matter?

Form a Hypothesis

After a physical change, matter looks different but is still the same kind of matter. During a chemical change, matter changes to become a different type of matter. How can physical and chemical changes affect chalk? Write a hypothesis.

Test Your Hypothesis

1. **Observe** Break a piece of chalk in half. Use a hand lens to look at the broken end of the chalk. Record your observations. Is this a chemical or physical change?

2. **Experiment** Use one of the chalk pieces and rub it on a piece of black paper. Using the hand lens look at the chalk on the paper. Record your observations. Is this a chemical or physical change?

Step 2

3. **Experiment** Use an eyedropper to add 1 drop of vinegar to the chalk on the black paper. Record your observations. Is this a chemical or physical change?

Draw Conclusions

4. **Analyze Data** What did you observe? Which changes were physical changes? Was there a chemical change?

Step 3

5 **Infer** Describe what happened to the chalk during the chemical change. What caused this to happen?

6 **Communicate** Use your observations to write your own definitions of chemical and physical change.

What are the signs of a chemical change?

Form a Hypothesis

How can you tell a chemical change has occurred? Write a hypothesis.

Test Your Hypothesis

Design an experiment to investigate chemical changes. Use the materials shown. Write the steps you plan to follow. Record your results and observations.

Materials

plastic cups

spoon

milk

steel wool

vinegar

baking soda

Draw Conclusions

What changes did you observe? Did your experiment support your hypothesis? Why or why not?

What else would you like to know about physical and chemical change? Come up with a question to investigate. For example, how do pennies turn green? Design an experiment to answer your question.

Remember to follow the steps of the scientific process.

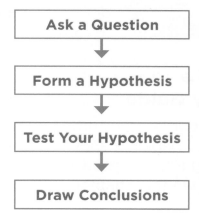

Ask a Question

↓

Form a Hypothesis

↓

Test Your Hypothesis

↓

Draw Conclusions

 3 IE 5.b. Differentiate evidence from opinion and know that scientists do not rely on claims or conclusions unless they are backed by observations that can be confirmed.

Summarize the Main Ideas

Three states of matter are solids, liquids, and gases. Each of these states of matter has its own properties. (pp. 260–269)

All matter is made up of elements. An atom is the smallest unit of an element that has the properties of that element. (pp. 272–279)

Physical changes cause matter to look different. Chemical changes cause a different kind of matter to form. (pp. 284–291)

Make a FOLDABLES™ Study Guide

Tape your lesson study guides on a piece of paper as shown. Use your study guide to review what you have learned in this chapter.

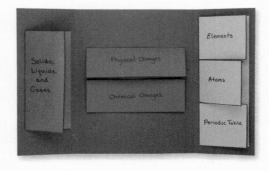

Fill each blank with the best word from the list.

chemical change, p. 288

condense, p. 268

elements, p. 274

evaporate, p. 267

gas, p. 265

liquid, p. 264

physical change, p. 286

solid, p.264

1. Matter that has a definite volume and takes the shape of its container is a _____. 3 PS 1.e

2. All matter is made up of _____. 3 PS 1.i

3. A change that causes a different kind of matter to form is a _____. 3 PS 1.g

4. Matter that does not have a definite shape or volume is a _____. 3 PS 1.e

5. When a liquid gains heat energy, it will _____ or turn into a gas. 3 PS 1.f

6. A change in the way matter looks is a _____. 3 PS 1.g

7. Matter that has a definite shape and volume is a _____. 3 PS 1.e

8. When a gas loses heat energy, it will _____ or become a liquid. 3 PS 1.f

Discuss or write about each of the following.

9. Main Idea How are matter, atoms, and elements related? 3 PS 1.h

10. Expository Writing What kind of changes occur as you blend pancake mix, milk, and an egg and then heat the batter to make pancakes? 3 PS 1.g

11. Measure Name the measurement tool shown in the photo. What property of matter does it measure? 3 PS 1.h

12. Critical Thinking Explain what kind of information you could discover by reading this table. 3 PS 1.i

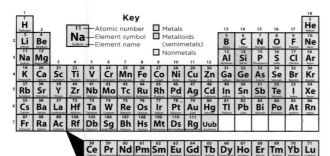

Periodic Table

Answer each of the following in a complete sentence.

13. What are two things that can occur when matter takes in heat energy? 3 PS 1.f

14. How are liquids and gases alike? How do they differ? 3 PS 1.e

15. How has our understanding of matter changed over time? 3 PS 1.i

16. What kind of change is shown in the photo? What causes this change? 3 PS 1.g

burning logs

17. What are some signs that show matter has gone through a chemical change? 3 PS 1.g

 What are some forms of matter and how can they change? 3 PS 1

Make a Matter Book

- Make a book about matter. Begin by drawing pictures that show ten different kinds of matter.

- Next to each picture, list five properties of the matter shown. Include the matter's state in your list.

- Include a page that illustrates what ancient people thought matter was made up of.

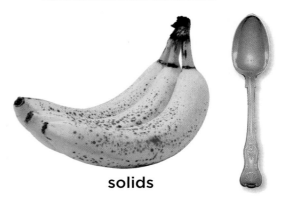

solids

liquids

gases

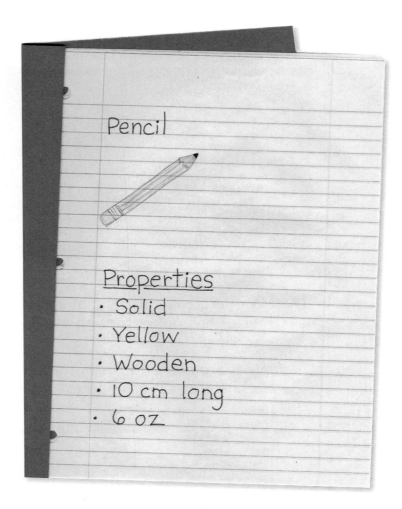

Pencil

Properties
- Solid
- Yellow
- Wooden
- 10 cm long
- 6 oz

1 Which of the following would show water changing from a solid to a liquid? 3 PS 1.f

A a pot of water on the stove

B an ice pop left in the Sun

C an ice pop left in the freezer

D a glass of water left by an open window

2 If you leave a half-filled glass of lemonade on a table for one week, what might happen to the water in the lemonade? 3 IE 5.e

A The water will boil in the sunlight.

B Someone will drink the lemonade.

C The water will evaporate.

D The water will combine with the sugar in the lemonade.

3 What happens when an ice cube changes its form? 3 PS 1.f

A A solid becomes a liquid.

B A liquid becomes a gas.

C It freezes.

D It evaporates.

4 Some students mixed butter, flour, sugar, and eggs in a bowl.

What type of change happened to the ingredients? 3 PS 1.g

A chemical change

B physical change

C solid change

D melting change

5 A student made a poster showing examples of chemical changes. Which poster is his? 3 PS 1.g

A water melting

B bowl of fruit salad

C children making cookies

D bowl of cut up fruit

6 A student wrote about matter in her science lab book. Which of the following is correct? 3 PS 1.h

A Matter is too small to see with the naked eye.

B Matter comes from the Sun.

C Matter may be stored and converted to energy.

D Matter is made up of small particles called atoms.

7 The periodic table shows 3 PS 1.i

A the names of different things that are mixed together.

B matter changing from a liquid to a gas.

C the amount of space taken up by all objects.

D all of the elements with their names and symbols.

Energy

★ What are some forms of energy and how can they change?

Lesson 1

Energy All Around

PAGE 302

Lesson 2

Using Energy

PAGE 314

Lesson 3

Energy on the Move

PAGE 326

3 PS 1. Energy and matter have multiple forms and can be changed from one form to another.

Literature
Nonfiction Book

ELA R 3.2.5. Distinguish the main idea and details in expository text. **ELA W 3.2.3.** Write personal and formal letters, thank-you notes, and invitations.

Tehachapi Pass near Los Angeles

Wind Power

by Christine Petersen

If you drive through the Tehachapi Pass north of Los Angeles, California, you'll see an amazing sight. Nearly 5,000 tall wind turbines blanket the hillsides of this broad valley. Tehachapi is home to traditional propeller-style turbines and "eggbeater" turbines, all spinning wildly as they capture strong winds flowing through the Mojave Desert and the foothills of the Tehachapi Mountains. Together, the turbines at Tehachapi produce more energy than any other wind power plant in the world.

 Write About It

Response to Literature This article tells about wind farms that create electricity. What do you think people do with the energy that is produced? Write a letter to a friend. Describe the ways that you use energy.

 e-Journal Write about it online @ **www.macmillanmh.com**

Energy all Around

Look and Wonder

Have you ever wondered what causes hot air balloons to rise into the sky? Could it be the hot air? What happens to air as it is heated?

3 PS 1.a. Students know energy comes from the Sun to Earth in the form of light.

What happens to air as it is heated?

Make a Prediction

How does heat affect air? Does it make air expand and rise? Does it make air contract and sink? Write a prediction.

Test Your Prediction

1. Place a few drops of water along the edge of the bottle's opening. Place the plastic disk on top of the opening.

2. **Predict** What will happen to the disk as the air in the bottle is warmed?

3. **Observe** Rub your hands back and forth rapidly. When your hands begin to feel warm, place them on the bottle. Observe the disk.

Draw Conclusions

4. **Communicate** What happened to the disk? Did the results match your prediction?

5. **Infer** What happens to air when it is heated?

Experiment Place an empty plastic bottle in the refrigerator for several hours. Remove the bottle from the refrigerator and immediately put a balloon over the opening. Predict what will happen to the balloon.

 3 IE 5.d. Predict the outcome of a simple investigation and compare the result with the prediction.

Materials

empty
plastic bottle

water   plastic disk

Step 3

▶ **Main Idea** 3 PS 1.a

Energy is the ability to do work. Energy can make matter change. The Sun is Earth's major source of energy.

▶ **Vocabulary**

energy, p. 304

friction, p. 307

solar energy, p. 308

 **e-Glossary**

@ **www.macmillanmh.com**

▶ **Reading Skill**

Draw Conclusions

Text Clues	Conclusions

▶ **Technology**

 Explore energy with the Secret Agents.

What is energy?

What do you think of when you hear that something has a lot of energy (EN•uhr•jee)? You may think of an athlete hard at work on the basketball court or soccer field. You may think of batteries that make your mp3 player work. Whenever work is done, energy is involved. **Energy** is the ability to do work. Energy can make matter move, grow, or change.

Using Energy

Energy can make matter move, grow, or change. These animals use energy every day to survive in their environment.

Energy Makes Things Move

Look around. You probably see many examples of energy being used to make matter move. When a soccer player kicks a ball, energy moves from the player's foot to the ball. The ball moves to a new location. When a swimmer glides through water, the swimmer uses energy to move from one place to another.

Energy Makes Things Change and Grow

Energy can change matter physically or chemically. An ice cube melts when it gains energy from the air. It changes from a solid to a liquid. Its physical properties change. When air gains heat energy, it *expands*, or spreads out. A log burns in a fireplace when it gains energy from the fire. It changes from wood to smoke, gases, and ashes. A chemical change occurs.

Energy causes living things to grow. Plants need energy to make food and grow. Animals need energy to move and grow. Living things cannot survive without energy.

 Quick Check

Draw Conclusions How can energy affect matter? Give examples.

Critical Thinking Can work be done without energy? Tell why or why not.

Read a Photo

How are the penguins using energy?

Clue: Pictures tell a story.

What are some forms of energy?

There are many different forms of energy. Some common forms are shown in the chart below.

Forms of Energy

Chemical Energy

Chemical energy is energy stored in substances. The chemical energy in gasoline is used to move a car down a street. The chemical energy in foods you eat helps your body grow and stay warm. Batteries have chemical energy, too. This chemical energy is used to run a handheld video game or camera.

Electrical Energy

Electrical energy is another form of energy. Any item that is plugged into an electrical outlet runs on electrical energy. Televisions, computers, washing machines, and hair dryers are just a few items that use electrical energy.

Heat Energy

A stove, a candle, and a match give off *heat energy*. When you feel warm, you are actually feeling heat energy. Heat is given off when energy is transferred from a hot object to one that is cooler.

Mechanical Energy

Energy in moving objects is called *mechanical energy*. Wind that blows across Earth's surface has mechanical energy. Water that moves along a river has mechanical energy. When you ride your bicycle, you use mechanical energy to move from one place to another.

Energy Can Change Form

When we use energy, it does not disappear. We change it from one form of energy into another. Rub your hands together. What do you notice? They get warmer. Since your hands are moving, they have a certain amount of mechanical energy. As friction (FRIK•shuhn) slows your hands down, some of that energy is changed to heat energy. **Friction** is a force that acts when two surfaces rub against each other. Friction causes some mechanical energy to change into heat energy.

Friction causes mechanical energy from your moving hands to change into heat energy. This makes your hands feel warmer. ▼

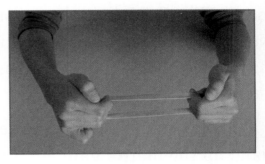

≡ *Quick Lab*

Forms of Energy

1. **Observe** Place a thick rubber band against the back of your hand. Does the rubber band feel warm, hot, or cold?

2. Stretch and release the thick rubber band 30 times.

3. **Observe** Repeat step 1. How does the rubber band feel? Is it warm, hot, or cold?

4. **Communicate** Describe how the rubber band changed.

5. **Draw Conclusions** How is energy being changed from one form to another?

✔ *Quick Check*

Draw Conclusions A car changes chemical energy in gasoline into what kind of energy?

Critical Thinking What are some objects in your home that use electrical energy?

What is Earth's main source of energy?

The Sun is Earth's main source of energy. Energy from the Sun is called **solar energy** (SOH•lahr EN•uhr•jee). Solar energy travels millions of miles through space as rays of light. Light is a form of energy. The Sun's rays do not strike all parts of Earth evenly. Some places get more direct rays of sunlight than other places. This happens because Earth is tilted on its axis.

As solar energy strikes matter, the atoms that make up the matter gain energy. They begin to move about and bump into one another. This movement produces heat energy. We see the Sun's energy as light and feel it as heat.

The Sun is Earth's main source of energy. You see the Sun's energy as light and feel it as heat.

Changing the Sun's Energy

Most forms of energy on Earth begin as energy from the Sun. Plants use solar energy to make food. This food contains chemical energy that plants use to grow. When animals eat plants, some of that energy is transferred to them.

Energy from the Sun heats Earth's air unevenly causing winds to form. The wind has mechanical energy. It can be used to turn the blades of a windmill or move a sailboat. It can even push a kite through the air. In the past, people used wind energy to grind corn and pump water. Today, wind energy turns generators to make electricity.

 Quick Check

Draw Conclusions Where does most of Earth's energy begin?

Critical Thinking How do you use energy from the Sun?

▲ The turning blades collect the wind's energy and put it to work.

Eating parts of a plant gives your body chemical energy. Your body uses this energy to grow, stay warm, and do work. ▶

How does the Sun's energy change matter?

Solar energy can cause matter to change. Solids, such as ice cream and chocolate, can melt when solar energy causes them to gain enough heat energy. Solar energy also causes liquids, such as ocean water, to evaporate and turn into a gas.

The Sun and the Water Cycle

Earth has had the same amount of water for billions of years. Water is used over and over by nature. The Sun provides energy to change snow and ice to liquid. It causes liquid water in oceans, lakes, and rivers to change to water vapor that becomes part of the air. Water vapor in the air cools and changes back into a liquid, forming clouds. The clouds get heavy and water falls back to Earth in the form of rain, hail, sleet, or snow.

▲ The Sun's energy can cause solid matter to change.

 Quick Check

Draw Conclusions What are some ways solar energy can change matter?

Critical Thinking Johnny left his glass of water in the Sun. After a few days, the glass was empty. What caused this change?

◄ Sunlight supplies the energy needed for water to evaporate, condense, and then fall back into Earth's oceans through the water cycle.

Summarize the Main Idea

Energy is the ability to do work. Energy can make matter move, change, or grow. (pp. 304–305)

Energy has many **forms.** Chemical, electrical, heat, and mechanical energy are a few forms of energy. (pp. 306–307)

The Sun is Earth's main source of energy. (pp. 308–310)

Make a FOLDABLES™ Study Guide

Make a three-tab book. Use it to summarize what you learned about energy.

Define Energy

Energy has many forms...

The Sun's Energy

Think, Talk, and Write

1. **Main Idea** What is energy? What are some forms of energy?

2. **Vocabulary** What is friction? Talk about it.

3. **Draw Conclusions** Plants get the chemical energy they need to survive from the food they make. Animals need chemical energy, too, but they cannot make their own food. How do they get energy?

Text Clues	Conclusions

4. **Critical Thinking** How is an apple like gasoline in a car?

5. **Test Practice** Earth's main source of energy comes from
   A water
   B the Sun
   C batteries
   D electricity

 Math Link

Solve a Problem
Heat energy from the Sun causes liquids to evaporate. Suppose it takes $1\frac{1}{2}$ days for 1 liter of lemonade to evaporate outside in summer. How long will it take 4 liters of lemonade to evaporate at the same rate?

 Art Link

Make a Collage
Cut out pictures of different types of energy from a magazine. Identify the type of energy being used. Paste your pictures onto a poster. Present your poster to the class.

Draw Conclusions

You just did an experiment about energy. And you read about different forms of energy. In this section, you will experiment with one of those forms of energy. Scientists do a lot of experiments. They test their ideas and then **draw conclusions** about what they observed and recorded.

❶ Learn It

When you **draw conclusions**, you interpret the results of an experiment to answer a question. You look at all the facts and decide what is true. As you gather facts and make observations, it is important to record everything on a chart. Then you will have all the data in one place to help you draw a conclusion.

◀ A water wheel is a device that uses the energy of flowing or falling water to power mills and factories.

② Try It

Now discover if water provides enough energy for a plastic plate to lift a paper clip! Gather facts and **draw conclusions** by following the steps below.

▶ Cut four 3 cm slits into a plastic plate. Then, bend the slits to create a pinwheel.

▶ Push a pencil through the center of the plate.

▶ Tie a piece of thread to a paper clip and the other end to the pencil, near the hole in the plate.

▶ Turn on the faucet so that the water runs slowly.

▶ Rest the pencil across the palms of your hands. Then, aim the edge of the plate 2 cm under the falling water. Record what you do and what you observe.

▶ Repeat with a faster stream of water. Record what you do and observe.

Now draw conclusions. Use the facts and your observations to answer these questions:

▶ What conclusion can you draw about water energy?

▶ What conclusion can you draw about the speed of water for supplying energy?

▶ What do you think would happen if you used a heavier paper clip?

③ Apply It

Now that you've learned to think like a scientist, gather facts and draw more conclusions. Do you think a paper-plate waterwheel could lift a wooden block? Test your idea, record your facts, and **draw conclusions**!

 3 IE 5.b. Differentiate evidence from opinion and know that scientists do not rely on claims or conclusions unless they are backed by observations that can be confirmed.

Using Energy

Look and Wonder

Have you ever been to a race like this one? What causes the cars to move? How can you make them go faster and farther?

3 PS 1.b. Students know sources of stored energy take many forms, such as food, fuel, and batteries. •**3 PS 1.c.** Students know machines and living things convert stored energy to motion and heat.

How can you increase the distance a toy car travels?

Form a Hypothesis

How will the steepness of a hill affect how far a car travels? Write a hypothesis.

Test Your Hypothesis

Materials

books

cardboard

masking tape

toy car

meterstick

1. Stack three books on top of one another. Tape one edge of the cardboard to the edge of the top book. Tape the bottom edge of the cardboard to the floor. The cardboard should look like a slide.

2. Put a car at the edge of the cardboard and let go.

3. **Measure** Place a piece of tape at the spot where the car stops moving. Use a meterstick to measure the distance from the bottom of the cardboard to the tape. Record your measurement.

4. **Use Variables** Add another book to the stack and repeat steps 2 and 3. Continue adding books until you have six. Compare the distances the car traveled each time.

Draw Conclusions

5. **Draw Conclusions** How did the steepness of the hill affect how far the car traveled? Did your results support your hypothesis?

Explore More

Experiment If you use a larger car, what will happen to the total distance traveled?

 3 IE 5.e. Collect data in an investigation and analyze those data to develop a logical conclusion.

Step 2

Step 3

▶ **Main Idea** 3 PS 1.b
3 PS 1.c

Potential energy is energy that is stored in objects. Kinetic energy is the energy of motion.

▶ **Vocabulary**

potential energy, p. 317

kinetic energy, p. 317

fuel, p. 318

LOG ON ⓔ **–Glossary**

@ www.macmillanmh.com

▶ **Reading Skill**

Make Inferences

Clues	What You Know	Inferences

What is potential energy and kinetic energy?

A toy car cannot move on its own. It needs a source of energy to move. Moving the car to the top of a ramp or hill can supply that energy. The taller the hill, the greater the amount of energy the car will have. The greater the amount of energy, the greater the distance the car will move.

◀ When a roller coaster is at the top of the track, it has stored energy.

When a car rests at the top of a hill, it has stored energy because of its position. Stored energy is energy that is available to be used. Stored energy is called **potential energy** (puh•TEN•shuhl EN•uhr•jee).

When a toy car moves down a ramp and across the floor, it uses potential energy. The potential energy is changed into kinetic energy. **Kinetic energy** (ki•NET•ik EN•uhr•jee) is the energy of motion. All moving objects— a toy car, a real car, even a basketball player running down a court—have kinetic energy.

▲ The swinging hammer has kinetic energy. The energy is transferred to the nail as the hammer strikes.

 Quick Check

Make Inferences What kind of energy does a rolling bowling ball have?

Critical Thinking When does a roller coaster have the most potential energy?

◄ When a roller coaster races down a track, it has kinetic energy.

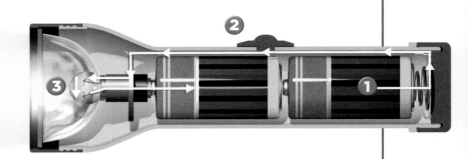

Stored Chemical Energy

1 Chemical energy is stored inside batteries.

2 When the flashlight is turned on, some of the stored chemical energy is changed to electrical energy.

3 Electrical energy is changed to light and heat by the bulb.

Read a Diagram

How does a flashlight work?

Clue: Look at the picture and read the captions.

What are some sources of stored energy?

The chemical energy stored in food, fuel, and batteries is potential energy. **Fuel** (FYEWL) is a substance such as gasoline, coal, or wood that we burn for energy. We depend on stored chemical energy for many things. We use it to heat homes and businesses. We use it to run most cars, planes, and trains. Even our bodies use chemical energy to move, grow, and stay warm.

A match has chemical energy. When you strike a match, the chemical energy is released. It changes to heat and light energy. When the chemical energy has all been used, the match goes out. Heat and light energy are no longer produced.

▲ The stored energy in a match is released as heat and light as it burns.

The food you eat contains stored chemical energy much like a match. Your body breaks down the food into simpler substances that are carried to your muscles. Here the stored energy is released. Your body uses it to grow and stay strong and healthy.

 Quick Check

Make Inferences A flashlight gives off a very low beam of light. What might this show about the batteries inside the flashlight?

Critical Thinking How does your body use stored chemical energy?

▲ **The stored energy in the food you eat helps you play and have fun.**

≡ *Quick Lab*

Using Energy

1. Your body needs energy. The table below shows how much energy is in some of the foods we eat.

Food	Energy in Calories
1 cup of 2% chocolate milk	220
1 cup of tuna salad	383
pizza slice	320

2. **Use Numbers** Using the table, plan a lunch. How many calories are in one lunch with those foods?

3. **Analyze Data** The table below shows some activities. Choose one. How long will you need to do that activity before you have used all the calories from your lunch? Choose another activity and follow the same procedure.

Activity	Calories Burned in 30 Minutes
biking (slow)	100
jogging	160
listening to music	17

4. **Compare** Which activity uses the most energy?

How is stored energy changed?

Many kinds of machines change stored energy into kinetic energy. A gas stove, oven, or furnace converts the energy stored in natural gas to heat energy. When you wind a toy, a spring in the toy tightens and potential energy is stored. This potential energy turns the gears and moves the toy when you release the spring. The moving toy has kinetic energy.

An automobile engine changes the chemical energy stored in gasoline to turn the car's wheels and move the car. Some of the stored energy is changed to heat energy. Too much heat energy can cause a car to overheat. That is why cars have a cooling system around the engine. The cooling system keeps the car from overheating.

Living things change stored energy into kinetic energy and heat energy, too. When you play outdoors with friends, you use the energy stored in foods to move about. If you move about very quickly, you might begin to feel warm. You might even begin to sweat! People sweat in order to cool their bodies.

▲ A car will stop working if too much heat energy builds up inside its engine.

If you begin to feel warm or sweaty while playing, you should stop and drink some water to cool your body off. ▼

Quick Check

Make Inferences Why are the wheels of a skateboard cool before a rider zooms down a ramp but warm after the ride?

Critical Thinking Why do you sweat when you play or exercise?

Lesson Review

Summarize the Main Idea

Potential energy is stored energy. Kinetic energy is the energy of motion. (pp. 316–317)

Foods, fuels, and batteries contain stored **chemical energy** that can be changed to other energy forms. (pp. 318–319)

Machines and living things are able to change stored energy into kinetic energy. (p. 320)

Make a **FOLDABLES**™ Study Guide

Make a trifold book. Use it to summarize what you learned about using energy.

Potential Energy | Chemical Energy | Machines and Living Things

Think, Talk, and Write

1 **Main Idea** What are some sources of potential energy?

2 **Vocabulary** What is kinetic energy?

3 **Make Inferences** Why is it important to eat a balanced meal every day?

Clues	What You Know	Inferences

4 **Critical Thinking** Why does a candle melt as it burns?

5 **Test Practice** Another name for stored energy is

A kinetic energy

B potential energy

C heat

D motion

 Writing Link

Explanatory Writing
How does a yo-yo convert potential energy into kinetic energy? Use a drawing to show when the yo-yo has the most potential energy and kinetic energy.

Math Link

Ordering Whole Numbers
Use the table on page 319 to order the activities from fewest to most calories burned. Make an Energy Number Line: On a number line from 0 to 200, put each activity in its correct place.

Turning the Power On

People use a lot of energy. We need it to power our cars, heat our homes, and run the many machines we use each day. Energy sources like coal or oil are limited. When they are used up, they are gone forever. Other sources of energy are renewable. *Renewable* means they can be used again and again. Here's a look at how people have used these alternative energy sources over time.

Wind Energy Wind turbines are invented in Denmark. These machines use the energy of the wind to create electricity.

1904

1890

1882

Hydropower Energy The river current turns a turbine. The turbine changes the river's energy into electricity.

Geothermal Energy Heat energy is harnessed from hot geysers in Italy. Steam from the geysers turns turbines that produce electricity.

ELA R 3.3.4. Determine the underlying theme or author's message in fiction and nonfiction text.

Renewable energy sources can be replaced in a short period of time. The five renewable sources used most often include hydropower (water), wind, geothermal, solar, and biomass. No matter what energy source you use, it's important to use less electricity. That means turning off the light when you leave a room.

When you draw a conclusion,

► you explain the answer to a question

► you use what you already know

► you look for clues in the article

1941

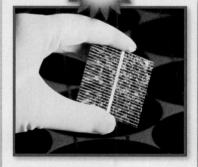

Solar Energy
Russell Ohl invents a solar cell. Solar cells transform light from the Sun into electricity.

1985

Biomass Energy The biomass power industry began to grow in California in 1985. Biomass consists of materials such as dead trees, leftover crops, and animal waste. These materials are burned to produce heat, steam, or electricity.

 ## Write About It

Draw Conclusions Why is it important for people to use renewable energy sources? Use what you already know and what you read in the article to draw a conclusion.

 e-Journal Write about it online @ **www.macmillanmh.com**

Save Gas

In this chapter you have learned that gasoline is a source of energy. Gasoline is used to make cars move and machines work. Gasoline is also used for making electrical energy. Gasoline is a fossil fuel. It is not a source of renewable energy. Once gasoline is used, it cannot be replaced. Do you think it is important to save gasoline? Why? What are some ways that people can save gasoline?

A good persuasive letter

▶ clearly states an opinion about a topic

▶ tries to persuade another person to agree with that opinion

▶ supports the opinion with convincing reasons, facts, and examples

▶ saves the best reason for last

Think about how each person is saving gasoline.

 ## Write About It

Persuasive Writing Write a persuasive letter to a community leader. Tell your opinion about why it is important to save gas. Give strong reasons, facts, and examples that will convince your reader. Save your best reason for last. Use examples to tell what will happen if your community does not save gas now. Be sure to follow the form of a formal letter.

 LOG ON **e-Journal** Write about it online @ **www.macmillanmh.com**

ELA W 3.2.3. Write personal and formal letters, thank-you notes, and invitations:
a. Show awareness of the knowledge and interests of the audience and establish a purpose and context.
b. Include the date, proper salutation, body, closing, and signature.

The Cost of Energy

The chart below shows the amount of energy used by several household appliances in a year. The energy used is measured in kilowatt-hours (kWh) and costs 10 cents ($0.10) per kWh. Multiply to find out how much it costs to use these appliances for a year.

How to multiply decimals

▶ To multiply a decimal number by a whole number, first multiply the same way you would with two whole numbers.

▶ Then count the number of decimal places. Place the decimal point that many places from the right.

3 x $1.50 (2 decimal places)

3 x 150 = 450 (count 2 decimal places $4.50)

3 x $1.50 = $4.50

 Solve It

Copy the chart and fill in the missing information. Then answer the questions below.

▶ A DVD player uses 24 kWh of energy in a year. If it costs $0.10 per kWh, what does it cost to use a DVD player for a year?

▶ If you save $0.50 per week for one year (52 weeks), how much will you have saved in one year?

Appliance	Energy Use (kWh)	Cost (per kWh)	Total Yearly Cost
clock radio	86	0.10	$8.60
refrigerator	2,088	0.10	$208.80
toaster	50	0.10	$5.00
vacuum cleaner	94	0.10	$_____
telephone answering machine	32	0.10	$_____
19-inch color television	238	0.10	$23.80
clothes washer	108	0.10	$10.80

 MA NS 3.3.3. Solve problems involving addition, subtraction, multiplication, and division of money amounts in decimal notation and multiply and divide money amounts in decimal notation by using whole-number multipliers and divisors.

Energy on the Move

Look and Wonder

Have you ever watched a buoy float up and down on the water as the waves pass by? What is happening? Why does the buoy move up and down?

 3 PS 1.d. Students know energy can be carried from one place to another by waves, such as water waves and sound waves, by electric current, and by moving objects.

Do waves carry energy?

Make a Prediction

Energy can be carried from one place to another by moving objects. Do waves transfer energy? Write a prediction.

Test Your Prediction

1 Pour water into the container so that it is nearly filled. Place the table tennis ball in the water.

2 **Predict** What will happen to the ball if you drop the rock into the container? Think about how the ball will move. Write down your prediction.

3 **Observe** Carefully drop the rock into the middle of the container. Observe the effect of the rock on the water and the ball.

4 **Compare** What was the water like before and after the rock was dropped into it?

Draw Conclusions

5 What caused the ball to move? How is the ball like a buoy in an ocean?

Explore More

How can you prove waves are transferring energy to the ball? Where does the energy come from?

Materials

deep container of water

table tennis ball

small rock

Step **3**

 3 IE 5.d. Predict the outcome of a simple investigation and compare the result with the prediction.

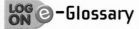
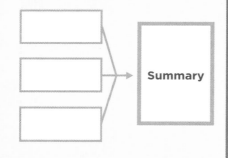

▲ **How does a bowler use energy to knock down all the pins?**

How can energy move through objects?

Have you ever gone bowling? If so, you saw that energy can move from one object to another. Kinetic energy from your arm and hand is transferred to the ball when you throw it down the lane. The kinetic energy of the moving ball is transferred to the first pin it hits. The kinetic energy of the pin moves to other pins that it hits. If you aim correctly, energy can help you get a strike!

Energy and Moving Objects

All moving objects have kinetic energy. The kinetic energy of moving objects is carried to any other objects that they bump into. The other objects then gain kinetic energy and may begin to move.

Many games that you play use the energy of moving objects. As a baseball player swings at a pitch, the bat is in motion. It has kinetic energy. When the bat strikes a ball, the energy is transferred. The ball gains kinetic energy. It moves away from the bat. When a soccer player kicks a soccer ball, her leg is in motion. This energy of motion is transferred to the ball. The ball gains kinetic energy. It moves away from the player's foot.

 Quick Check

Summarize How do moving objects transfer energy?

Critical Thinking How do you use the energy of moving objects to win a game of marbles?

▲ How is the energy of motion used to score a goal?

When you push the first domino, energy is transferred to start a chain reaction of falling dominoes. ▶

How is energy transferred by waves?

Waves are everywhere. Whether you recognize them or not, waves are all around you. Sound waves, visible light waves, seismic or earthquake waves, and ocean waves are a few of the examples of waves.

Have you ever enjoyed a swim in the ocean? If so, you know that waves carry energy from place to place. A **wave** is a disturbance that moves through matter or space. Waves move through ocean water in a regular pattern. The energy that moves along these waves is transferred to objects or people floating in the water.

Ocean waves transfer energy to objects in the water.

Wave Movement

Waves move in different ways. Ocean waves move partly up and down. Their energy is transferred to objects in the water. This causes the objects to bob up and down. Waves that move in an up and down motion are called *transverse waves*.

A wave affects the matter it moves through. As a wave moves through water, the water moves up and down, but then returns to its original position. The energy in the water, however, moves from one place to another.

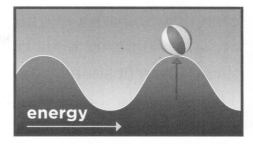

Transverse Wave

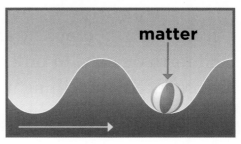

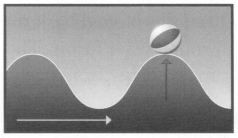

▲ Energy moves forward through a transverse wave, but the ball moves up and down.

Read a Diagram

As the wave moves from left to right, how do the water and the ball move?

Clue: Arrows show direction.

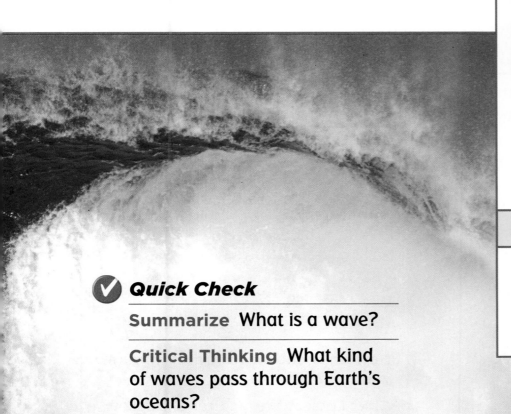

✔ *Quick Check*

Summarize What is a wave?

Critical Thinking What kind of waves pass through Earth's oceans?

How does sound energy move?

You hear many different kinds of sound each day. Some sounds are loud, others are soft. Some are high, others are low. All these different sounds are alike in one way. They are caused by sound energy. Sound is a type of mechanical energy. **Sound energy** is the energy made by objects that vibrate (VIGH•brayt). **Vibrate** means to move back and forth quickly. In order for a sound to be produced, something must move.

When an object vibrates, it pushes on the air around it. The air is squeezed together. Then it is pushed back to its original place. A sound wave forms. The sound wave carries energy from one place to another.

1. Sound waves enter the **outer ear**.

2. Sound waves travel to the **eardrum**, making it vibrate.

3. The vibrating eardrum makes the hammer, anvil, and stirrup vibrate in the **middle ear**.

4. The vibrating bones cause fluid in the **inner ear** to vibrate. The vibrating fluid causes tiny hairs to vibrate, too.

5. Vibrations are passed to a **nerve** that carries sound waves to the brain. The brain processes the sound waves, and you hear sound.

How Sound Energy Moves

Sound waves carry energy from one place to another.

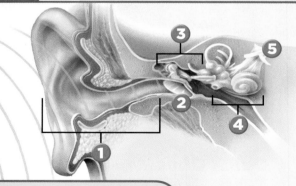

Read a Diagram

How do sound waves travel through your ear?

Clue: Look at the pictures and follow the path of the sound waves.

LOG ON *Science in Motion* Watch how sound energy moves @ **www.macmillanmh.com**

Sound waves have a different kind of motion than transverse waves. Sound waves do not move up and down. They move back and forth. That is because they form when air is quickly pulled together and then pushed apart. Waves that move back and forth are called *compression waves*.

Every sound that you hear is carried to your ear by a compression wave. As the wave strikes your ear, parts of your ear begin to vibrate. If the parts vibrate very quickly, you hear a high sound like a whistle. If the parts move slowly, you hear a low sound like a tuba.

 Quick Check

Summarize How does sound energy move from one place to another?

Critical Thinking What happens when you hear a sound?

When you pull one end of a spring toy, compression waves form. They move back and forth. Sound waves are compression

Quick Lab

How Sounds Are Made

1 Wrap several rubber bands around a cardboard box.

2 **Observe** Pluck the bands to make sounds. What do you see happening?

3 **Draw Conclusions** Can you make a sound without the rubber bands moving? Why or why not?

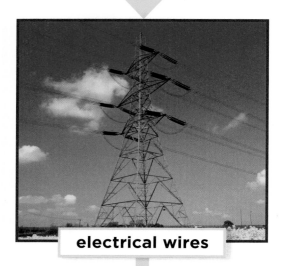

power plant

electrical wires

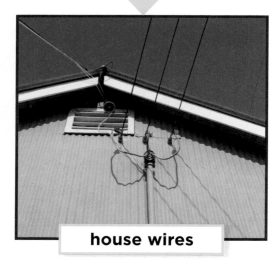

house wires

▲ The electrical energy made inside a power plant moves through wires. The wires run into your home.

How does electrical energy move?

Has the power ever gone off in your home? If so, you soon learned that many of your favorite things run on electrical energy. Your lights and refrigerator stopped working. That is because the electrical energy needed to run these things stopped flowing into your home.

Electrical energy is produced in power plants. A power plant is where potential or kinetic energy is changed into electrical energy.

The electrical energy made inside a power plant moves through wires. The wires run into your home. Electric sockets in your home connect to these wires. When you plug an electric cord into a socket, electrical energy moves through the cord. It then changes form and becomes the light energy of a lamp or the sound and light energy of a television set.

 Quick Check

Summarize How does electrical energy get to your home?

Critical Thinking Why do we need to use electrical outlets to run lights and refrigerators?

Lesson Review

Summarize the Main Idea

Energy can be carried from one place to another by **moving objects**. (pp. 328–329)

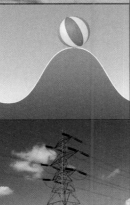
Waves carry energy from place to place. (pp. 330–333)

Electrical energy is moved from place to place through **wires**. (p. 334)

Make a FOLDABLES™ Study Guide

Make a three-tab book. Use it to summarize what you read about how energy moves.

Think, Talk, and Write

1 **Main Idea** What are three ways energy is carried from place to place?

2 **Vocabulary** What is a wave?

3 **Summarize** How are ocean and sound waves alike? How do they differ?

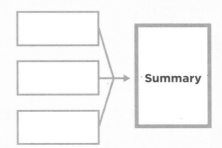
Summary

4 **Critical Thinking** Jon threw a large rock into a pond. Soon, flowers floating on the other side of the pond began to move up and down. Explain why.

5 **Test Practice** Waves that move back and forth are called
A electrical waves
B transverse waves
C kinetic waves
D compression waves

Math Link

Make a Bar Graph
The data table lists the loudness of some sounds. Use the data to construct a bar graph.

Sound	Loudness in Decibels
whisper	20
talking	60
city street	80
thunder	110

Health Link

Write a Research Report
Too much noise can harm your ears. It is important to protect your ears from loud noises. How might you protect your ears? What are some places where you need to protect your ears?

Be a Scientist

Materials

plastic bag

water

tuning fork

wooden block

How does sound energy move through different materials?

Form a Hypothesis

Sound is a form of energy. It travels in waves through air, water, and solid objects. Traveling through some objects can slow down sound waves. Sound can be stopped, or absorbed, by other objects. What happens when sound travels through solids, liquids, and gases? Write a hypothesis.

Test Your Hypothesis

1 **Record Data** Fill a plastic bag with water and seal it. Hold it to your ear. In your journal, describe how sounds in the classroom change when you place the bag near your ear.

2 **Experiment** Hold the bag of water against your ear. Gently tap the tuning fork on a desk and hold it close to the bag. Record what you hear. Touch the tuning fork to the bag. Does that change the sound? Record your answer.

Matter	Sound Description
solid	
liquid	
gas	

Step **1**

3 **Experiment** Hold a wooden block to your ear. Tap the tuning fork and hold it near the block. Record what you hear. Touch the tuning fork to the block. Record any change that you hear.

4 **Experiment** Tap the tuning fork and hold it near your ear. Record what you hear. Have a partner walk across the room and tap the fork. Record any differences you heard.

Step **2**

Draw Conclusions

⑤ Compare What did the tuning fork sound like when it traveled through water? Was that different than what it sounded like when it traveled through air?

⑥ Analyze Data Which material blocked more sound energy, air, wood, or water? Why do you think the sound energy was blocked?

⑦ Infer What materials would you use to build a room, such as a library, that needs to block sound?

Inquiry Guided

How can wind energy change?

Form a Hypothesis

How can you change wind energy into another form of energy? Write a hypothesis.

Test Your Hypothesis

Design an experiment to investigate how wind energy can be changed. Write out the steps you plan to follow. Record your results and observations.

Draw Conclusions

Did your experiment support your hypothesis? Why or why not?

Inquiry Open

What else could you test about energy waves? For example, what can cause changes in waves on water? Design an experiment to find out.

Remember to follow the steps of the scientific process.

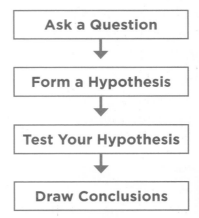

Ask a Question

↓

Form a Hypothesis

↓

Test Your Hypothesis

↓

Draw Conclusions

3 IE 5.e. Collect data in an investigation and analyze those data to develop a logical conclusion.

Summarize the Main Ideas

Energy is the ability to do work. Energy can make matter change. The Sun is Earth's major source of energy. (pp. 302–311)

Food, fuel, and batteries contain stored energy. Machines and living things change stored energy into motion and heat. (pp. 314–321)

Energy is carried from one place to another by moving objects, by waves, and by electric current that flows through wires. (pp. 326–335)

Make a **FOLDABLES**™ Study Guide

Tape your lesson study guides on a piece of paper as shown. Use your study guide to review what you have learned.

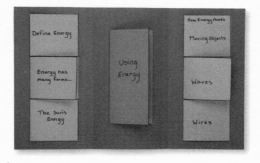

Fill each blank with the best word from the list.

energy, p. 304

friction, p. 307

fuel, p. 318

kinetic energy, p. 317

potential energy, p. 317

solar energy, p. 308

sound energy, p. 332

wave, p. 330

1. All moving objects have the energy of motion or _____. 3 PS 1.c

2. A disturbance that moves through matter or space is a _____. 3 PS 1.d

3. The ability to do work is called _____. 3 PS 1.a

4. Energy made by objects that vibrate is _____. 3 PS 1.d

5. Energy that is stored or waiting to be used is _____. 3 PS 1.b

6. Gasoline is a _____, which is a source of stored energy. 3 PS 1.b

7. When you rub your hands together, you are using _____ to keep them warm. 3 PS 1.c

8. Energy from the Sun is called _____. 3 PS 1.a

LOG ON **e-Review** Summaries and quizzes online @ **www.macmillanmh.com**

Discuss or write about each of the following.

9. Draw Conclusions What is causing this matter to change? 3 PS 1.a

10. Expository Writing How does a baseball player hitting a home run show that energy can move from one object to another? 3 PS 1.d

11. Draw Conclusions How will this roller coaster convert potential energy into kinetic energy? How will it move along this track? 3 PS 1.b

12. Critical Thinking Both a car and a person need energy to move. How is the way they obtain this needed energy alike? 3 PS 1.c

Answer each of the following in a complete sentence.

13. Name four forms of energy. 3 PS 1.d

14. How does energy from the Sun change matter? 3 PS 1.a

15. What kind of energy change is shown in the photograph? 3 PS 1.b

16. How are transverse waves and compression waves alike? Different? 3 PS 1.d

17. What must happen for the listeners to hear the sound of a guitar? 3 PS 1.d

 What are some forms of energy and how can they change? 3 PS 1

CHAPTER 7

Make an Energy Poster

- Make a poster about energy. Begin by drawing a picture that shows Earth's main source of energy. Beneath the picture, write a sentence that tells how this energy reaches Earth.

- Then, draw pictures that show four different forms of energy. Label each of your pictures.

- Next, draw two pictures that show energy changing form. Beneath each picture, write a sentence that describes the change.

chemical energy

kinetic energy

heat energy

1 **How are a lamp and the Sun alike?** 3 PS 1.a

A both give daylight

B both give off heat

C both produce electricity

D both reflect light

2 **Sound energy is carried by** 3 PS 1.d

A noise.

B waves.

C wires.

D ears.

3 **Which of the following has the most potential energy?** 3 PS 1.c

A roller-coaster car at the bottom of a hill

B roller-coaster car half way up a hill

C roller-coaster car at the top of a hill

D roller-coaster car half way down a hill

4 **When you switch on a flashlight, you are converting** 3 PS 1.d

A food energy into heat

B stored energy into light

C kinetic energy into motion

D potential energy into speed

5 **How does energy travel from the Sun to Earth?** 3 PS 1.a

A as wind

B as light

C as matter

D as water

6 **Look at the graph below.**

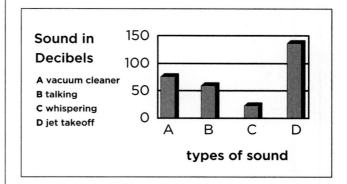

Sound in Decibels

A vacuum cleaner
B talking
C whispering
D jet takeoff

types of sound

Based on the data, which sound is loudest? 3 IE 5.e

A sound from a vacuum cleaner

B sound from talking

C sound from whispering

D sound from a jet takeoff

7 **A bowling pin falls over when it is hit by a bowling ball because the ball is transferring** 3 PS 1.d

A energy of motion to the bowling pin.

B heat energy to the bowling pin.

C chemical energy to the bowling pin.

D stored energy to the bowling pin.

Light

 What is light and how does it travel?

342

Lesson 1

How Light Moves

PAGE 346

Lesson 2

Seeing Light and Color

PAGE 356

Lesson 3

Shadows

PAGE 368

 3 PS 2. Light has a source and travels in a direction.

Literature

Poem

 ELA R 3.2.3. Demonstrate comprehension by identifying answers in the text.
ELA W 3.2.1. Write narratives: **a.** Provide a context within which an action takes place. **b.** Include well-chosen details to develop the plot. **c.** Provide insight into why the selected incident is memorable.

A prism separates white light into all the colors of the rainbow.

Crystal Vision

by Lawrence Schimel

The prism bends a beam of light
And pulls it into colored bands.
My fingers tremble with delight:
I hold a rainbow in my hands.

Write About It

Response to Literature The poet tells about
an experience he had with light. How did the
experience make him feel? Write a personal
narrative about an experience you have had
with light. It might be a rainbow, a sunrise,
or a sunset. Tell how you felt about the
experience and why it is memorable.

LOG ON **e-Journal** Write about it online
@ **www.macmillanmh.com**

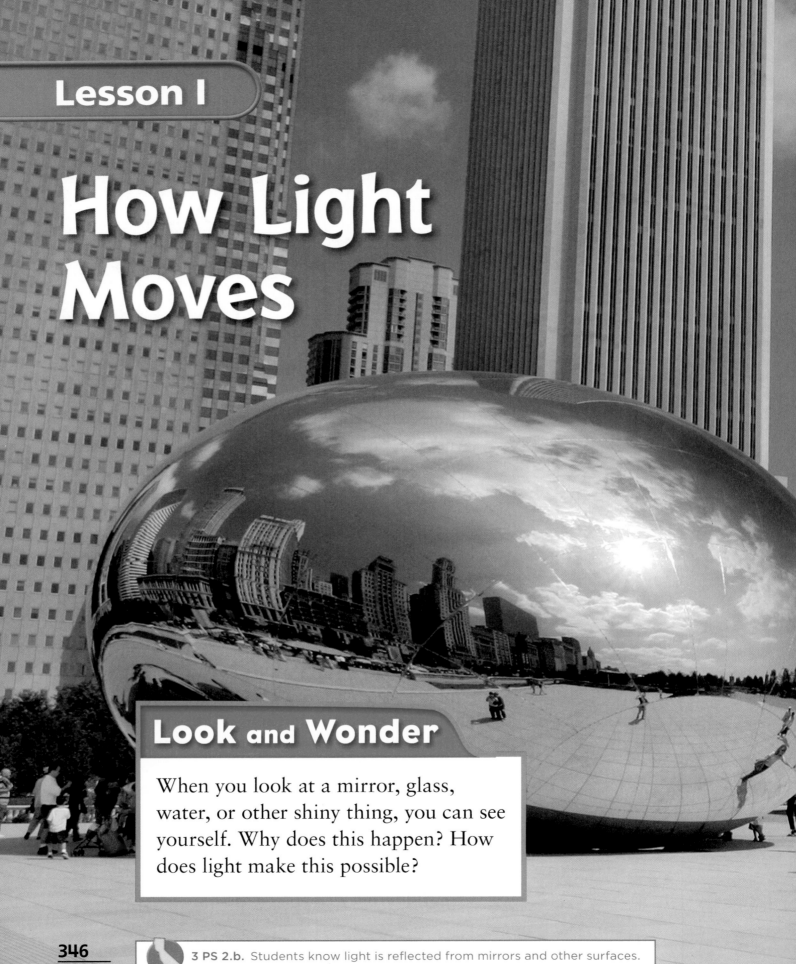

How Light Moves

Look and Wonder

When you look at a mirror, glass, water, or other shiny thing, you can see yourself. Why does this happen? How does light make this possible?

3 PS 2.b. Students know light is reflected from mirrors and other surfaces.

How does light move?

Make a Prediction

What happens to light when it hits a mirror?

Test Your Prediction

1 Hold a mirror in front of you. Have a partner shine the flashlight onto the mirror.

2 **Observe** What happens to the flashlight's beam?

3 **Experiment** Pick a spot on the wall or chalkboard. Can you make light bounce off the mirror and shine on that spot? How? Do you have to move the mirror, the flashlight, or both?

Draw Conclusions

4 What happened to the beam of light when it hit the mirror? What happened when you moved the mirror? What happened when you moved the flashlight?

5 **Communicate** Make a drawing to show how light moves.

Explore More

Experiment Sit next to your partner and hold the mirror so that you can see your partner. Can your partner see you in the mirror? Can you see yourself and your partner in the mirror at the same time?

 3 IE 5.e. Collect data in an investigation and analyze those data to develop a logical conclusion.

Materials

mirror

flashlight

Step 1

Step 3

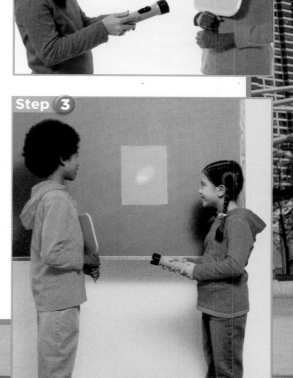

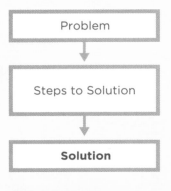

What is light?

From blue skies to green grass and golden sunshine, you live in a world of color. What is color? Why do we see color? To understand color, you must learn about light. **Light** is a form of energy. Light is made up of transverse waves that move up and down.

Visible Light

You can see some waves of light energy. Color is light energy we can see. Light you can see is called *visible light*. The beam of a flashlight and flash of a camera are visible light. Everything you see with your eyes is because of visible light.

Forms of Light Energy

▼ **Radio waves** are used to transmit signals for cellular phones, radios, and televisions.

Infrared waves are felt as heat. This photo was taken with film that shows infrared light.

▼ **Microwaves** are used to cook food.

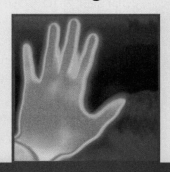

radio waves   microwaves   infrared waves

Invisible Light

Other forms of light energy are not visible. X-ray waves are a form of light energy that you cannot see. We use X-ray waves to take pictures of bones and teeth. The waves given off inside a microwave oven are another form of invisible light energy. You cannot see microwaves but you can see how they change uncooked foods.

 Quick Check

Problem and Solution You fell and hurt your ankle. How can you find out if you broke it?

Critical Thinking How are light and sound similar?

Visible light waves are the only light energy we can see. We see these waves as the colors of the rainbow.

Ultraviolet waves tan your skin but can also give you a sunburn. ▶

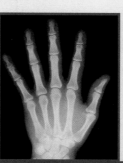

An **X-ray wave** is invisible light energy used to take pictures of bones. ▼

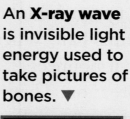

High-energy **gamma waves** are used in nuclear power plants. ▼

CAUTION RADIOACTIVE MATERIALS

| visible waves | ultraviolet waves | X-ray waves | gamma waves |

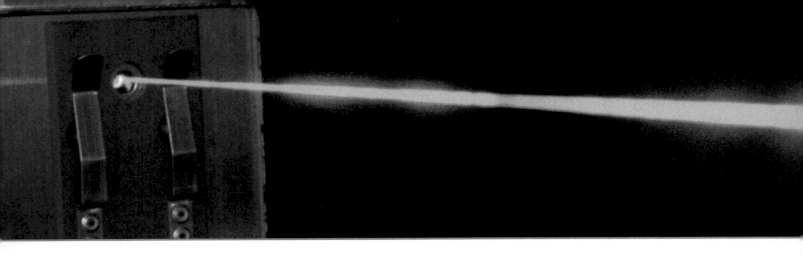

How does light travel?

All forms of light energy are alike in one way. Light always travels in a straight path. Visible light moves outward from a lamp in a straight path. The microwaves in a microwave oven move in a straight path. Even light energy from the Sun travels millions of miles through space in straight paths.

Reflection

Have you ever played tennis? After you hit the ball toward the ground, it bounces upward. Light acts much like a tennis ball. When light hits an object, it bounces off in a different direction. Then it continues moving in a straight path. The bouncing of light waves off an object is called **reflection** (ri•FLEK•shuhn).

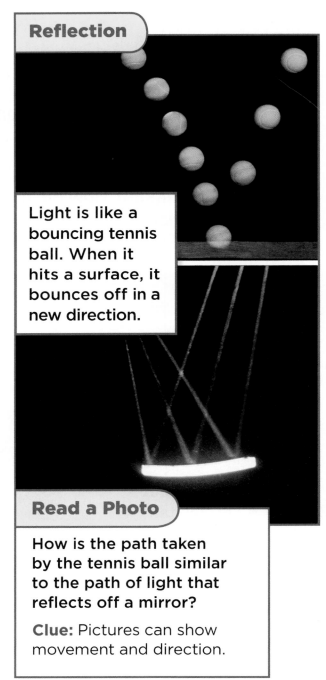

Reflection

Light is like a bouncing tennis ball. When it hits a surface, it bounces off in a new direction.

Read a Photo

How is the path taken by the tennis ball similar to the path of light that reflects off a mirror?

Clue: Pictures can show movement and direction.

What do you notice about the path of the laser light?

Smooth, shiny surfaces reflect almost all the light that strikes them. These surfaces can be used as mirrors. Light bounces off them in one direction and forms a picture called an *image*.

 Quick Check

Problem and Solution How can you see yourself if you do not have a mirror?

Critical Thinking Is it possible to see in the dark? Explain.

Movement of Light

1. Use a pencil and carefully poke a hole in two index cards. Hold the cards upright on a flat surface so that the holes are lined up.

2. **Observe** Place a lit flashlight directly behind the last card. Then bend your body so that you are eye level with the first card. Can you see the flashlight's beam?

3. **Predict** What will happen if you move one of the cards? Will you still be able to see the light? Write down your prediction and make a drawing of how you think the light will move.

4. **Observe** Move the second card a little to the right. Again bend your body so that you are eye level with the first card. Can you see the flashlight's beam now?

5. **Draw Conclusions** What caused differences in your observations? Make another sketch to explain how light travels.

◀ **When you look in a mirror you see an image of yourself.**

What happens when light hits a rough surface?

A smooth, shiny mirror reflects light very well and shows a clear image. A mirror with a scratched surface will not reflect a clear image. Why?

When light hits a rough surface, it bounces off in different directions. Because of this, a clear image does not form. You can see yourself on the surface of a calm pond. If the water is rough and swirling, a clear image does not form. This is because the light is reflected in many different directions.

▲ When light hits a rough pond, it bounces off in different directions. You cannot see a clear image on the surface.

▲ Light that hits a rough surface is reflected in different directions.

 Quick Check

Problem and Solution If you were planning a building that reflects the sky, what kind of material would you use?

Critical Thinking Have you ever looked at your reflection in a pool of water? Why do you think a pool of water can act like a mirror?

Lesson Review

Summarize the Main Idea

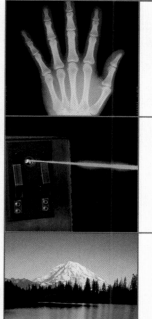

Light is a **form of energy**. Some light energy is visible. Some is invisible. (pp. 348–349)

Light travels in a straight path. The light that bounces off an object is a **reflection**. (p. 350–351)

If light hits a **smooth surface**, a clear image forms. Light that hits a **rough surface** scatters. (pp. 350–352)

Make a FOLDABLES™ Study Guide

Make a layered-look book. Use it to summarize what you read about light.

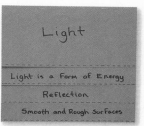

Think, Talk, and Write

1. **Main Idea** What is light?

2. **Vocabulary** What is a reflection?

3. **Problem and Solution** Why can you see yourself in the base of a silver spoon but not at the bottom of a plastic bowl?

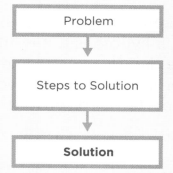

Problem

↓

Steps to Solution

↓

Solution

4. **Critical Thinking** How is a reflection in a mirror different from the object in front of the mirror?

5. **Test Practice** How does light travel?
   - **A** in a zigzag path
   - **B** in a curved path
   - **C** in a circular path
   - **D** in a straight path

 **Writing Link**

Write a Paragraph
Count the number of mirrors in your home. Are there many? We don't think about mirrors, but they are very useful tools. Write a paragraph listing at least five uses for mirrors.

 Math Link

Solve a Problem
One side of a rectangular mirror is 8 feet long. Another side of the rectangular mirror is 10 feet long. What are the lengths of the other two sides of the mirror?

Experiment

You just read that light moves in a straight path. How did scientists figure this out? They did an **experiment**, recorded what they observed, and analyzed the data to draw a conclusion.

① Learn It

When you **experiment**, you make and follow a procedure to test a hypothesis. It is important to record what you observe during an experiment. Once you have enough information, you can decide whether your hypothesis is supported or disproved.

② Try It

In the following **experiment**, you will test the hypothesis that light moves in a straight path. Follow the steps of the procedure. Then use your observations to draw a conclusion.

Procedure

❶ Draw a target on a sheet of white paper. Hang it on a wall near your desk or table.

❷ Stand two mirrors in clay as shown. Then shine a flashlight into one mirror. Draw or write your observations on a chart.

❸ Move the light or the mirror until the light is reflected in the other mirror. Record your observations.

❹ Continue to move the light or mirrors until the light is reflected off your target.

❺ Shine the flashlight from a higher, then a lower angle. Record your observations.

Draw Conclusions

▶ How did you make the light hit the target? Does light always move in a straight path?

▶ Did your observations support or disprove the hypothesis?

❸ Apply It

Now do another **experiment**. Put the mirrors back in place. Place a small object between them. How many reflections do you see? Move the mirrors closer together, then farther apart. How many reflections do you see each time? Remember to record your observations.

What I Did	What I Observed
shine the light in one mirror	
made light reflect in the other mirror	
shine the light from a higher angle	
shine the light from a lower angle	

3 PS 2.b. Students know light is reflected from mirrors and other surfaces.

355
EXTEND

Seeing Light and Color

Look and Wonder

Have you ever looked through colored glass? How does colored glass change the way an object looks?

3 PS 2.c. Students know the color of light striking an object affects the way the object is seen. •**3 PS 2.d.** Students know an object is seen when light traveling from the object enters the eye.

How does light affect the color you see?

Form a Hypothesis

Will the color of an object appear to be different if you look at it through a colored filter?

Test Your Hypothesis

1 Predict Look at a sheet of white paper and a few sheets of colored paper. What color will each sheet of paper appear to be if you observe it through the blue filter? The red? The green? Write down your predictions.

2 Experiment Look at the white paper and the colored paper through the red filter. Repeat for each of your colored filters. Make a list of all the colors that you see.

Draw Conclusions

3 Compare How do your observations compare to your predictions? How do they differ?

4 Analyze Data Why did you see different colors?

Explore More

Experiment What color will a white object be if you look at it through a blue filter? What if you look through both a blue and a red filter at the same time? Try it and explain what you see.

 3 IE 5.d. Predict the outcome of a simple investigation and compare the result with the prediction.

Materials

sheets of colored paper

sheets of colored plastic

Step **2**

Main Idea 3 PS 2.c 3 PS 2.d

You see an object when reflected light enters your eyes. The color of light that bounces off an object gives the object its color.

Vocabulary

cornea, p. 358

pupil, p. 358

iris, p. 358

lens, p. 359

prism, p. 360

absorb, p. 360

LOG ON ⊜-Glossary
@ www.macmillanmh.com

Reading Skill

Main Idea

How do you see?

You know that light reflects or bounces off objects it strikes. If the reflected light enters your eyes, you see an image of the object. The light first strikes the cornea. The **cornea** is the clear outer covering of the eye. After light passes through the cornea, it enters the pupil. The **pupil** is an opening into the eye.

Your pupils change size to let in more or less light. Your pupils are small when there is a lot of light. They grow larger and let in more light as the amount of light around you decreases. This change in your pupil's size is caused by the iris. The **iris** is the colored circle that surrounds the pupil. It controls how much light enters the eye by changing the size of the pupil.

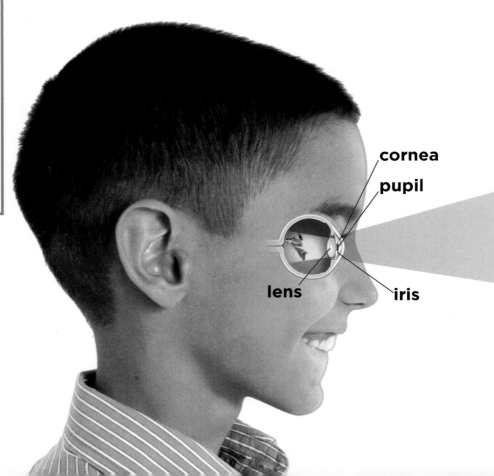

cornea

pupil

lens

iris

Light that moves into your eye must be focused. This is just like light from a movie projector that must be focused on a screen. The part of the eye that focuses incoming light is the **lens**. It is located behind the pupil and iris. The lens focuses light on the back of the eyeball. Information about the picture that forms is sent to the brain. The brain then makes sense out of the picture.

 Quick Check

Main Idea How does reflected light allow you to see?

Critical Thinking Why does the size of a pupil change?

How Light Affects Your Pupils

1. **Predict** Does the amount of light in a room affect your pupils? Write down your prediction.

2. **Observe** Dim the classroom lights. Look at your pupils in a mirror. Make a sketch of what you see.

3. **Observe** Turn on the classroom lights. Again, look at your pupils in the mirror. Make a sketch of what you see.

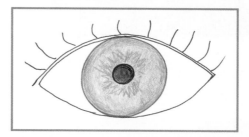

4. **Compare** How do your sketches differ?

5. **Draw Conclusions** What caused differences in your sketches? What does this show about the amount of light that enters your eyes?

◀ Light entering the eye passes through the cornea, the pupil, and the lens. The light is focused on the eyeball to form an image.

Why can you see colors?

Have you ever seen a rainbow? If so, you probably saw bands of different colors. This happens when white light is separated by an object called a prism (PRIZ•uhm). A **prism** is a special lens that separates white light. Drops of water in the sky can act like prisms and separate sunlight. When this happens, a rainbow forms. A rainbow has seven different colors. That is because white light is made up of seven different colors of light.

When white light strikes an object, some colors of light are **absorbed**, or taken in. Some colors of light are reflected. If you look at the object, some of the reflected light enters your pupils. You see the object as the color of this reflected light.

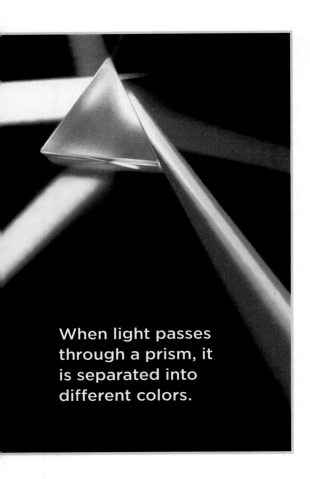

When light passes through a prism, it is separated into different colors.

Red, orange, yellow, green, blue, indigo, and violet are the colored lights that form white light.

The leaf looks green.

The flower looks red.

White light that strikes a leaf is made up of seven different colors. The leaf absorbs all of the colors except for green. Only green light bounces off the leaf. It is reflected to your eyes. You see the leaf as green.

Something quite different happens when the same white light strikes a red flower. Now the green light is absorbed. All of the colors are absorbed except for red. Only the red light is reflected to your eyes. You see the flower as red.

 Quick Check

Main Idea What happens when white light passes through a prism?

Critical Thinking Why does a banana appear to be yellow?

Why do objects appear black or white?

When white light hits a tar-covered road, all the colors of light are absorbed. Almost no light is reflected. This is why the road looks black. When white light strikes a snowman, all the colors of light are reflected. No light is absorbed. The snowman looks white.

What happens when you view a white object through a colored filter? Because a white object reflects all the colors of light, the object will look the same color as the filter. If you shine a red light on a white sheet of paper the paper will look red. The filter only allows red light to pass through it. It absorbs all other colors of light. If you look at the same sheet of paper through a blue filter, it will look blue. Only blue light can pass through the blue filter. All the other colors of light are absorbed. An object's color is affected by the light shining on it.

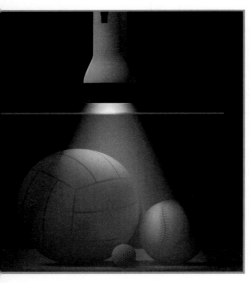

▲ Why do the objects appear to be the same color as the filter?

 Quick Check

Main Idea Why does a tar-covered road look black?

Critical Thinking What color do you see if you look at a white sheet of paper through a yellow filter? Why?

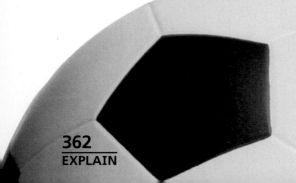

◀ Light is absorbed by the black sections and reflected off the white sections.

Lesson Review

Summarize the Main Idea

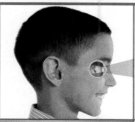

When reflected light enters **your eye**, you see an image. (pp. 358–359)

White light is made up of seven **colors**. (pp. 360–361)

Black objects absorb all colors. **White** objects reflect all colors. (p. 362)

Make a FOLDABLES™ Study Guide

Make a trifold book. Use it to summarize what you learned about color.

Think, Talk, and Write

1 **Main Idea** What must happen for an object to be seen? Talk about it.

2 **Vocabulary** What is a prism?

3 **Main Idea** Why does a school bus appear yellow and a fire truck appear red?

4 **Critical Thinking** A chalkboard appears black whether you shine red light or white light on it. But, an index card appears red in red light and white in white light. What causes this to happen?

5 **Test Practice** How many colors make up white light?
A four
B five
C six
D seven

Writing Link

Write a Story
Is color important? Write a story about a world without color. What would life in your story be like?

Math Link

Make a Chart
A spinner landed on "Red" 6 times, "Blue" 4 times, and "Green" 5 times. Construct a tally chart to show these results.

A BEAM OF LIGHT

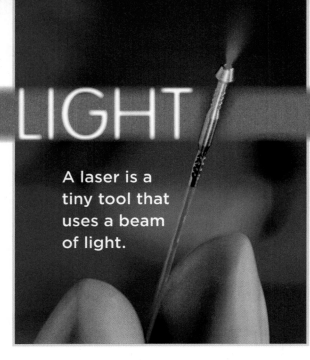

A laser is a tiny tool that uses a beam of light.

Surgeons are doctors who perform operations to fix injuries or treat diseases. They use scalpels, special tools with sharp blades, to cut through tissues such as skin, muscles, and organs. Today, they have another tool they can use to do operations that were impossible in the past. That tool is a beam of light!

This beam of light is called a laser. Not many people know that LASER stands for Light Amplification by Stimulated Emission of Radiation. Lasers are very powerful and precise. Lasers can cut though tissue without causing a lot of blood loss.

Lasers were first used to fix marks on children's skin. Today, surgeons use lasers to treat injuries to the brain, the heart, and many other parts of the human body. Lasers are even used to help people see better.

Doctors perform laser eye surgery on people who have vision problems. The laser is tapped, or "pulsed," on the surface of the eye to change its shape. After the surgery, the patient's vision is improved. The patient usually does not have to wear glasses or contact lenses.

AMERICAN MUSEUM ᵒᶠ NATURAL HISTORY

ELA R 3.2.6. Extract appropriate and significant information from text, including problems and solutions.

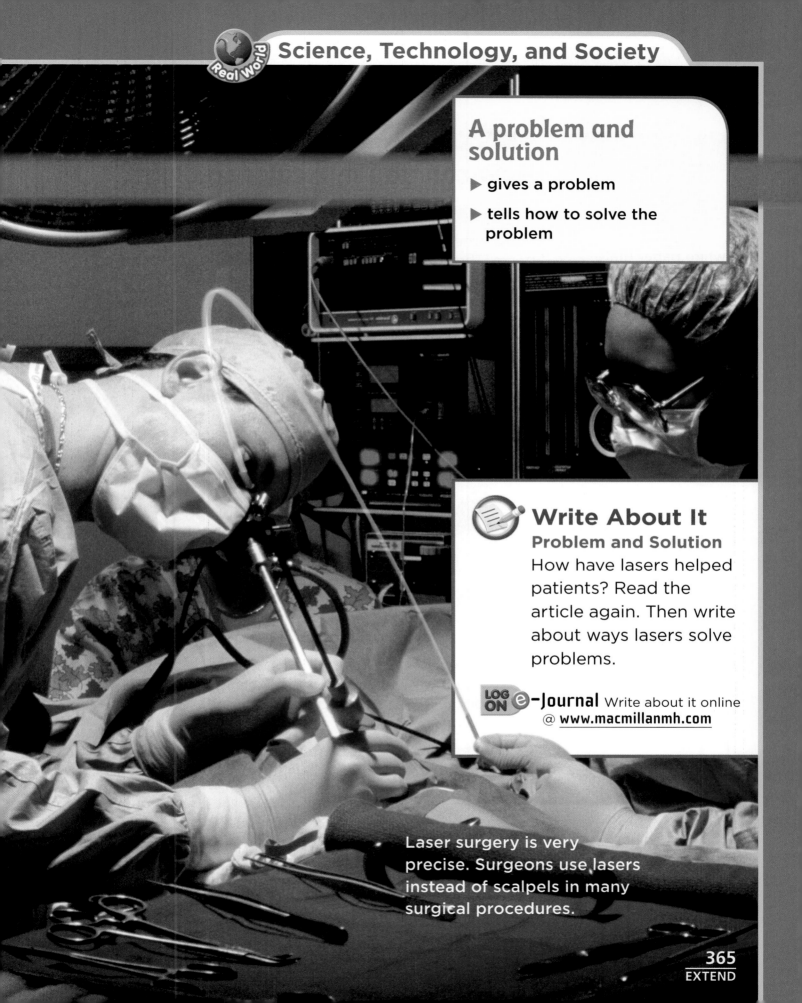

A problem and solution

▶ gives a problem

▶ tells how to solve the problem

Write About It

Problem and Solution
How have lasers helped patients? Read the article again. Then write about ways lasers solve problems.

LOG ON e-Journal Write about it online @ **www.macmillanmh.com**

Laser surgery is very precise. Surgeons use lasers instead of scalpels in many surgical procedures.

Be a Scientist

How can you mix colors of light?

Materials

white paper plate

colored crayons

pencil

Form a Hypothesis

You learned that drops of water in the sky can act like a prism. The prism separates white light into bands of color. Can you mix bands of color to get white light? Write a hypothesis. Start with, "If I mix the right colors, then . . ."

Test Your Hypothesis

❶ Divide the white paper plate into eight equal sections by folding the plate three times. Color each section of the spinner in a different color.

Step ❶

❷ **Observe** Carefully push a pencil into the center of the plate. Spin your spinner away from your body. What color do you see while the spinner is spinning?

❸ **Experiment** Repeat steps 1–3 to make another spinner. This time choose colors that you think will make the spinner appear white when you spin it. If necessary, make several spinners to find the color combinations that work best.

Draw Conclusions

4 What colors did you mix together to make the best white?

5 **Infer** What is white light made up of?

How are the colors of the rainbow arranged?

Form a Hypothesis

Rainbows often don't last very long. Sometimes we even miss seeing them! What colors are in a rainbow? In what order do the colors appear?

Test Your Hypothesis

Design an experiment to test your hypothesis. Use the materials shown. Write out the steps you plan to follow. Record your results and observations.

Draw Conclusions

If you were asked to draw a rainbow, in which order would you put the colors? Does every rainbow have these specific colors? Are these colors always arranged in the same order?

What other questions do you have about light or rainbows? Talk with your classmates about questions you have. How might you find the answers to your questions?

Remember to follow the steps of the scientific process.

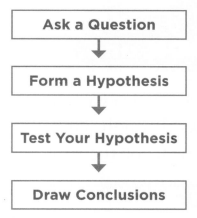

Ask a Question
↓
Form a Hypothesis
↓
Test Your Hypothesis
↓
Draw Conclusions

Materials

white paper   flashlight   prism

 3 IE 5.d. Predict the outcome of a simple investigation and compare the result with the prediction.

Shadows

Look and Wonder

Have you ever wondered why sunlight flows through windows but not through the walls or the roof of a building?

3 PS 2.a. Students know sunlight can be blocked to create shadows.

How do materials affect light?

Make a Prediction

Do all materials allow light to pass through them? What kinds of materials block light?

Test Your Prediction

① **Predict** Which of the materials listed will allow light to pass through them? Which ones will not? Record your predictions.

② **Experiment** Turn off the lights. Have a partner hold up a plastic cup. Shine the flashlight on the cup. Does the light pass through it? Shine the flashlight on the paper cup, plastic wrap, and aluminum foil.

③ **Record Data** Make a two-column chart and record your results.

④ **Classify** Classify the items as those that light passed through and those that blocked light.

Draw Conclusions

⑤ How are the items that light passed through alike? How are the items that blocked light alike?

Explore More

Experiment Does the brightness of light affect how well light passes through materials? Make a plan to find out.

 3 IE 5.a. Repeat observations to improve accuracy and know that the results of similar scientific investigations seldom turn out exactly the same because of differences in the things being investigated, methods being used, or uncertainty in the observations.

Materials

plastic cup

flashlight

paper cup

plastic wrap

aluminum foil

Step **②**

Main Idea 3 PS 2.a

Different materials affect light energy differently. Some materials block light energy and form shadows. Other materials allow light energy to pass through them.

Vocabulary

opaque, p. 370

shadow, p. 370

transparent, p. 374

translucent, p. 374

e-Glossary

@ **www.macmillanmh.com**

Reading Skill

Compare and Contrast

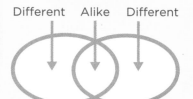

Different   Alike   Different

How are shadows formed?

How do you stay dry on a rainy day? You stand under an umbrella! The raindrops hit the open umbrella. They slide down its sides. Since the raindrops do not pass through the umbrella, they do not reach you.

Opaque (oh•PAYK) materials act somewhat like an umbrella to light energy. **Opaque** materials absorb some light energy. They reflect some of it as well. In this way, opaque objects block light energy from passing through them. Because the light energy is blocked, a **shadow**, or dark space, forms.

Opaque Objects

Raindrops do not pass through the umbrella. They do not reach you.

Opaque objects, such as a brick wall, a tree, a dog, or even you, do not let light pass through them. All opaque objects cast shadows. The shadows are formed on the opposite side of the light source.

Opaque materials can stop you from seeing objects behind them. Remember, you see an object when light that reflects from the object enters your eyes. Opaque materials block light, so you do not see the object.

 Quick Check

Compare and Contrast How are all shadows alike?

Critical Thinking Why do opaque materials stop you from seeing objects?

▲ Shadows always form on the opposite side of a light source.

Read a Photo

How is an umbrella like an opaque object?

Clue: Compare the pictures.

◄ Opaque objects block light from passing through them. This causes shadows to form.

What affects the shape and size of shadows?

A shadow is the dark area that forms when an opaque object blocks light energy. If you have ever played outside on a sunny day, you have probably seen your shadow. Your body blocked sunlight. The shadow that formed had an outline similar to your body. If your bicycle blocked sunlight, then another shadow formed. It looked like the bicycle.

Shadows differ in size and shape. That is because a shadow is like a copy of the object that is blocking light energy. Objects with different shapes form shadows with different shapes.

▲ The rock hammer blocks the sunlight. A shadow forms that looks like the hammer.

Your shadow follows you everywhere you go. It looks like you!

The size of a shadow depends on where the light source is. The closer an object is to a light source, the bigger the shadow. Light coming from above an object creates a shorter shadow. Light coming from the side of an object creates a longer shadow.

A *sundial* is a device that measures time by the position of the Sun. As the Sun moves across the sky, the sundial casts a shadow. The shadow's length and position show the time of day. At noon, when the Sun is directly overhead, the sundial casts its shortest shadow. At sunrise and sunset, the sundial casts its longest shadow.

✔ Quick Check

Compare and Contrast How do shadows differ?

Critical Thinking Why is your shadow not always the same size?

You can tell time by reading the shadows on a sundial. The shadow on this sundial tells us it is 10 A.M. ▼

≡ Quick Lab

What causes a shadow to change size?

1 Predict Can the position of light change the size of a shadow? Write down your ideas.

2 Observe Tape paper to a smooth wall. Have a classmate hold an object in front of the paper. Shine a flashlight on the object. Have another classmate trace the shadow that forms. Measure the size of the shadow.

3 Experiment What will happen to the size of the shadow if the person with the flashlight moves farther away? Closer? Try it and find out.

4 Compare Measure the outline of the shadows each time. How do they differ?

5 Experiment What will happen to the size of the shadow if you move the object and not the light? Try it and find out.

6 Draw Conclusions Why did the size of the shadows change?

What are transparent and translucent materials?

The walls of your home are made of opaque materials. Opaque materials block light energy. You cannot see through them. However, you can see through the windows of your home. That is because the glass in your window is a transparent material. **Transparent** materials allow light energy to pass through them. You can see objects outside a glass window because most of the light reflected from those objects passes through the glass.

Translucent (trans•LEW•suhnt) materials absorb some light energy and let some light energy pass through. A small amount is also reflected. Clear colored glass is a translucent material. You can faintly see an object through colored glass. That is because some of the light the object reflects is absorbed and some passes through to reach your eyes.

 Quick Check

Compare and Contrast How are transparent and translucent materials alike? How are they different?

Critical Thinking Why does sunlight pass through a car's windshield but not its metal roof?

Glass is a transparent material. Colored glass is a translucent material. ▶

Lesson Review

Summarize the Main Idea

Opaque materials block light energy and cause shadows or dark areas to form. (pp. 370–371)

The size and shape of a **shadow** depends on the object's shape and its distance from the light source. (pp. 372–373)

Transparent materials allow light to pass through. **Translucent** materials let some light through. (p. 374)

Make a FOLDABLES™ Study Guide

Make a four-door book. Use it to summarize what you learned about light and shadows.

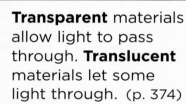

Opaque Materials | Shadow

Transparent Materials | Translucent Materials

Think, Talk, and Write

1 **Main Idea** What causes a shadow to form? Talk about it.

2 **Vocabulary** What is a shadow?

3 **Compare and Contrast** How do opaque, transparent, and translucent materials differ?

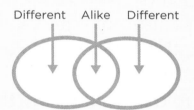

Different   Alike   Different

4 **Critical Thinking** How could you make the shadow of a small child have the same height as the shadow of an adult?

5 **Test Practice** A sheet of aluminum foil is an example of what type of material?

  A translucent

  B shadow

  C transparent

  D opaque

 **Math Link**

Solve a Problem

In the morning, the shadow of a tree is 12 meters long. At midday it is 2 meters long. Write a number sentence that shows, the difference between the two shadows.

 **Art Link**

Hand Shadows

Use your hands and a flashlight or lamp to make shadows. Try to make different shapes and animals. Move your hand closer and farther away from the light. What happens to the shadow?

How Lasers Help People to See Better

Lasers are helping people to see better. First, doctors place the patient in a reclining chair. Next, they numb the eye with a drop of liquid. Once the eye is numb, they place a ring around it. After this, they cut a flap in the cornea and fold it back. Then, they use the tiny, powerful beam of light from a laser to change and correct the curve of the cornea. Finally, they complete the operation. All this takes less than 30 minutes.

A good explanation

▶ tells how to do or make something

▶ begins with a topic sentence that is supported by facts and details

▶ gives step-by-step instructions

▶ uses time-order words, such as first, next, then, and finally, to make instructions clear

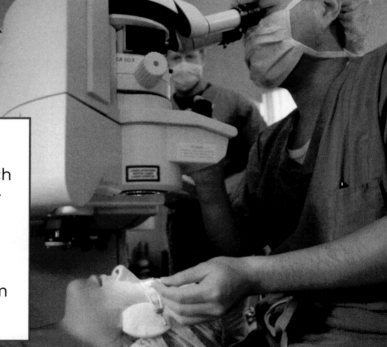

 Write About It

Expository Writing Use research materials to learn about another way that lasers are used to help people. Write a paragraph to explain what you learned. Organize the steps in order, from first to last.

 e-Journal Write about it online @ **www.macmillanmh.com**

 ELA W 3.1.1. Create a single paragraph:
a. Develop a topic sentence.
b. Include simple supporting facts and details.

Keeping Time by Sunlight

A sundial in front of Park Side Elementary School in Sebastopol, California, tells the time from 8 A.M. to 4 P.M. A sundial is a type of clock that casts different shadows at different times of the day. How many minutes are there between 8 A.M. and 4 P.M.?

How to convert hours to minutes

▶ An hour has 60 minutes.

▶ To find how many minutes there are in 2 hours, add 60 minutes twice: 60 minutes + 60 minutes = 120 minutes; or multiply 60 minutes x 2 = 120 minutes.

▶ There are 8 hours between 8 A.M. and 4 P.M. To find how many minutes there are in 8 hours, add 60 minutes eight times or multiply 60 minutes x 8.

 Solve It

1. How many minutes are in your school day?
2. How many minutes do you usually sleep at night?
3. If a movie is $2\frac{1}{2}$ hours long, how many minutes will the movie run?
4. How many hours are in a soccer match that is 90 minutes?

◀ This tower at Sundial Bridge in Redding, California, acts like a giant sundial.

 MA MG 3.1.4. Carry out simple unit conversions within a system of measurement (e.g., centimeters and meters, hours and minutes).

Summarize the Main Ideas

Light is a form of energy that travels in a straight path. When light strikes an object, it is reflected off the object. (pp. 346–353)

If reflected light enters the eye, you see an image. The color of reflected light gives an object its color. (pp. 356–363)

Light can pass through some materials. Other materials block light energy. When light energy is blocked, a shadow forms. (pp. 368–375)

Make a **FOLDABLES**™ Study Guide

Tape your lesson study guides on a piece of paper as shown. Use your study guide to review what you have learned.

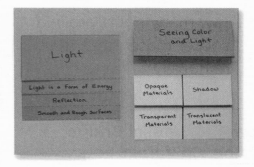

Fill each blank with the best word from the list.

lens, p. 359   **pupil**, p. 358

light, p. 348   **reflection**, p. 350

opaque, p. 370   **shadow**, p. 370

prism, p. 360   **transparent**, p. 374

1. Whenever light energy is blocked, a _____ forms. 3 PS 2.a

2. The _____ is an opening into the eye. 3 PS 2.d

3. Light energy passes through _____ materials such as glass. 3 PS 2.a

4. The part of the eye that focuses incoming light is the _____. 3 PS 2.d

5. A tree is an _____ material that blocks the movement of light energy. 3 PS 2.a

6. Like sound, _____ is a form of energy. 3 PS 2

7. A special lens that separates white light is called a _____. 3 PS 2.c

8. The bouncing of light waves off an object is called _____. 3 PS 2.b

Discuss or write about each of the following.

9. Problem and Solution Why do the wheels of a fire truck appear black but the sides of the truck appear red? 3 PS 2.c

10. Expository Writing Explain what must happen for you to see the object shown in the photo? 3 PS 2.d

How You See

11. Predict Predict what you would observe if you viewed a sheet of white paper through a red filter. Give reasons for your prediction. 3 PS 2.c

12. Critical Thinking You want to check out your new haircut. But you do not have a mirror. Name two items you could use to see your reflection. 3 PS 2.b

Answer each of the following in a complete sentence.

13. How are light and sound alike? How do they differ? 3 PS 2.d

14. What happens when light strikes this surface? 3 PS 2.b

light striking a rough surface

15. What causes the size of your pupils to change? 3 PS 2.d

16. What happens when white light strikes a red rose? 3 PS 2.c

17. What happens when sunlight strikes an object? 3 PS 2.a

 What is light and how does it travel? 3 PS 2

CHAPTER 8

Classify Objects

- Gather an assortment of twelve objects or cut pictures of twelve objects from magazines.

- Think about how each object interacts with light energy. Does the object block light? Does the object allow light to move through it? What colors of light does the object absorb? What colors of light does the object reflect?

- Use the answers to these questions to classify the objects into at least four different groups.

- Label index cards with the trait shared by all objects in each group. Place the card in front of the objects or pictures.

opaque objects

transparent objects

objects that absorb all colors of light

objects that reflect one color of light

380

1 Some students tested light on objects and recorded their findings below.

Amount of Light Passing Through	Number of Objects
all light	⊬⊬
some light	‖
no light	⊬⊬ ‖

What conclusions can you make from the data? 3 IE 5.d

A Less than half the objects absorb light.

B Half of the objects can make shadows.

C Most of the objects are made of clear material.

D Some objects are transparent.

2 The chart below shows the results of looking at white paper through different-colored sheets of cellophane. 3 PS 2.c

Cellophane	Red	Blue	Green	Yellow	Orange
How the white paper looks	Red	Blue	Green	Yellow	?

What will the white paper look like through orange cellophane?

A purple

B black

C white

D orange

3 What happens when the seven colors in white light hit a piece of black construction paper? 3 PS 2.c

A The colors are reflected back to our eyes.

B The colors pass through the construction paper.

C The colors are absorbed by the paper.

D The colors are separated by the paper.

4 Which sequence follows the path of reflected light in our eyes? 3 PS 2.d

A lens, iris and pupil, cornea

B iris and pupil, cornea, lens

C cornea, lens, iris and pupil

D cornea, iris and pupil, lens

5 Which shadow is caused by the Sun around noon? 3 PS 2.a

A very long shadow

B medium long shadow

C short shadow

D dark shadow

6 What happens to the beam of a flashlight when it hits a mirror? 3 PS 2.b

A It stops moving in a straight line.

B It becomes a new form of energy.

C It is reflected off the mirror.

D It goes into the mirror.

The Shocking Story of ELECTRIC EELS

People use electrical energy for many things. Electrical energy turns on the lights, charges the telephone, and powers the toaster when you make breakfast. The energy we use often comes from burning fossil fuels. It may also come from capturing the power of water, wind, or the Sun. But if you were an electric eel, you could make your own electricity!

▲ Electric eels zap fish with 650 volts of electricity.

Electric eels use their own electrical signals to find their way around the ocean. ▼

An electric eel is a freshwater fish that lives in South America. Special body parts work like built-in batteries to produce an electric current. Why? An electric eel uses electricity for some of the same reasons you do, but not in the same way.

An electric eel can't turn on a light to see better in the dark water where it lives. Instead, the eel sends out a weak electric signal as it swims. This works as a "sixth sense" that helps the eel find its way around. It also uses electrical pulses to communicate with other eels.

What about breakfast? Well, an eel doesn't use a toaster, but electricity still comes in handy. When its "sixth sense" detects a fish to eat, the eel turns on its electricity full power. That can be up to 650 volts! (The electricity that powers your home is only 110 volts.) *Zap*! The prey is stunned or killed, and the eel gets a meal. How shocking!

3 PS 1 Energy and matter have multiple forms and can be changed from one form to another. **ELA R 3.2.6.** Extract appropriate and significant information from the text, including problems and solutions.

Lighting Technician

Have you ever watched a motion picture awards show? If so, you may have heard actors thank members of the film crew. An important part of the film crew is the chief lighting technician.

The chief lighting technician designs the lighting for the scenes of a movie. The lighting must create a mood that matches the action of the scene. The chief lighting technician uses different combinations of lights for different scenes. The technician also changes the location of the light sources to create different moods.

To become a chief lighting technician, you need to know about light and electrical energy. You also should have some experience in drama or filmmaking. Many chief lighting technicians start off as basic crew members and work their way up over time.

▲ This technician is lighting a set for a motion picture.

▲ A lighting technician knows about light and electrical energy.

Here are some other Physical Science careers:

- electrician
- engineer
- chemist
- car designer

Reference

California Science Content Standards 386

Science Handbook

Units of Measurement 388

Measure Time 390

Measure Length and Area 391

Measure Mass 392

Measure Volume 393

Measure Weight/Force 394

Measure Temperature 395

Use a Hand Lens 396

Use a Microscope 397

Use Calculators 398

Use Computers 400

Make Graphs 402

Make Maps 404

Make Tables 405

Make Charts 406

FOLDABLES 407

Glossary 411

Index 425

▶ **You can use a hand lens to observe the details of an object.**

Science Content Standards

Physical Sciences

1. **Energy and matter have multiple forms and can be changed from one form to another. As a basis for understanding this concept:**

   a. *Students know* energy comes from the Sun to Earth in the form of light.

   b. *Students know* sources of stored energy take many forms, such as food, fuel, and batteries.

   c. *Students know* machines and living things convert stored energy to motion and heat.

   d. *Students know* energy can be carried from one place to another by waves, such as water waves and sound waves, by electric current, and by moving objects.

   e. *Students know* matter has three forms: solid, liquid, and gas.

   f. *Students know* evaporation and melting are changes that occur when the objects are heated.

   g. *Students know* that when two or more substances are combined, a new substance may be formed with properties that are different from those of the original materials.

   h. *Students know* all matter is made of small particles called atoms, too small to see with the naked eye.

   i. *Students know* people once thought that earth, wind, fire, and water were the basic elements that made up all matter. Science experiments show that there are more than 100 different types of atoms, which are presented on the periodic table of the elements.

2. **Light has a source and travels in a direction. As a basis for understanding this concept:**

   a. *Students know* sunlight can be blocked to create shadows.

   b. *Students know* light is reflected from mirrors and other surfaces.

   c. *Students know* the color of light striking an object affects the way the object is seen.

   d. *Students know* an object is seen when light traveling from the object enters the eye.

Life Sciences

3. **Adaptations in physical structure or behavior may improve an organism's chance for survival. As a basis for understanding this concept:**

   a. *Students know* plants and animals have structures that serve different functions in growth, survival, and reproduction.

   b. *Students know* examples of diverse life forms in different environments, such as oceans, deserts, tundra, forests, grasslands, and wetlands.

   c. *Students know* living things cause changes in the environment in which they live: some of these changes are detrimental to the organism or other organisms, and some are beneficial.

   d. *Students know* when the environment changes, some plants and animals survive and reproduce; others die or move to new locations.

   e. *Students know* that some kinds of organisms that once lived on Earth have completely disappeared and that some of those resembled others that are alive today.

Earth Sciences

4. **Objects in the sky move in regular and predictable patterns. As a basis for understanding this concept:**

    a. *Students know* that patterns of stars stay the same, although they appear to move across the sky nightly, and different stars can be seen in different seasons.

    b. *Students know* the way in which the Moon's appearance changes during the four-week lunar cycle.

    c. *Students know* telescopes magnify the appearance of some distant objects in the sky, including the Moon and the planets. The number of stars that can be seen through telescopes is dramatically greater than the number that can be seen by the unaided eye.

    d. *Students know* that Earth is one of several planets that orbit the Sun and that the Moon orbits Earth.

    e. *Students know* the position of the Sun in the sky changes during the course of the day and from season to season.

Investigation and Experimentation

5. **Scientific progress is made by asking meaningful questions and conducting careful investigations. As a basis for understanding this concept and addressing the content in the other three strands, students should develop their own questions and perform investigations. Students will:**

    a. Repeat observations to improve accuracy and know that the results of similar scientific investigations seldom turn out exactly the same because of differences in the things being investigated, methods being used, or uncertainty in the observation.

    b. Differentiate evidence from opinion and know that scientists do not rely on claims or conclusions unless they are backed by observations that can be confirmed.

    c. Use numerical data in describing and comparing objects, events, and measurements.

    d. Predict the result of a simple investigation and compare the result with the prediction.

    e. Collect data in an investigation and analyze those data to develop a logical conclusion.

Measurement

Units of Measurement

Temperature

▶ The temperature on this thermometer reads 83 degrees Fahrenheit. That is the same as 30 degrees Celsius.

Length and Area

▶ This student is 3 feet plus 9 inches tall. That is the same as 1 meter plus 14 centimeters.

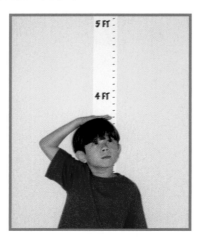

Mass

▶ You can measure the mass of these rocks in grams.

Volume of Fluids

▶ This bottle of water has a volume of 1 liter. That is a little more than 1 quart.

Weight/Force

▶ This pumpkin weighs 7 pounds. That is a force of 31.5 newtons.

Rate

▶ This student can ride her bike 100 meters in 50 seconds. That means her speed is 2 meters per second.

Table of Measurements

SI (International System) of Units	English System of Units
Temperature Water freezes at 0 degrees Celsius (°C) and boils at 100°C.	**Temperature** Water freezes at 32 degrees Fahrenheit (°F) and boils at 212°F.
Length and Distance 10 millimeters (mm) = 1 centimeter (cm) 100 centimeters = 1 meter (m) 1,000 meters = 1 kilometer (km)	**Length and Distance** 12 inches (in.) = 1 foot (ft) 3 feet = 1 yard (yd) 5,280 feet = 1 mile (mi)
Volume 1 cubic centimeter (cm^3) = 1 milliliter (mL) 1,000 milliliters = 1 liter (L)	**Volume of Fluids** 8 fluid ounces (fl oz) = 1 cup (c) 2 cups = 1 pint (pt) 2 pints = 1 quart (qt) 4 quarts = 1 gallon (gal)
Mass 1,000 milligrams (mg) = 1 gram (g) 1,000 grams = 1 kilogram (kg)	**Weight** 16 ounces (oz) = 1 pound (lb) 2,000 pounds = 1 ton (T)
Area 1 square kilometer (km^2) = 1 km x 1 km 1 hectare = 10,000 square meters (m^2)	**Rate** mph = miles per hour
Rate m/s = meters per second km/h = kilometers per hour	
Force 1 newton (N) = 1 kg x 1m/s^2	

Measurement

Measure Time

You use timing devices to measure how long something takes to happen. Some timing devices you use in science are a clock with a second hand and a stopwatch. Which one is more accurate?

Comparing a Clock and a Stopwatch

1️⃣ Look at a clock with a second hand. The second hand is the hand that you can see moving. It measures seconds.

2️⃣ Get an egg timer with falling sand. When the second hand of the clock points to 12, tell your partner to start the egg timer. Watch the clock while the sand in the egg timer is falling.

3️⃣ When the sand stops falling, count how many seconds it took. Record this measurement. Repeat the activity, and compare the two measurements.

4️⃣ Look at a stopwatch. Click the button on the top right. This starts the time. Click the button again. This stops the time. Click the button on the top left. This sets the stopwatch back to zero. Notice that the stopwatch tells time in hours, minutes, seconds, and hundredths of a second.

5️⃣ Repeat the activity in steps 2 and 3, but use the stopwatch instead of a clock. Make sure the stopwatch is set to zero. Click the top right button to start timing. Click the button again when the sand stops falling. Do this twice.

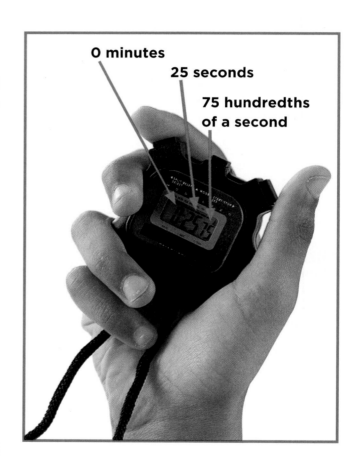

0 minutes

25 seconds

75 hundredths of a second

More About Time

1️⃣ Use the stopwatch to time how long it takes your heart to beat 100 times. Then run in place for 3 minutes. How long does it take for your heart to beat 100 times now?

2️⃣ Estimate how long it would take you to walk 100 meters. Then time yourself and try it.

Measure Length

You measure length to find out how long something is or how far away something is.

Find Length with a Ruler

1 Look at the ruler below. Each number represents 1 centimeter (cm). Each centimeter is divided into 10 millimeters (mm). How long is the beetle?

2 The length of the beetle is 1 centimeter plus 5 millimeters. You can write this length as 1.5 centimeters.

3 Place a ruler on your desk. Lay a pencil against the ruler so that one end of the pencil lines up with the 0 on the ruler. Record the length of the pencil in centimeters.

4 Measure the length of another object in centimeters. Then ask a partner to measure the same object.

5 Compare your measurements. Explain how two scientists can record slightly different measurements even if the item measured is the same.

Measure Area

Area is the amount of surface something covers. To find the area of a rectangle, multiply the rectangle's length by its width. For example, the rectangle here is 3 centimeters long and 2 centimeters wide. Its area is 3 cm x 2 cm = 6 square centimeters. You write the area as 6 cm^2.

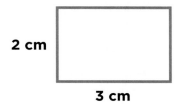

2 cm

3 cm

Find Area with a Ruler

1 Find the area of your science book. Measure the book's length to the nearest centimeter. Measure its width.

2 Multiply the book's length by its width. Remember to put the answer in cm^2.

Measurement

Measure Mass

Mass is the amount of matter an object has. You use a balance to measure mass. To find the mass of an object, you balance it with objects whose masses you know.

Measure the Mass of a Box of Crayons

① Place the balance on a flat, level surface.

② The pointer should point to the middle mark. If it does not, move the slider a little to the right or left to balance the empty pans.

③ Gently place a box of crayons on the left pan. Add gram masses to the right pan until the pans are balanced.

④ Count the numbers on the masses that are in the right pan. The total is the mass of the box of crayons in grams.

⑤ Record this number. After the number, write a *g* for "grams."

More About Mass

What would happen if you replaced the box of crayons with a paper clip or a pineapple? You may not have enough masses to balance the pineapple. It has a mass of about 1,000 grams. That's the same as 1 kilogram, because *kilo* means "1,000." Measure other objects and record your measurements.

Measure Volume

Have you ever used a measuring cup? Measuring cups measure the volume of liquids. Volume is the amount of space something takes up. In science you use special measuring cups called beakers and graduated cylinders. These containers are marked in milliliters (mL).

Measure the Volume of a Liquid

1 Fill a beaker and a graduated cylinder so they are each half full with water.

2 The surface of the water in the graduated cylinder curves up at the sides. You measure the volume by reading the height of the water at the flat part. Compare the height of the water to the marks on the measuring device. What is the volume of water in the graduated cylinder? How much water is in the beaker?

3 Pour 50 mL of water from a pitcher into a graduated cylinder. The water should be at the 50-mL mark on the graduated cylinder. If you go over the mark, pour a little water back into the pitcher.

4 Pour the 50 mL of water into a beaker.

5 Repeat steps 3 and 4 using 30 mL, 45 mL, and 25 mL of water.

6 Measure the volume of water you have in the beaker. Do you have about the same amount of water as your classmates?

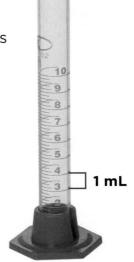

▲ This graduated cylinder can measure volumes up to 10 mL. Each number on the cylinder represents 1 mL.

□ 1 mL

▲ A beaker is a tool you can use to measure volume.

393

Measurement

Measure Weight/Force

You use a spring scale to measure weight. An object has weight because the force of gravity pulls down on the object. Therefore, weight is a force. Like all forces, weight is measured in newtons (N).

Measure the Weight of an Object

1. Look at a spring scale to see how many newtons it measures. See how the measurements are divided. The spring scale shown here measures up to 20 N. It has a mark for every 0.5 N.

2. Hold the spring scale by the top loop. Put a small object on the bottom hook. If the object will not stay on the hook, place it in a net bag. Then hang the bag from the hook.

3. Let go of the object slowly. It will pull down on a spring inside the scale.

4. Wait for the spring to stop moving. Read the number of newtons next to the tab. This is the object's weight.

More About Spring Scales

You probably weigh yourself by standing on a bathroom scale. This is a spring scale. The weight of your body stretches a spring inside the scale. The dial on the scale is probably marked in pounds—the English unit of force. One pound is equal to about 4.5 newtons.

The scale in a grocery store is also a spring scale. ▶

Measure Temperature

Temperature is how hot or cold something is. You use a thermometer to measure temperature. A thermometer is made of a thin tube with colored liquid inside. When the liquid gets warmer, it expands and moves up the tube. When the liquid gets cooler, it contracts and moves down the tube. You may have seen most temperatures measured in degrees Fahrenheit (°F). Scientists measure temperature in degrees Celsius (°C).

Read a Thermometer

1. Look at the thermometer shown here. It has two scales—a Fahrenheit scale and a Celsius scale. Every 20 degrees on the Celsius scale has a number. Every 40 degrees on the Fahrenheit scale has a number.

2. What is the temperature shown on the thermometer? Give your answers in °F and in °C.

How Is Temperature Measured?

1. Fill a large beaker about half full of cool water. Put the thermometer in the water. Do not let the thermometer bulb touch the beaker. Use a clamp if necessary.

2. Wait until the liquid in the thermometer stops moving— about a minute. Read and record the temperature. Record the temperature scale you used.

3. Remove the thermometer. Place the beaker on a hot plate and warm the beaker for two minutes. Be careful of the hot plate and warm water.

4. Put the thermometer in the water. Record the temperature of the water. Use the same temperature scale you chose in Step 2.

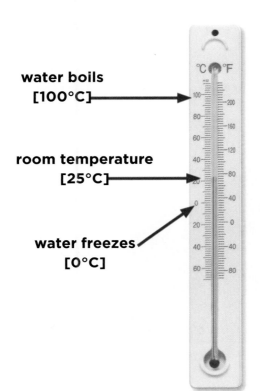

water boils [100°C]

room temperature [25°C]

water freezes [0°C]

Collect Data

Use a Hand Lens

You use a hand lens to magnify an object or make the object look larger. With a hand lens, you can see details that would be hard to see without the hand lens.

Magnify a Rock

1. Look at a rock carefully. Draw a picture of it.

2. Hold the hand lens so that it is just above the rock. Look through the lens, and slowly move it away from the rock. The rock will look larger.

3. Keep moving the hand lens until the rock begins to look blurry. Then move the lens a little closer until you can see the rock clearly.

4. Draw a picture of the rock as you see it through the hand lens. Fill in details that you did not see before.

5. Repeat this activity using objects you are studying in science. They might include a plant, some soil, a seed, or something else.

Use a Microscope

Hand lenses make objects look several times larger. A microscope, however, can magnify an object to look hundreds of times larger.

Examine Salt Grains

1 Place the microscope on a flat surface. Always carry a microscope with both hands. Hold the arm with one hand, and put your other hand beneath the base.

2 Look at the photo to learn the different parts of the microscope.

3 Move the mirror so that it reflects light up toward the stage. Never point the mirror directly at the Sun or a bright light. Bright light can cause permanent eye damage.

4 Place a few grains of salt on a slide. Put the slide under the stage clips on the stage. Be sure that the salt grains are over the hole in the stage.

5 Look through the eyepiece. Turn the focusing knob slowly until the salt grains come into focus.

6 Draw what the grains look like through the microscope.

7 Look at other objects through the microscope. Try a piece of leaf, a strand of hair, or a pencil mark.

8 Draw what each object looks like through the microscope. Do any of the objects look alike? If so, how? Are any of the objects alive? How do you know?

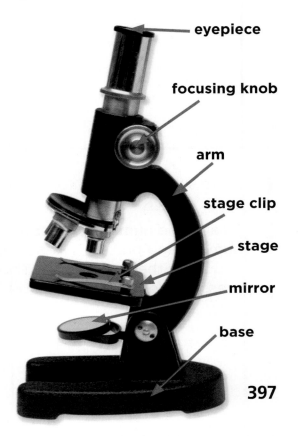

eyepiece

focusing knob

arm

stage clip

stage

mirror

base

397

Use Technology

Use Calculators: Add and Subtract

Sometimes after you make measurements, you have to add or subtract your numbers. A calculator helps you do this.

Add and Subtract Rainfall Amounts

The table shows the amount of rain that fell in a town each week during the summer.

Week	Rain (cm)
1	3
2	5
3	2
4	0
5	1
6	6
7	4
8	0
9	2
10	2
11	6
12	5

1 Make sure the calculator is on. Press the ON key.

2 To add the numbers, enter a number and press +. Repeat until you enter the last number. Then press =. Your total should be 36.

3 What if you found out that you made a mistake in your measurement? Week 1 should be 2 cm less, week 6 should be 3 cm less, week 11 should be 1 cm less, and week 12 should be 2 cm less. Subtract these numbers from your total. You should have 36 displayed on the calculator. Press −, and enter the first number you want to subtract. Repeat until you enter the last number. Then press =.

Use Calculators: Multiply and Divide

Sometimes after you make measurements, you have to multiply or divide your measurements to get other information. A calculator helps you multiply and divide, especially if the numbers have decimal points.

Multiply Decimals

What if you are measuring the width of your classroom? You discover that the floor is covered with tiles and the room is exactly 32 tiles wide. You measure a tile, and it is 22.7 centimeters wide. To find the width of the room, you can multiply 32 by 22.7.

1 Make sure the calculator is on. Press the ON key.

2 Press 3 and 2.

3 Press X.

4 Press 2, 2, ·, and 7.

5 Press =. Your total should be 726.4. That is how wide the room is in centimeters.

Divide Decimals

Now what if you wanted to find out how many desks placed side by side would be needed to reach across the room? You measure one desk, and it is 60 centimeters wide. To find the number of desks needed, divide 726.4 by 60.

1 Turn the calculator on.

2 Press 7, 2, 6, ·, and 4.

3 Press ÷.

4 Press 6 and 0.

5 Press =. Your total should be about 12.1. This means you can fit 12 desks across the room with a little space left over.

Suppose the room was 35 tiles wide. How wide would the room be? How many desks would fit across it? Use a calculator to multiply and divide.

Use Technology

Use Computers

A computer has many uses. The Internet connects your computer to many other computers around the world, so you can collect all kinds of information. You can use a computer to show this information and write reports. Best of all, you can use a computer to explore, discover, and learn.

You can also get information from compact discs (CDs) and digital videodiscs (DVDs). They are computer disks that can hold large amounts of information. You can fit a whole encyclopedia on one DVD.

Use Computers for a Project

Here's a project that uses computers. You can do the project in a group.

1. Use a collecting net to gather a soil sample from a brook or stream. Collect pebbles, sand, and small rocks. Keep any small plants also. Return any fish or other animals to the stream right away.

2. After the sample has dried, separate the items in the sample. Use a camera to photograph the soil, pebbles, small rocks, and plants.

3. Each group can use one of the photos to help them start their research. Try to find out what type of rocks or soil you collected.

4. Use the Internet for your research. Find a map and mark your area on it. Identify the type of soil. What types of plants grow well in that type of soil?

400

5 Find Web sites from an agency such as the Department of Environmental Protection. Contact the group. Ask questions about samples you collected.

6 Use DVDs or other sources from the library to find out how the rocks and soil in your sample formed.

7 Keep the information you have gathered in a folder. Review it with your group and use it to write a group report about your sample.

8 Each group will present and read a different part of the report. Have an adult help you to record your reports on a video recorder. Show your photographs in the video and explain what each represents. If you'd like, use music or other sounds to accompany the voices on the video recorder.

9 Make a list of computer resources you used to make your report. List Web sites, DVD titles, or other computer resources. Show or read the list at the end of your presentation.

10 Discuss how the computer helped each group to do their report. What problems did each group encounter using the computer? How were the problems solved?

Represent Data

Make Graphs

Graphs can help organize data. Graphs make it easy to notice trends and patterns. There are many kinds of graphs.

Bar Graphs

A bar graph uses bars to show information. For example, what if you are growing a plant? Every week you measure how high the plant has grown. Here is what you find.

The bar graph at the bottom right organizes the measurements so you can easily compare them.

Week	Height (cm)
1	1
2	4
3	7
4	10
5	17
6	20
7	22
8	23

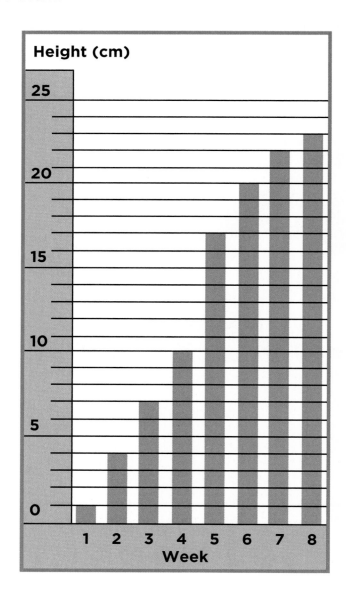

1. Look at the bar for Week 2. Put your finger at the top of the bar. Move your finger straight over to the left to find how many centimeters the plant grew by the end of Week 2.

2. Between which two weeks did the plant grow most?

3. Look at the 0 on the graph. Is it just a label on a scale or does it have a meaning in the graph? Explain.

Pictographs

A pictograph uses symbols, or pictures, to show information. What if you collect information about how much water your family uses each day? Here is what you find.

Water Used Daily (liters)	
drinking	10
showering	100
bathing	120
brushing teeth	40
washing dishes	80
washing hands	30
washing clothes	160
flushing toilet	50

You can organize this information into a pictograph. In the pictograph below each bucket means 20 liters of water. A half bucket means half of 20, or 10 liters of water.

1 Which activity uses the most water?

2 Which activity uses the least water?

Water Used Daily	
drinking	☖
showering	☖☖☖☖☖
bathing	☖☖☖☖☖☖
brushing teeth	☖☖
washing dishes	☖☖☖☖
washing hands	☖☖
washing clothes	☖☖☖☖☖☖☖☖
flushing toilet	☖☖☖

☖ = 20 liters of water

Line Graphs

A line graph shows how information changes over time. What if you measure the temperature outdoors every hour starting at 6 A.M.? Here is what you find.

Time	Temperature (°C)
6 A.M.	10
7 A.M.	12
8 A.M.	14
9 A.M.	16
10 A.M.	18
11 A.M.	20

Now organize your data by making a line graph. Follow these steps.

1 Make a scale along the bottom and side of the graph. Label the scales.

2 Plot points on the graph.

3 Connect the points with a line.

4 How do the temperatures and times relate to each other?

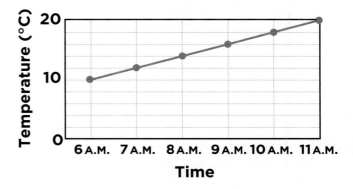

403

Represent Data

Make Maps

Locate Places

A map is a drawing that shows an area from above. Most maps have numbers and letters along the top and side. What if you wanted to find the Crocker Art Museum on the map below? It is located at D2. Place a finger on the letter D along the side of the map and another finger on the number 2 at the top. Then move your fingers straight across and down the map until they meet. The art museum is located where D and 2 meet.

1. What building is located at B4?

2. The U.S. District Court is located two blocks west and one block north of the library. What is its number and letter?

3. Make a map of an area in your community. It might be a park or the area between your home and school. Include numbers and letters along the top and side. Use a compass to find north, and mark north on your map. Exchange maps with a classmate.

Idea Maps

The map on the left shows how places are connected to each other. Idea maps, on the other hand, show how ideas are connected to each other. Idea maps help you organize information about a topic.

Look at the idea map below. It connects ideas about water. This map shows that Earth's water can be fresh water or salt water. The map also shows three sources of fresh water. You can see that there is no connection between "rivers" and "salt water" on the map. This reminds you that salt water does not flow in rivers.

Make an idea map about a topic you are learning in science. Your map can include words, phrases, or even sentences. Arrange your map in a way that makes sense to you and helps you understand the connection between ideas.

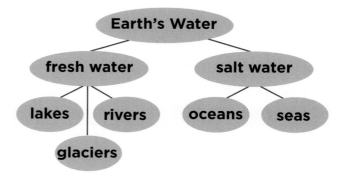

Make Tables

Tables help to organize data during experiments. Most tables have columns that run up and down, and rows that run across. The columns and rows have headings that tell you what kind of data go in each part of the table.

A Sample Table

What if you are going to do an experiment to find out how long different kinds of seeds take to sprout? Before you begin the experiment, you should set up your table. Follow these steps.

1 In this experiment you will plant 20 radish seeds, 20 bean seeds, and 20 corn seeds. Your table must show how many of each kind of seed sprouted on days 1, 2, 3, 4, and 5.

2 Make your table with columns, rows, and headings. You might use a computer. Some computer programs let you build a table with just the click of a mouse. You can delete or add columns and rows if you need to.

3 Give your table a title. Your table could look like the one here.

Types of Seeds	Number of Seeds that Sprout				
	Day 1	Day 2	Day 3	Day 4	Day 5
radish seeds					
bean seeds					
corn seeds					

Make a Table

Plant 20 bean seeds in each of two trays. Keep each tray at a different temperature and observe the trays for seven days. Make a table to record, examine, and evaluate the information of this experiment. How do the columns, rows, and headings of your table relate to one another?

Represent Data

Make Charts

A chart is simply a table with pictures as well as words. Charts can be useful for recording information during an experiment. They are also useful in communicating information.

Make a Chart

Make a chart that shows the information from the bean seed experiment on page 405. Make your chart with columns and rows. Remember to include labels.

Change	Living Thing	What Might Happen	Why
warmer climate	 saber-toothed cat	becomes extinct	unable to find food; unable to survive in warm climate
volcanic eruption	 short-tailed albatross	survives	flies to new environment
colder climate	 bear	survives	grows thicker fur

▲ This chart shows how changes can affect living things. It provides information using both pictures and words.

Folding Instructions

So how do you make a Foldables study guide? The following pages offer step-by-step instructions—where and when to fold, where to cut—for making 11 basic Foldables study guides. The instructions begin with the basic shapes, such as the hot dog fold.

Half-Book

Fold a sheet of paper ($8\frac{1}{2}''$ x 11") in half.

1. This book can be folded vertically like a hot dog or …
2. … it can be folded horizontally like a hamburger.

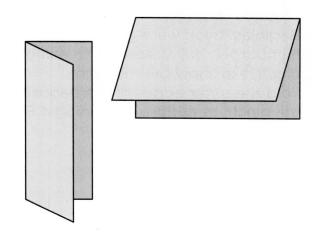

Folded Book

1. Make a Half-Book.
2. Fold in half again like a hamburger. This makes a ready-made cover and two small pages inside for recording information.

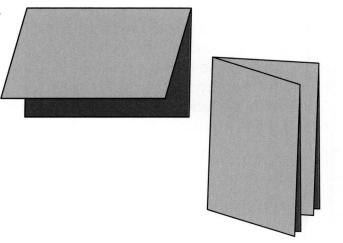

Trifold Book

1. Fold a sheet of paper ($8\frac{1}{2}''$ x 11")
   into thirds.
2. Use this book as is, or cut
   into shapes.

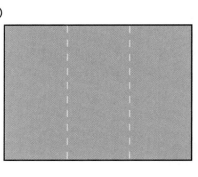
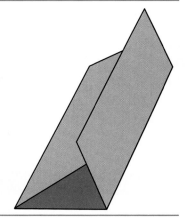

Shutter Fold

1. Begin as if you were going to make a
   hamburger, but instead of creasing the paper,
   pinch it to show the midpoint.
2. Fold the outer edges of the paper to meet at
   the pinch, or midpoint, forming a Shutter Fold.

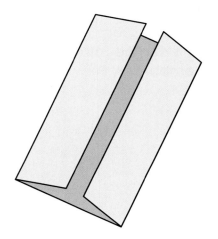

Pocket Book

1. Fold a sheet of paper ($8\frac{1}{2}''$ x 11") in half like
   a hamburger.
2. Open the folded paper and fold one of the
   long sides up two inches to form a pocket.
   Refold along the hamburger fold so that the
   newly formed pockets are on the inside.
3. Glue the outer edges of the two-inch fold
   with a small amount of glue.

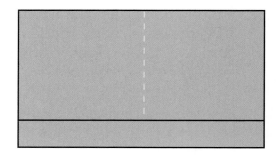

Two-Tab Book

Take a Folded Book and cut up the valley of the inside fold toward the mountain top. This cut forms two large tabs that can be used on the front and back for writing and illustrations.

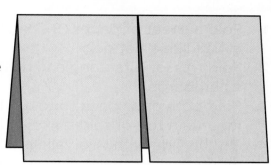

Three-Tab Book

1. Fold a sheet of paper like a hot dog.
2. With the paper horizontal and the fold of the hot dog up, fold the right side toward the center, trying to cover one half of the paper.
3. Fold the left side over the right side to make a book with three folds.
4. Open the folded book. Place one hand between the two thicknesses of paper and cut up the two valleys on one side only. This will create three tabs.

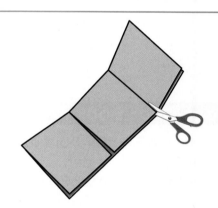

Layered-Look Book

1. Stack two sheets of paper ($8\frac{1}{2}''$ x 11") so that the back sheet is one inch higher than the front sheet.
2. Bring the bottoms of both sheets upward and align the edges so that all of the layers or tabs are the same distance apart.
3. When all the tabs are an equal distance apart, fold the papers and crease well.
4. Open the papers and glue them together along the valley, or inner center fold, or staple them along the mountain.

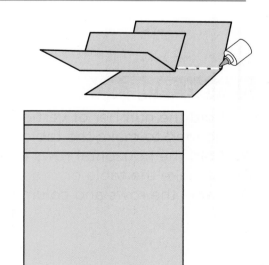

Four-Tab Book

1. Fold a sheet of paper ($8\frac{1}{2}''$ x 11'') in half like a hot dog.
2. Fold this long rectangle in half like a hamburger.
3. Fold both ends back to touch the mountain top or fold it like an accordion.
4. On the side with two valleys and one mountain top, make vertical cuts through one thickness of paper, forming four tabs.

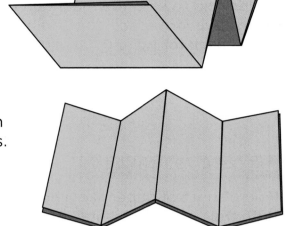

Four-Door Book

1. Make a Shutter Fold using 11'' x 17'' or 12'' x 18'' paper.
2. Fold the Shutter Fold in half like a hamburger. Crease well.
3. Open the project and cut along the two inside valley folds. These cuts will form four doors on the inside of the project.

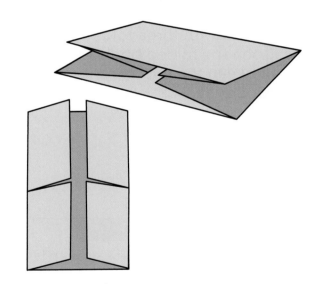

Folded Table or Chart

1. Fold the number of vertical columns needed to make the table or chart.
2. Fold the horizontal rows needed to make the table or chart.
3. Label the rows and columns.

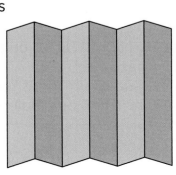
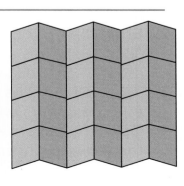

Glossary

Use this glossary to learn how to pronounce and understand the meanings of Science Words used in this book. The page number at the end of each definition tells you where to find that word in the book.

absorb (əb sôrb′) To take in. (pp. 113, 360) *Some materials absorb more light than others.*

adaptation (a′dap′tā′shən) A special trait that helps a living thing survive in its environment. (p. 32) *A fish's gills are an example of adaptation.*

air bladder (âr bla′dər) A balloonlike structure in plants and animals for holding gases. (p. 103) *Kelp has air bladders that help it float.*

algae (al′jē) Tiny one-celled organisms that use water, air, and sunlight to make food. (p. 102) *Algae are plantlike living things often found in shallow water.*

amphibian (am fib′ē ən) An animal that spends part of its life in water and part on land. (p. 116) *Frogs and salamanders are amphibians.*

analyze data (an′ə līz   da′tə) To use information that has been gathered to answer a question or solve a problem. (p. 11) *You can analyze data to find how daylight hours change throughout the year.*

arctic tundra (ärk′tik   tən′drə) A cold biome above the Arctic Circle. (p. 70) *Winters on the arctic tundra are long and dark.*

asteroid (as′tə roid′) A large piece of rock or metal in space. (p. 224) *Many asteroids orbit the Sun.*

astronaut (as′trə not) A person who travels into space. (p. 208) *Astronauts traveled to the Moon to study it up close.*

Pronunciation Key

The following symbols are used throughout the Macmillan McGraw-Hill Science Glossaries.

a	**a**t	e	**e**nd	o	h**o**t	u	**u**p	hw	**wh**ite	ə	**a**bout
ā	**a**pe	ē	m**e**	ō	**o**ld	ū	**u**se	ng	so**ng**		tak**e**n
ä	f**a**r	i	**i**t	ôr	f**or**k	ü	r**u**le	th	**th**in		penc**i**l
âr	c**a**re	ī	**i**ce	oi	**oi**l	u̇	p**u**ll	th	**th**is		lem**o**n
ô	l**a**w	îr	p**ier**ce	ou	**ou**t	ûr	t**ur**n	zh	mea**s**ure		circ**u**s

′ = primary accent; shows which syllable takes the main stress, such as **kil** in **kilogram** (kil′ e gram′).

′ = secondary accent; shows which syllables take lighter stresses, such as **gram** in **kilogram**.

astrophysicist (as′trō fi′zi sist) Someone who studies how objects in the universe interact. (p. 244) *An astrophysicist can explain how the planets move around the Sun.*

atom (at əm) The smallest unit of an element that has the properties of that element. (p. 276) *Atoms are too small to see on your own.*

axis (ak sis) A real or imaginary line through the center of a spinning object. (p. 184) *The geographic north and south poles are the ends of Earth's axis.*

B

binary stars (bī′nə rē stârz) Two stars that act as a pair. (p. 244) *If one of the binary stars weakens, the other one might absorb it.*

biomass (bī′ō mas) Plant materials and animal waste. (p. 323) *Biomass can be used as fuel to create energy.*

biome (bī′ōm) An area of land or water that has certain kinds of living and nonliving things. (p. 26) *A desert biome is very different from an ocean biome.*

blubber (blə′bər) A thick layer of fat found in large mammals. (p. 74) *Whale blubber allows the animal to stay warm in cold waters.*

bog (bog) A freshwater wetland filled with moss and rich soil. (p. 114) *The ground in bogs is usually wet and spongelike.*

brackish environment (brak′ish en vī′rən mənt) The living and nonliving things that exist in a place with a mixture of fresh and salt water. (p. 91) *Many marine animals lay their eggs in a brackish environment.*

buttress (bə′trəs) Something that supports or strengthens. (p. 60) *Some trees have special root structures called buttresses that spread out from the trunk and support the tree.*

calorie (ka′lə rē) A measure of the energy stored in a substance, such as food. (p. 319) *Rich foods, such as ice cream and fried dough, have many more calories than others.*

camouflage (kam′ə fläzh′) An adaptation that allows an animal to blend into its surroundings. (p. 42) *Camouflage might help an insect look like a leaf.*

canopy (ka′nə pē′) The part of a forest just below the uppermost branches of the tallest trees. (p. 60) *Most rain-forest animals live in the canopy because of the sunlight and food found there.*

carbon (kär'bən) One of the basic elements. (p. 60) *All living matter on Earth contains carbon.*

chemical change (kem'i kəl chānj) A change that causes a new kind of matter to form with different properties. (p. 288) *When food burns, the chemical change makes it taste different.*

chemical energy (kem'i kəl en'ər jē) Energy that is stored in a substance. (p. 306) *Your body uses chemical energy stored in sugar and other foods.*

classify (klas'ə fī) To place similar materials together in a group. (p. 5) *The periodic table classifies elements that share the same properties.*

climate (klī'mit) The average weather patterns of a region. (p. 27) *Most people prefer a warm climate.*

comet (kom'it) A chunk of ice mixed with rocks and dust moving through space. (p. 224) *A comet may have a glowing tail.*

communicate (kə mū'ni kāt') To share information. (p. 13) *Writing helps you to communicate your ideas to others.*

community (kə mū'ni tē) All the different populations in an ecosystem. (p. 146) *A rural community may include people, cows, and grasses.*

compare (kəm pār') To see what is the same and what is different between two or more things. (p. 34) *You can begin to classify things after you compare them.*

competition (kom'pi tish'ən) The struggle among living things. (p. 132) *There is great competition for water in the desert.*

compression wave (kəm presh'ən wāv) A wave that moves in a back and forth motion. (p. 333) *Sound waves are examples of compression waves.*

condense (kən dens') What happens when matter changes state from gas to liquid. (p. 268) *When water vapor in the air condenses, it can form dewdrops.*

coniferous (kon i'fər əs) A kind of temperate forest that stays green all year. (p. 61) *Pines, firs, and spruces grow in coniferous forests.*

constellation (kon ste lā'shun) A group of stars that forms a pattern or picture. (p. 240) *The Big Dipper is a major constellation.*

coral (kar'əl) Colorful rocklike formations created by certain marine animals. (p. 101) *Coral reefs are some of the most beautiful parts of the ocean.*

cornea (kôr'nē ə) The clear, outer covering of the eye. (p. 358) *A contact lens rests on the cornea and assists with vision.*

crescent moon (kreʹsənt mün) The phase of the moon in which the lighted side has almost disappeared. (p. 201) *A crescent moon is either just beginning to wax or almost done waning.*

deciduous (di siʹjə wəs) A kind of forest biome with many trees that lose their leaves each winter. (p. 61) *Maples, birches, and oaks can be found in deciduous forests.*

depth (depth) The distance away from the surface. (p. 92) *Water temperature in the ocean grows colder with depth.*

desert (deʹzərt) A hot, dry place with very little rain. (p. 38) *The Mojave Desert is a hot desert.*

dew (dü) Water vapor that has condensed into liquid on a cool object. (p. 268) *Small drops of dew often appear overnight as the moist air cools.*

dinosaur (dīʹnə sor′) An extinct kind of large reptile. (p. 162) *The word dinosaur comes from Greek words meaning "fearfully great lizard."*

draw conclusions (drô kən klüʹzhənz) To arrive at possible answers based on information you have gathered. (p. 13) *After you analyze the data from an experiment, you can draw conclusions about what you observed.*

ecosystem (ekʹō sisʹtəm) All the living and nonliving things that interact in an environment. (p. 146) *The desert and the forest are different ecosystems.*

electrical energy (i lekʹtrik əl enʹər jē) Energy produced by the movement of small particles called electrons. (p. 306) *A light bulb uses electrical energy to create light.*

electron microscope (i lekʹtron mīʹkrə skōp′) A tool that allows us to see very small objects. (p. 276) *Atoms can only be seen using an electron microscope.*

element (elʹə mənt) A basic building block of matter. (p. 274) *Oxygen, carbon, and iron are all elements.*

emergent layer (i mərʹjənt lār) The highest level in a forest biome. (p. 60) *The tops of the tallest trees form the emergent layer of the rain forest.*

energy (en′ər jē) The ability to do work. (p. 304) *Matter needs energy to move, grow, or change its state.*

environment (en vī′rən mənt) All the living and nonliving things that surround a living thing. (p. 26) *Plants need an environment in which they can get sunlight, water, carbon dioxide, and other nutrients.*

equator (i kwā′tər) The imaginary line that divides Earth into the north and south hemispheres. (p. 194) *Sunlight strikes Earth most directly at the equator.*

evaporate (i vap′ə rāt′) What happens when matter slowly changes state from liquid to gas. (p. 267) *Water can evaporate into a gas in direct sunlight.*

expand (ek spand′) To spread out. (p. 305) *Pumping air into a balloon causes the material to expand.*

experiment (ek sper′ə ment′) A test designed to support or disprove a hypothesis. (p. 9) *Most experiments are designed and carried out very carefully.*

extinct (ek stingkt′) All dead, no more left alive on Earth. (p. 154) *The mammoths became extinct after a change in climate killed them all.*

force (fôrs) A push or pull. (p. 307) *You use force when you make an object move.*

forest (fôr′əst) A biome that has many trees. (p. 58) *Different types of forests exist in different parts of the world.*

forest floor (fôr′əst flôr) The ground level of a forest biome. (p. 60) *Very little sunlight reaches the forest floor.*

fossil (fos′əl) The hardened remains of a living thing. (p. 156) *Most fossils are buried deep in the ground.*

fossil fuel (fos′əl fū′əl) A source of energy that comes from the breakdown of animal and plant remains. (p. 324) *Gasoline is a fossil fuel.*

freeze (frēz) What happens when matter changes state from liquid to solid. (p. 268) *When water freezes, it becomes ice.*

freshwater environment (fresh′wô′tər en vī′rən mənt) The living and nonliving things that exist in a place where the water is not salty. (p. 91) *Most ponds and most rivers are freshwater environments.*

friction (frik′shən) The force created when surfaces rub against each other. (p. 307) *Friction from rubbing your hands makes them warm.*

fuel (fū′əl) A source of stored energy. (p. 318) *Cars use fuel called gasoline to make their engines run.*

galaxy (gal′ək sē) A very large group of stars. (p. 238) *Our galaxy is called the Milky Way.*

gamma waves (ga′mə wāvz) An invisible form of light with high energy. (p. 349) *Gamma waves are used in nuclear power plants.*

gas (gas) Matter in a state that has no definite shape or volume. (p. 265) *The air we breathe is made up of gases such as oxygen and carbon dioxide.*

geothermal (jē′ə thər′məl) Using heat from inside the Earth. (p. 322) *Steam from a hot spring that turns a turbine is an example of geothermal energy.*

gibbous (gi′bəs) More than half but not yet full. (p. 200) *A gibbous moon can be waxing toward full or waning toward half.*

gills (gilz) Body parts in fish and other animals that allows them to breathe in water. (p. 104) *Gills collect oxygen from the water.*

grassland (gras′land) A biome that is covered with grass. (p. 48) *Grasslands provide a great deal of food for many animals.*

habitat (hab′i tat) The place where a living thing makes its home. (p. 144) *Whales live in an ocean habitat.*

heat energy (hēt en′ər jē) Energy that causes the temperature of something to rise. (p. 306) *The Sun is the main source of heat energy on Earth.*

hibernate (hī′bər nāt) To sleep through the winter. (p. 64) *Bears hibernate in caves from late fall until spring.*

horizon (hə rī′zən) The distant line where the land seems to meet the sky. (p. 180) *The Sun rises over the eastern horizon.*

humus (hū′məs) Leftover decomposed plant or animal material in soil. (p. 27) *Each layer of soil has different amounts of rock and humus.*

hydropower (hī′drə pou′ər) Using water to create energy. (p. 322) *Many dams turn a river's current into hydropower.*

hypothesis (hī poth′ə sis) A suggested statement or explanation that can be tested to answer a question. (p. 7) *An experiment can help you to test a hypothesis.*

image (i′mij) A picture produced by the reflection of light. (p. 351) *A mirror shows you an image of yourself.*

infer (in fûr′) To come up with an idea based on facts or observations. (p. 7) *The data from an experiment can help you infer what happened.*

infrared waves (in′freə red′ wāvz) A form of light energy that we feel as heat. (p. 348) *Devices that detect infrared waves can be used to "see" in the dark.*

inner planets (in′ər plan′itz) The four planets closest to the Sun. (p. 222) *Mercury, Venus, Earth, and Mars are the inner planets.*

iris (ī′rəs) In the eye, the colored circle around the pupil. (p. 358) *The iris changes the size of the pupil in different light conditions.*

kelp (kelp) A type of algae that groups together. (p. 103) *Kelp has large, brown leaflike structures.*

kinetic energy (ki net′ik en′ər jē) Energy in the form of movement or motion. (p. 317) *A falling leaf has kinetic energy.*

laser (lā′zər) A tool that uses a very thin beam of light. (pp. 364, 376) *Doctors can use lasers to perform surgery.*

lens (lenz) A piece of clear material that affects the path of light rays. (pp. 230, 359) *The lens in your eye focuses incoming light.*

light (līt) A form of energy made up of transverse waves. (p. 348) *Color is light energy we can see.*

liquid (lik′wid) Matter in a state that has a definite volume but not a definite shape. (p. 264) *Water in its liquid state takes the shape of its container.*

lunar cycle (lü′nər sī′kəl) The full sequence of the Moon's phases. (p. 202) *The lunar cycle takes about four weeks.*

lunar eclipse (lü′nər ē klips′) A period of time when the Moon moves into Earth's shadow. (p. 204) *The Moon may appear to be dark red during a total lunar eclipse.*

mangrove (man′grōv) A kind of tropical tree often found in swamps. (p. 118) *Mangrove roots provide shelter for fish and shrimp.*

marine environment (mə rēn′ en vī′rən mənt) Another name for a saltwater environment. (p. 91) *Whales and dolphins live in a marine environment.*

marsh (märsh) A type of wetland featuring soft plants such as grasses. There are no trees in marshes. (p. 114)

mass (mas) A measure of the amount of matter in an object. (p. 262) *Mass is often measured in grams.*

matter (ma′tər) Anything that takes up space. (p. 262) *The Earth is made up of all kinds of matter.*

measure (mezh′ər) To find the size, volume, area, mass, weight, or temperature of an object, or to find how long an event occurs. (p. 5) *When you measure something, you gather data or information about it.*

mechanical energy (mi ka′ni kəl en′ər jē) The energy in moving objects. (p. 306) *The rushing water in a river has mechanical energy.*

melt (melt) What happens when matter changes state from solid to liquid. (p. 266) *When ice melts, it becomes liquid water.*

meteor (mē′tē ər) A small piece of ice, rock, or metal that has broken off a comet or asteroid. (p. 224) *Most shooting stars are also meteors.*

meteorite (mē′tē ə rīt′) A meteor that hits the Earth. (p. 224) *Some meteorites create huge holes where they hit the ground.*

microscope (mī′krə skōp′) A tool that allows us to make small objects seem larger. (p. 397) *You can see some plant cells using a microscope.*

microwaves (mī′krō wāvz) A form of light energy. (p. 348) *The energy in microwaves can be used to cook food.*

migrate (mī′grāt) To move from one place to another. (p. 76) *Some birds migrate to new homes each fall and spring.*

mimicry (mim'i krē) When one thing imitates the traits of another. (p. 62) *Some insects use mimicry to look like other insects and fool predators.*

mixture (miks'chər) Different kinds of matter blended together. (p. 287) *Soda is a mixture of sugar, water, and other ingredients.*

model (mo'dəl) Something that represents another object or event. (p. 9) *A spinning ball can serve as a model to show the rotation of a planet.*

nocturnal (näk tər'nəl) Active during the night. (p. 42) *Nocturnal animals usually sleep during the day and hunt for food at night.*

observe (əb zûrv') To use one or more of your senses to identify or learn about an object or event. (p. 5) *You conduct an experiment to observe what happens in a particular situation.*

ocean (ō'shən) A large body of salt water. (p. 101) *The Atlantic and the Pacific are both oceans.*

opaque (ō pāk') Unable to let light pass through. (p. 370) *A piece of heavy construction paper is opaque.*

orbit (ôr'bit) The path an object takes as it travels around another object. (p. 190) *Earth's orbit around the Sun takes about 365 days.*

ornithologist (or'nə thâ'lə jist) A scientist who studies birds. (p. 54) *An ornithologist will often record the flight paths of birds.*

outer planets (out'ər plan'itz) The four planets farthest from the Sun. (p. 222) *Jupiter, Saturn, Uranus, and Neptune are the outer planets.*

oxygen (ok'sə jən) A common gas found in air and water that many animals need to survive. (p. 102) *When you breathe, your body is taking in oxygen.*

periodic table (pîr'ē od'ik tā'bəl) A chart that lists all of the known elements and their properties. (p. 278) *The periodic table helps us to group and classify elements.*

permafrost (pər'mə frost) A layer of soil that is always frozen. (p. 71) *Most permafrost can be found in arctic and antarctic regions.*

phase (fāz) A temporary state of being. (p. 200) *The Moon has many phases based on its appearance, including full, half, and gibbous.*

physical change (fiz'i kəl chānj) A change in which matter looks different but is still the same matter. (p. 286) *Breaking an ice cube into pieces is a physical change because it is all still water.*

planet (plan'it) A large sphere in space that orbits a star. (p. 220) *Our planet moves around the Sun.*

pollution (pə lü'shən) What happens when harmful materials get into the air, water, or land. (p. 136) *Litter is a kind of pollution.*

population (pop'yə lā'shən) All the members of a single type of living thing in an ecosystem. (p. 146) *Population might go down if an area's resources are used up.*

potential energy (pə ten'shəl en'ər jē) Energy that is stored up inside of matter. (p. 317) *You release the potential energy in a lifted object when you drop it.*

prairie (prer'ē) A temperate grassland. (p. 49) *Prairies have soil that is rich in humus.*

predator (pred'ə tər) An animal that hunts another animal for food. (p. 87) *Sharks are the ocean's fiercest predators.*

predict (pri dikt') To state likely results of an event or experiment. (p. 9) *You might be able to predict the weather by looking at clouds in the sky.*

prey (prā) An animal that is hunted by another animal for food. (p. 106) *Mice are prey to hawks.*

prism (pri'zəm) A special lens that can break light into many parts and colors. (pp. 344, 360) *Some telescopes use prisms to alter the light coming in.*

property (prop'ər tē) A trait of something that can be observed and measured. (p. 263) *The properties of matter include size, color, and state.*

pupil (pyü'pəl) The central opening into the eye. (p. 358) *The pupil grows larger in dark conditions to let in more light.*

radio waves (ra'dē ō wāvz) An invisible form of light energy. (p. 348) *Radio waves are used to transmit signals for phones, radios, and televisions.*

record data (rē côrd da′tə) To make note of an observation in a permanent way, as in writing. (p. 11) *When you record data on a chart, you organize your observations.*

recycle (rē sī′kəl) To turn an old thing into something new. (p. 136) *Paper can be recycled in many ways, including the creation of more paper.*

reduce (rē düs′) To use less of something. (p. 136) *When you reduce the amount of napkins you use during a meal, you conserve paper-making resources.*

reflection (rē flek′shən) Light bouncing off an object. (p. 350) *Your reflection in a mirror is light bouncing back at you.*

renewable energy (rē nü′ə bəl en′ər jē) Energy that can be replaced once it is used. (p. 322) *Wind power is a source of renewable energy.*

reuse (rē ūz′) To use something again. (p. 136) *When you refill a water bottle on a hiking trip, you are reusing the bottle.*

revolve (ri volv′) To move around another object in a circular way. (p. 190) *The Earth revolves in a regular path around the Sun.*

rotate (rō′tāt) To turn. (p. 182) *Earth rotates from the west to the east. Each complete rotation takes 24 hours.*

saltwater environment (sôlt′wô′tər en vī′rən mənt) The living and nonliving things that exist in a place where the water is salty. (p. 91) *Oceans and seas are saltwater environments.*

savanna (sə va′nə) A tropical grassland. (p. 49) *Africa's Serengeti Plain is a savanna.*

scientific method (sī ən tif′ik me′thud) The procedure for finding out how something works by controlled experiments. (p. 13) *You can test a hypothesis by using the scientific method.*

sequoia (si kwoi′ə) A kind of huge tree that grows in California. (p. 23) *Sequoias are sometimes called redwoods.*

shadow (sha′dō) The darkened area that results when light energy is blocked. (pp. 181, 370) *If you face away from the Sun, your shadow will appear in front of you.*

shelter (shel′tər) A place or object that protects an animal and keeps it safe. (p. 30) *During a rainstorm, you might seek shelter under a tree.*

soil (soil) A mixture of tiny rock particles, minerals, and decayed plant and animal matter. (p. 27) *Every biome has a certain kind of soil.*

solar energy (sō′lər en′ər jē) Energy that comes from the Sun. (p. 308) *On Earth, we see solar energy as light and feel it as heat.*

solar system (sō′lər sis′təm) The Sun and the objects in orbit around it. (p. 220) *Our solar system is in the Milky Way galaxy.*

solid (sol′id) Matter in a state that has a definite shape and volume. (p. 264) *You can measure a solid using both meters and liters.*

sound energy (sound en′ər jē) Wav es of energy created when an object vibrates. (p. 332) *When you hit a drum hard, your ear responds to the sound energy.*

sphere (sfēr) A body that has the shape of a ball or globe. (p. 184) *Most planets are spheres.*

star (stär) A hot, glowing ball of gases in space. (p. 220) *The nearest star to the Earth is the Sun.*

state (stāt) One of three categories of matter that has certain properties. (p. 264) *The three states of matter are solid, liquid, and gas.*

structure (strək′chər) A thing that is developed or built for a particular use. (p. 29) *Fish have structures called gills to help them breathe in the ocean.*

sundial (sən′dī əl) A device that shows time using a shadow cast by the Sun. (pp. 373, 377) *The shadows cast on a sundial are shorter around noon.*

surgeon (sər′jən) A kind of doctor who works inside the body to treat problems. (p. 364) *Many eye surgeons today use lasers to fix vision problems.*

swamp (swomp) A wetland with many trees or shrubs. (p. 114) *Cypress and willow trees grow well in swamps.*

telescope (tel′ə skōp′) A tool to make distant objects appear closer and larger. (p. 230) *The Hubble telescope helps us to see planets and stars more clearly.*

temperate (tem′pər ət) Having few or no extremes. (p. 49) *A temperate environment has a mild climate and four seasons.*

temperate forest (tem′pər ət fôr′əst) A forest biome with four distinct seasons. (p. 59) *Temperate forests are found in North America, Europe, and Asia.*

tentacle (ten′tə kəl) A long, thin, armlike structure. (p. 98) *Jellyfish use their tentacles to capture food.*

translucent (trans lü'sənt) A material that absorbs some light energy but lets some through. (p. 374) *Colored glass is a translucent material.*

transparent (trans per'ənt) A material that does not absorb or reflect much light energy. (p. 374) *A clear glass window is transparent.*

transverse waves (trans vərs' wāv) A wave that moves in an up and down motion. (p. 331) *Light is made up of transverse waves.*

tropical (trä'pi kəl) Coming from a region near the equator with warm temperatures all year long. (p. 49) *Tropical fish live in a warm marine environment.*

tropical rain forest (rān fôr'əst) A hot, wet forest biome found near the equator. (p. 58) *There are more kind of living things in tropical rain forests than any other land biome.*

turbine (tər'bīn) A machine that turns and produces energy. (p. 322) *A simple turbine looks like an electric fan that moves when steam, water, or air pushes against the blades.*

ultraviolet waves (əl'trə vī'ə lət wāvz) An invisible form of light that can cause a reaction in the skin. (p. 349) *Tans and sunburns are caused by ultraviolet waves from the Sun.*

understory (ən'dər stôr'ē) The area in a forest between the canopy and the ground. (p. 60) *Leopards, frogs, and many insects live in the understory of the rain forest.*

variable (vâr'ē ə bəl) Something that can be changed or controlled. (p. 9) *In a plant-growing experiment, the amounts of light and water you provide are variables.*

vibrate (vi'brāt) To move back and forth quickly. (p. 332) *A guitar string vibrates when you pull and release it.*

visible light (vi'zə bəl līt) The range of light energy that humans can see. (p. 348) *Visible light includes all of the colors you see.*

volume (vol'ūm) The amount of space that an object takes up. (p. 264) *Volume is often measured in liters or cubic meters.*

waning (wān′ing) In the process of getting smaller. (p. 200) *A waning Moon may go from full to half.*

water vapor (wô′tər vā′pər) The gas state of water. (p. 267) *You cannot see water vapor in the air.*

wave (wāv) A disturbance that moves through matter or space. (p. 330) *If you jostle water in a glass, you create small waves.*

waxing (wax′ing) In the process of getting larger. (p. 200) *A waxing Moon may go from half to full.*

wetland (wet′land) Environments where water covers the soil for most of the year. (p. 112) *Bogs, swamps, and marshes are all wetland environments.*

wind power (wind pou′ər) A renewable kind of energy that uses the energy of the wind. (p. 322) *Windmills are actually turbines that can gather wind energy and create electricity.*

X-ray waves (eks′rā wāvz) An invisible form of light energy that can pass through objects. (p. 349) *X-ray waves are used to take pictures of bones inside the body.*

Index

A

Absorption, 360
    of color of light, 360–62
    of light by translucent materials, 374
Adaptations, 32
    animal, 44*–45*
        to arctic tundra, 74–75*, 76
        to desert, 42
        to forest, 62–63*, 64
        to grasslands, 52
        to water environments, 94, 99*,
            104–6
        to wetlands, 116
    camouflage, 42, 44*–45*, 54, 76, 87, 105
    to environment changes, 145
    hibernation, 64
    migration, 76
    mimicry, 62
    plant
        to arctic tundra, 72–73
        to desert, 37*, 40–41*
        to forest, 60–61
        to grassland, 50–51
        to water environments, 94, 102–3*
        to wetlands, 114–15
    to protect against predators, 62, 63, 64
    survival through, 160
    of woodpeckers, 170–71
African American slaves, following stars to
    freedom, 246*
Air
    effect of heat on, 303*, 305
    sound wave in, 332, 333
Air bladders, 103
Aldrin, Buzz, 209
Algae, 92, 102–3
    kelp, 103
Alternative energy sources, 322–23
Amber fossils, 164

Amphibians, 116
Analyzing data, skill of, 186*–87*
Andrews, Roy Chapman, 162
Angler fish, 106
Animal rescue workers, 172
Animals
    in arctic tundra, 68, 69*, 71, 74–75*, 76
        adaptations to, 74–75*, 76
    camouflage of, 42, 44*–45*, 54, 76, 87,
        105
    changes in environment affecting,
        144–45
        response to, 154–55
    changes in environment caused by, 132,
        133, 134–35
    colors and survival of, 45*, 62, 76
    comparing fossils with living, 158–59*,
        160, 162–63
    in desert, 42, 45*
        adaptations to, 42
    ecosystem balance upset by new, 148
    energy from eating plants, 309
    energy needs, 305
    forest, adaptations of, 62–63*, 64
    fossils, 156–60, 162–63, 164
    in grasslands, 47*, 52
        adaptations to, 52
    as living things, 26
    needs of, 30–31
    nocturnal, 42
    response to changes in day length,
        252–53
    structures, 30–31
    in water environments
        adaptations to, 94, 99*, 104–6, 116
        ocean, 89*, 94, 103, 104–6
        wetlands, 116
Antelopes, 52
Arctic forget-me-nots, 73
Arctic fox, 76
Arctic tundra, 68–77
    animals in, 68, 69*, 71

adaptations of, 74–75*, 76
plants in, 71
adaptations of, 72–73
Area, estimating, 79*
Armstrong, Neil, 209
Asteroids, 224
Astronauts, 209, 217
Astrophysicist, 280
Atoms, 276–77
model of, 277*
Axis, 184
of Earth, 184, 190, 191, 308

Bacteria, 132
Baking, chemical changes in, 284, 289
Baobab tree, 51
Bar graph, 187*
Bark of tree, 51
Batteries, 318
Beaks of birds, 30, 31
Bears, 32
polar, 68, 74
Beavers, 134–35*
Big Dipper constellation, 240, 246*
Binary stars, 244–45
Biomass energy, 323
Biomes, 26–27, 82*
arctic tundra, 68–77
desert, 26, 36–43
forest, 56–65
temperate forest, 59, 61, 64
tropical rain forest, 58–59, 60, 62–63
grasslands, 27, 46–55
Birds, 54–55, 146
beaks of, 30, 31
as living dinosaurs, 163
nests, 31
wetland, 116

woodpecker adaptations, 170–71
Blubber, 74, 94
Bogs, 114
Bones, fossil, 156
Brackish environments, 91
Breathing
gills for, 31, 104, 144
lungs for, 31
oxygen, 30, 31, 102, 104, 275
Burrows, animal, 52
Buttresses, 60

Cactuses, 32
prickly pear, 41
saguaro, 40
California
climate, 32
new plants and animals upsetting
ecosystem of, 148
seasons in, 192–93, 196
California condors, 165
Camouflage, 42, 44*–45*, 54, 76, 87, 105
Canada geese, 76
Canopy of tropical rain forest, 60, 66*–67*
Can We Save the Peregrine Falcon
(Dobson), 129
Car, stored energy used by, 320
Carbon, 275
atoms, 276
as nonmetal, 278
Carbon dioxide, 28, 29
Careers in science
lighting technician, 384
map maker, 254
wildlife manager, 172
Catfish, 116
Cernan, Gene, 209
Changes. *See also* Environment, changes in

* Indicates an activity related to this topic.

chemical, 288–89*, 290, 292*–93*, 305
    physical, 286–87, 292*–93*, 305
Cheetahs, 52
Chemical changes, 288–89*, 290, 292*–93*
    energy and, 305
    signs of, 290, 293*
Chemical energy, 306, 309
    sources of stored, 318–19*
    use of, 320
Classification
    compare and classify skill, 34*–35*
    of matter, 264–65*
Claws, 75
Climate, 27, 32. *See also* Temperature
    change, 154–55
    of desert, 38
    of grasslands, 49
    of temperate forest, 59
    of tropical rain forest, 58
Clock, sundial as type of, 373, 377
Clouds, formation of, 310
Cold environment. *See* Arctic tundra
Color change, as sign of chemical change,
    290
Colors
    animal survival and, 45*, 62, 76
    of arctic plants, 73
    light and seeing, 357*, 360–62
    mixing colors of light, 366*–67*
    rainbow, 360, 367*
    as visible light energy, 348
Comets, 224
Community, 146
    prairie, 146–47
Compare and classify skill, 34*–35*
Competition, 132–33
Compression waves, 333
Conclusions, drawing, 312*–13*, 323
Condensation, 268, 310
Condors, California, 165
Coniferous trees, 61
Conservation of electricity, 323
Constellations, 240–41*, 242, 246*

Copernicus, 232
Coral reef, 101
Cornea, 358
Coyotes, 42
Crescent Moon, 200, 201
Crocodiles, 160
Crystal Vision (Schimel), 345
Cube, 283*
Cushion plants, 73

Dams, beaver, 134–35
Day and night, 178–85
    cause of, 182–83*
    hours of daylight, 186*–87*, 197*
    length of full day, 182
    seasons and length of, 191, 252–53
    Sun's position in sky and, 180–81
    temperature change in, 39
DDT, 129
Death Valley, 36
Deciduous trees, 61
Decimals, multiplication of, 325
de Marco, Orsola, 244–45
Depth of water environments, 92, 93, 101
Desert, 26, 36–43
    adaptations to, 37*, 40–41*, 42
    animals in, 42, 45*
    plants in, 37*, 40–41*
Dew, 268
Dinosaurs, 156, 158, 159, 162–63
Dobson, David, Can We Save the Peregrine
    Falcon by, 129
Dragons of the Sea (Schleichert), 87
Drawing conclusions, 312*–13*, 323
Drought, 142
Dry environment. *See* Desert
Dwarf fireweed, 73

Eagles, 146, 147
Ear, path of sound waves in, 332, 333
Earth
    history told by fossils, 157
    lunar eclipse and, 204
    model of, 183*
    orbit (revolution) around Sun, 190–91,
        232
    as planet, 220, 223
    rotation of, 182, 183*, 190, 192
        stars and, 239, 240
    seasons on, 188–95, 189*, 196
    as sphere, 184
    Sun as main source of energy on,
        308–10
    tilted axis of, 184, 190, 191, 308
    water supply of, 90–91, 121
Earthquakes, 142
Eclipse, lunar, 204
Ecosystem, 146–47*. *See also* Biomes
    new plants and animals upsetting
        balance of, 148
Eelgrass, 102
Einstein, Albert, 275
Electrical energy, 306, 318
    movement of, 334
Electrical wires, 334
Electricity
    alternative energy sources for, 322–23
        biomass energy, 323
        geothermal energy, 322, 323
        hydropower, 322, 323
        solar energy, 308–10, 323
        wind energy, 301, 309, 322, 323,
            337*
    conserving, 323
Electric sockets, 334
Electron microscopes, 276
Elements, 274–75
    ancient beliefs about, 274
    atoms in, 276–77*
    chemical change and, 288
    examples of, 275
    formation of, 280
    matter made up of more than one, 275
    periodic table of, 278
    physical change and, 286
    symbols for, 278
Elephant, woolly mammoth compared to,
    158–59
Emergent layer of tropical rain forest, 60
Endangered habitats, 118
Energy, 298–341, 340*. *See also* Heat
    energy; Light
    change and growth from, 305
    chemical, 306, 309, 318–19*
    cost of, 325*
    definition of, 304
    Earth's main source of, 308–10
    electrical, 306, 318, 334
    forms of, 306–7*, 309, 312*–13*
    kinetic, 315*, 317, 320, 328–29
    movement and, 305
    moving objects and, 329
    potential, 315*, 316, 317, 318–19*
    renewable sources of, 322–23
        biomass energy, 323
        geothermal energy, 322, 323
        hydropower, 322, 323
        solar, 308–10, 323
        wind, 301, 309, 322, 323, 337*
    sound, 332–33*, 336*–37*
    transferred by waves, 327*, 330–33
    using, 304, 314–25, 319*
Environment, changes in, 126–49. *See also*
    Fossils
    caused by living things, 130–39, 131*
        animals, 132, 133, 134–35
        people, 136
        plants, 132, 133
    damaging, 142–43

* Indicates an activity related to this topic.

effect on living things, 129, 140–49,
141*, 150*–51*
animals, 144–45, 154–55
causes of change, 142–43, 148
plants, 141*, 144–45, 150*–51*
people and, 136, 143
recovery from, 143
sudden, 154–55
Environments, 26–27
adaptations to. See Adaptations
biomes, 26–27, 82*
arctic tundra, 68–77
desert, 26, 36–43
forest, 56–65
grasslands, 27, 46–55
describing your, 78*
fossils and ancient, 157
protecting, 136, 138*–39*
water. See Oceans; Water
environments; Wetlands
Equator, 194
tropical grasslands near, 49
tropical rain forests near, 58
water temperature near, 93
Eucalyptus trees, 148
Evaporation, 267, 310
Expanded notation, using, 165
Experimenting, skill at, 354*–55*
Extinction, 154–55
species saved from, 165
Eyes
of deep ocean animals, 106
laser eye surgery on, 364, 376
parts of, 358–59
seeing color with, 360–62

Falcons, peregrine, 129
Fall season, 191

changing day length in, 253
path of Sun in, 193
Fat
blubber, 74, 94
survival in cold environment and, 69*,
74
Feet of arctic animals, 75
Fictional narrative, 120
Filter
looking through colored, 357*, 362
wetlands as, 111*, 113
Fires in grasslands, 49, 50, 51
First quarter Moon, 200, 203
Fish, 94
adaptations to ocean environment, 87,
104, 106
fossils, 157
gills, 31, 104, 144
Floods, 140, 142
beaver dams causing, 135
effect on plants, 141*
wetlands and, 113
Food
animal structure for getting, 30
chemical changes in, 288–89, 290
chemical energy stored in, 309, 319,
319*
use of, 320
Forests, 56–65
adaptations to, 60–63*, 64
animals in, 62–63*, 64
kelp, 103
mangrove, 115, 118–19
permanent changes in, 143
plants in, 57*, 60–61
temperate, 59, 61, 64
tropical rain forest, 58–59, 60, 62–63,
66*–67*
Fossil fuel, 324
Fossils, 152, 153*, 156–60
amber, 164
comparing living things to, 158–59*, 160,
162–63

F

Fractions, 121
Frank, John, 259
Freezing, 268, 286
Freezing Rain (Frank), 259
Fresh water, 90
    plants, 94
    supply of, 90, 121
    uses of, 121
Freshwater environments, 91, 92, 94
Friction, 307
Frilled lizard, 158, 159
Frogs, 62, 116, 145, 146
Fuel, 320, 324
Full Moon, 201, 203
Fungi, 132
Fur, 74, 75

Galaxy, 238
Galileo, 232
Gamma waves, 349
Gases, 265, 265*
    condensation of, 268, 310
    formation, as sign of chemical change,
        290
    liquid evaporation to, 267, 310
Gasoline, 318, 320, 324
    saving, 324
Geothermal energy, 322, 323
Geysers, heat energy from, 322
Giant Sequoias (Alarcón), 23
Giant squid, 106
Gibbous Moon, 200, 201
Gills, 31, 104, 144
Glass
    colored, 356, 374
    as transparent, 374
Glassy-winged sharpshooters, 148
Gleick, Peter, 121

Granger, Walter, 162
Grasses, 48, 50, 51*, 143
Grassland, 27, 46–55
    adaptations to, 50–52
    animals in, 47*, 52
    Pampas, 54–55
    plants in, 48, 50–51, 143
    prairies, 48, 49, 146–47*
    recovery from environmental damage,
        143
    types of, 48, 49, 51
Growth, energy and, 305

Habitat, 144
    effect of changes in, 144–45
    endangered, 118
Heat, adaptations to conserve, 74
Heat energy, 306, 320
    effect on air, 303*, 305
    friction and, 307
    renewable source of, 322
    as sign of chemical change, 290
    solar energy felt as, 308
    states of matter changed by, 266–68
    using chemical energy for, 318
Herons, 116
Hibernation, 64
History of Science
    To the Moon!, 208–9
    Turning the Power on, 322–23
Horizon, 180
Horseshoe crab, 159
Hours, converting into minutes or seconds,
    197*
Hubble Space Telescope, 231
Humus, 27, 39, 49, 59
Hydrogen, 275, 280
Hydropower energy, 322, 323

* Indicates an activity related to this topic.

Ice, melting, 305
Ice age, 154
Iguanas, 63
Image, 351, 352
Infrared waves, 348
Inner planets, 222–23
Inquiry skills
    analyzing data, 186*–87*
    compare and classify, 34–35*
    drawing conclusions, 312*–13*
    experimenting, 354*–55*
    measuring, 270*–71*
    observation, 226*–27*
    predicting, 96*–97*
    recording data, 138*–39*
Insects
    preserved in amber, 164
    woodpecker adaptations for catching, 171
Invisible light, 349
Iris, 358
Iron, 278
    rusting, 290

Jackrabbits, 42
Jellyfish, 98, 99*
Jupiter, 220, 221, 222

Kangaroo, 31
Kelp forests, 103
Kinetic energy, 315*, 317, 320, 328–29
    changing stored energy into, 320

Lakes, 91
Landfills, 136
Laron, Elaine, 177
Lasers, 364, 376
    used in surgery, 364–65, 376
Leafy seadragons, 87
Leaves of plants, 29, 130
    in desert, 40
    estimating area of, 79*
    in grasslands, 51
    in temperate forest, 61
    in tropical rain forest, 60
Lens, 230, 231*
    of eye, 359
    prism, 360
    telescope, 230
Lichen, 72
Light, 346–84
    definition of, 348
    in eyes, seeing and, 358–59
    forms of light energy, 348–49
    invisible, 349
    lasers, 364–65, 376
    materials affecting, 369*, 370–71, 374
    mixing colors of, 366*–67*
    movement of, 347*, 350–51*, 355*
    path traveled by, 350–51
    reflection of, 350–51, 352, 355*, 358, 371
    on rough surface, 352
    seeing color and, 357*, 360–62
    shadows and, 368–75
    as sign of chemical change, 290
    solar energy seen as, 308
    using chemical energy for, 318
    visible, 348, 349, 350
Light Amplification by Stimulated Emission of Radiation (LASER), 364–65, 376
Light energy, 334, 348–49
Lighting technician, 384

Lightning, 142
Light years, 247*
Lion, 30
Liquids, 264, 265*
adding heat to, 267
evaporation of, 267, 310
freezing of, 268, 286
Literature
magazine articles, 86–87, 300–301
nonfiction book, 128–29
personal narrative, 216–17
poems, 22–23, 176–77, 258–59, 344–45
Little Dipper constellation, 240
Living things. *See also* Animals; Plants
adaptations for survival. *See*
Adaptations
dependence on each other, 146–47
environments of, 26–27. *See also*
Environment, changes in
of past. *See* Fossils
stored energy used by, 320
Lizards, compared to dinosaurs, 158, 159
Lodges, beaver, 134–35
Lunar cycle, 202–3. *See also* Moon
Lunar eclipse, 204
Lungs, 31
Lynx, 75

Machines, stored energy used by, 320
Magazine articles
Dragons of the Sea (Schleichert), 87
Mammoth, woolly, 154, 157, 158–59
Mangroves, 115, 118–19
Map maker, 254
Marine environment, 91. *See also* Oceans
Mars, 220, 223
Marshes, 114
Mass
definition of, 262
measuring, 263, 270*–71*
Math in Science
cost of energy, 325
Earth's water, 121*
estimating the area of leaves, 79*
finding the distance between stars, 247*
identifying a cube or rectangular solid, 283*
keeping time by sunlight, 377
Matter, 256–97, 282*, 296*
changing, 284–93, 285*
chemical changes, 288–89*, 290, 292*–93*
energy and, 305, 310
physical changes, 286–87, 292*–93*
classifying, 264–65*, 273*
definition of, 262
elements as building blocks of, 274–75
mixture of different kinds of, 287
properties of, 263, 287
states of, 264–65*, 283*. *See also* Gases; Liquids; Solids
changes in, 266–68, 286, 287, 310
Measurement, 263
of distance between stars, 247*
skill, 270*–71*
Mechanical energy, 306, 309
change to heat energy, 307
sound energy, 332–33*, 336*–37*
wind energy, 301, 309, 322, 323, 337*
Meet a Scientist
Ana Luz Porzecanski, 54–55
Neil deGrasse Tyson, 280–81
Orsola de Marco, 244–45
Melting, 266, 310
Mercury, 220, 222
Mesquite tree, 40
Metals, 278
Meteorite, 224
Meteors, 224
Microscope, 274

* Indicates an activity related to this topic.

electron, 276
Microwaves, 348, 349, 350
Midday, Sun at, 180, 181
Migration, 76
    habitat change and, 145
Milky Way galaxy, 238
Mimicry, 62
Mirrors, 351, 352
Mixtures, 287
Moon, 198–205
    changing shape of, 199*, 200–203,
        206*–7*
    eclipse of, 204
    orbit around Earth, 202–3
    phases of, 200–203, 202*, 212*
    position in sky, 207*
    as sphere, 202
    travel to, 208–9
Moss, 114
Motion. *See* Movement
Mount St. Helens, 143
Movement
    energy and, 305
    kinetic energy of moving objects, 315*,
        317, 320, 328–29
    of light, 347*, 350–51*, 355*
    under water, adaptations for, 104
    of waves, 331
Multiplication of decimals, 325
Musk oxen, 74

Narrative
    fictional, 120
    personal, 196, 216–17
NASA, 209
Neptune, 220, 221, 223
Nests
    bird, 31

dinosaur, 162
New Moon, 200, 203
Night. *See* Day and night
Nocturnal animals, 42
Nonfiction books, 128–29, 300-01
Nonliving things, 26. *See also* Sunlight;
    Water
Nonmetals, 278
Northern Hemisphere, 192, 194
North Pole, 184, 190, 191
Numbers
    expanded notation to represent, 165
    multiplying decimals, 325
    subtracting 3-digit, 247*
Nutrients, 28. *See also* Food

Objects, describing, 261*
Observation skill, 226*–27*
Oceans, 91, 98–107
    adaptations to, 102–3*, 104–6
    animals in, 89*, 94, 103, 104–6
    definition of, 101
    depth of, 92, 101
    names of, 101
    plants in, 102–3*
    very deep, 106
Ocean waves, 330, 331
Ohl, Russell, 323
Okie, Susan, 217
Opaque materials, 370–71, 372, 374
Orbit
    of asteroids, comets, and meteors, 224
    of Earth around Sun, 190–91, 232
    of Moon around Earth, 202–3
    of planets around Sun, 219*, 220, 221
Orchid mantis, 62
Orion, 242
Ornithologist, 54

Outer planets, 222–23
Owen, Richard, 162
Oxygen, 30, 102, 104, 275
    animal structures for getting, 30, 31, 104

Pacific Ocean, 101, 103
Pampas, 54–55
Pan balance, 263, 270*
Park ranger, 172
Paws, arctic animal, 75
Peregrine falcons, 129
Performance assessment
    biomes, 82*
    classifying objects, 380*
    energy, 340*
    making postage stamp about
        environment, 168*
    matter, 296*
    phases of the Moon, 212*
    solar system, 250*
    water environments, 124*
Periodic table of elements, 278
Permafrost, 71
Personal narrative, 196, 216–17
    To Space & Back (Ride and Okie), 217
Petersen, Christine, Wind Power by, 301
Phases of Moon, 200–203, 202*, 212*
    lunar cycle, 202–3
    Sun and, 202
Physical changes, 286–87, 292*–93*
    energy and, 305
Pine cones, 61
Planets, 219*, 220–23. *See also* Solar
    system
    definition of, 220
    Earth as, 220, 223
    inner, 222–23

orbit around Sun, 219*, 220, 221
    outer, 222–23
    position in sky, 239
    as spheres, 220
Plants
    adaptations of, 37*, 40–41*, 50–51,
        60–61, 72–73, 102–3*, 114–15
    in arctic tundra, 71, 72–73
    changes in environment affecting, 141*,
        144–45, 150*–51*
    changes in environment caused by, 132,
        133
    in desert, 37*, 40–41*
    ecosystem balance upset by new, 148
    effect of shade on, 151*
    energy needs, 305
    flood's effect on, 141*
    as food, 309
    forest, 57*, 60–61
    fossils, 156–60
    in grasslands, 48, 50–51, 143
    growth toward light, 57*
    leaves of, 29, 40, 51, 60, 61, 79*, 130
    as living things, 26
    needs of, 25*, 28
    responses to changes in day length,
        252–53
    roots of, 28, 40, 50, 60, 72, 115, 143
    salt water and, 109*
    solar energy used by, 309
    stems of, 28, 40, 114
    structures of, 29, 29*
    in water environments, 94
        ocean, 102–3*
        wetlands, 113, 114–15*
Pluto, 220, 221, 223
Poems
    Crystal Vision (Schimel), 345
    Freezing Rain (Frank), 259
    Giant Sequoias, (Alarcón), 23
    Sun and the Moon, The (Laron), 176–77
Poisonous arrow frog, 62
Polar bears, 68, 74

* Indicates an activity related to this topic.

Polaris, 240
Pollution, 136, 143
Ponds, 91, 94
    depth of, 92
Population, 146
    extinction of, 155
Porcupines, 31, 64
Porzecanski, Ana Luz, 54–55
Potential energy, 315*, 316, 317
    changed to kinetic energy, 317, 320
    chemical energy as source of, 318–19*
Power plants, 334
Prairie dogs, 52, 146–47
Prairies, 48, 49
    community, 146–47*
Predators, adaptations to protect against, 62, 63, 64, 87
Prediction, skill at, 96*–97*
Prickly pear cactus, 41
Prism, 345, 360
Properties, 263
Pupil (eye), 358, 359*

Quills, porcupine, 64

Radio telescopes, 231
Radio waves, 231, 348
Rain
    in desert, 38
    flooding and, 140, 142
    freezing, 2259
    in grasslands, 49
    in temperate forests, 59

    in tropical rain forests, 58
Rainbow, 360, 367*
Rain forest, tropical, 58–59, 60, 62–63, 66*–67*
Ranger Rick
    What a Difference Day Length Makes, 252–53
Rattlesnakes, 42
Recording data, 138*–39*
Rectangular solid, identifying, 283*
Red foxes, 148
Reduce, reuse, recycle (3 Rs), 136, 138*–39*
Redwoods, 32
Reef, coral, 101
Reflection of light, 350–51, 352, 355*, 358, 371
    by planets, 221
    seeing color and, 360–62
Renewable energy sources, 322–23
    biomass energy, 323
    geothermal energy, 322, 323
    hydropower, 322, 323
    solar energy, 308–10, 323
    wind energy, 301, 309, 322, 323, 337*
Revolving Earth, 190. *See also* Orbit
Ride, Sally, To Space & Back by, 217
Rivers, 91
Roots of plants, 28
    in arctic tundra, 72
    in desert, 40
    in grasslands, 50, 143
    mangrove, 115
    of tropical rain forest, 60
    in wetlands, 115
Rotation of Earth, 182, 183*, 190, 192
    stars and, 239, 240
Rust, 290

Saguaro cactus, 40
Salt, 283*
Salt water, 90
Saltwater environments, 91. *See also*
    Oceans
    animals of, 94
    floating in, 108*–9*
    plants in, 109*
Saturn, 220, 221, 222
Savannas, 49, 51, 145
Schimel, Lawrence, Crystal Vision by, 345
Schleichert, Elizabeth, Dragons of the Sea
    by, 87
Schmitt, Harrison, 209
Science, Technology, and Society
    Beam of Light, A, 364–65
    Mail Call, 118–19
Seas, 91. *See also* Oceans
Seasons, 188–95, 189*, 196
    change of, 189*, 190–91
    changes in day length with, 191, 252–53
    in Northern and Southern Hemispheres,
        194
    path of Sun and, 192–93
    stars and, 242
    in temperate forest, 59
    temperature and, 191, 193, 194
Sea turtles, 88
Seeds, mangrove, 115
Sequence, 209
Sequoias, 23
Serengeti Plain, 46, 49
Shadows, 368–75
    definition of, 370
    formation of, 370–71
    lunar eclipse and, 204
    materials blocking light, 369*, 370–71,
        372
    shape and size of, 372–73*

Sun and, 178, 179*, 181, 373
    translucent vs. transparent materials
        and, 374
Shelters, 30
    animal, 31
    beaver lodges, 134–35
Shrimp, 160
Sight, 358–59, 371
    color, 357*, 360–62
    laser eye surgery for, 364, 376
Size of arctic plants, 73
Skill Builder. *See* Inquiry skills
Skunks, 64
Snow in arctic tundra, 70, 71
Soil, 27
    changes caused by living things in, 132,
        133
    in desert, 39
    in grasslands, 49, 50
    humus in, 27, 39, 49, 59
    permafrost in arctic tundra, 71
    in temperate forest, 59
    in tropical rain forest, 59
    in wetland, 112, 113
Solar energy, 308–10, 323
    matter changed by, 310
Solar system, 214–33. *See also* Stars
    asteroids in, 224
    comets in, 224
    definition of, 220
    early beliefs about, 232
    meteors in, 224
    in Milky Way galaxy, 238
    planets in, 219*, 220–23
    Sun in, 173, 220, 221
    using telescopes to learn about, 228–
        232
Solids, 264, 265*, 283*
    adding heat to, 266
    melting of, 310
Sonoran Desert, 38
Sound energy, movement of, 332–33*,
    336*–37*

* Indicates an activity related to this topic.

Sound wave, 332–33, 336*–37*
Southern Hemisphere, 194
South Pole, 184, 191
Space. *See also* Solar system
    using telescopes to learn about, 231, 232
Spacecrafts
    space shuttle launch, 217
    travel to Moon, 208–9
Spectacular Science, poem from, 345
Speed of animals, 52
Sphere, 184, 202, 220
Spines on plants, 40
Spring, 190
    changing day length in, 253
    path of Sun in, 193
Squid, giant, 106
Stars, 221, 236–48, 237*
    binary, 244–45
    constellations of, 240–41*, 242, 246*
    during daytime, 237*, 238
    elements formed inside, 280
    finding distance between, 247*
    galaxy of, 238
    position in sky, 235*, 239
    seasons and, 242
    Sun as, 221, 238
States of matter, 283*. *See also* Gases;
    Liquids; Solids
    changes in, 286, 287, 310
        heat and, 266–68
    classifying matter by, 264–65*
Stems of plants, 28
    in desert, 40
    in wetlands, 114
Stingray, 105
Story, elements of good, 120
Streams, 91
Structures, 29
    animal, 30–31
    plant, 29, 29*
Succulents, 41
Sugar, 275, 283*
Summer, 190, 193

    in arctic tundra, 70
    constellations seen in, 242
    path of Sun in, 192
Sun
    day and night and, 178–85
    energy from, 308–10, 323, 350
    lunar eclipse and, 204
    orbit of Earth around, 190–91, 232
    orbit of planets around, 219*, 220, 221
    path from season to season, 192–93
    phases of Moon and, 202
    position in sky, 180–81
    shadows and, 178, 179*, 181, 372, 373
    in solar system, 173, 220, 221
    as star, 173, 221, 238
    water cycle and, 310
Sundial, 373, 377
Sunlight
    angle of, 181
    direct, 190–91
    at equator, 194
    in water environments, 92, 93
Sunrise, 180, 181, 186*
    shadows cast at, 373
Sunset, 180, 181, 186*, 193*
    shadows cast at, 373
Surgeons, lasers used by, 364–65, 376
Survival. *See* Adaptations
Swamps, 114
    mangroves, 115, 118–19
Sweat, 320

Teeth
    fossil, 156
    of grassland animals, 52
Tehachapi, turbines at, 301
Telescope, 228–35
    how it works, 230

learning about distant objects with, 229*, 230, 232, 234*–35*
types of, 231
Temperate forests, 59
    animals in, 64
    plants in, 61
Temperate grasslands, 49
Temperature. *See also* Climate; Heat energy
    in arctic tundra, 70
    in day and night, 39
    in desert, 39
    near equator, 194
    seasons and, 191, 193, 194
    in temperate forest, 59
    in tropical rain forest, 58
    in water environments, 93, 93*
Test practices, 83, 125, 169, 213, 251, 297, 341, 381
Third quarter Moon, 203
Thorns on plants, 40
Three-dimensional shape, 283*
Time
    converting hours to minutes, 377*
    sundial to tell, 373, 377
Tinamous, 54, 55
To Space & Back (Ride and Okie), 217
Translucent materials, 374
Transparent materials, 374
Transverse waves, 331, 348–49
Trash, 136, 138*–39*, 143
Trees. *See also* Forests
    coniferous, 61
    deciduous, 61
    eucalyptus, 148
    mangrove, 115, 118–19
    of temperate forest, 61
    in tropical grasslands, 51
    in tropical rain forest, 60
Trilobite, 159
Tropical grasslands, 49, 51
Tropical rain forest, 58–59, 60, 62–63, 66*–67*

animals in, 62–63*
layers of, 60
plants in, 60
Tube worms, 106
Tundra, arctic. *See* Arctic tundra
Turbines, 322
    wind, 301, 322
Turtles, sea, 88
Tyson, Neil DeGrasse, 280–81

Ultraviolet waves, 349
Understory of tropical rain forest, 60
Uranus, 220, 221, 223

Venus, 218, 220, 222
Vibration, 332, 333
Viperfish, 106
Visible light, 348, 349, 350
Vision. *See* Sight
Volcanic eruptions, changes in environment and, 142, 143
Volume
    definition of, 264
    states of matter and, 264, 265

Waning Moon, 200
Water
    animal structures for getting, 30

* Indicates an activity related to this topic.

change of state, 286
cleaned by wetlands, 113
elements in, 275
gas state of. *See* Water vapor
hydropower energy and, 322, 323
mass of liquid vs. solid, 270*–71*
Water cycle, 310
Water environments, 88–97, 96*–97*, 124*.
   See also Oceans; Wetlands
   adaptations to
      of animals, 94, 99*, 104–6
      of plants, 94, 102–3*
   differences between, 92–93
   temperature of, 93, 93*
   types of, 90–91
Watering holes, 144, 145
Water lilies, 94
Water supply, 90–91, 121
Water vapor, 267, 310
   condensation forming dew, 268
Waves
   compression, 333
   definition of, 330
   energy transferred by, 327*, 330–33
   examples of, 330
   forms of light energy, 348–49
   movement of, 331
   ocean, 330, 331
   radio, 231, 348
   sound, 332–33, 336*–37*
   transverse, 331, 348–49
Waxing Moon, 200
Weather, change in environment and, 142
Wetlands, 110–20
   adaptations to, 114–16
   animals in, 116
   beaver dams causing, 135
   definition of, 112
   plants in, 113, 114–15*
   types of, 114
   as water filter, 111*, 113
Whales, 94
White light

colors forming, 360–62
   seeing black or white, 362
Wildlife manager, 172
Wind energy, 301, 309, 322, 323, 337*
Wind farms, 301
Wind Power (Petersen), 301
Wind turbines, 301, 322
Winter, 191, 193
   adaptations to survive, 64
   in arctic tundra, 70
   constellations seen in, 242
   path of Sun in, 192
Wires, electrical, 334
Wood, burning, 318
   chemical change in, 288, 305
Woodpecker, 170–71
Woolly mammoth, 154, 157, 158–59
Work, energy as ability to do, 304
Worms, 131*, 132
Writing in Science
   descriptive writing, 78*
   expository writing, 164, 246*, 282, 376
   fictional narrative, 120
   personal narrative, 196
   persuasive letter, 324

X-ray wave, 349

Year, days in, 190

Zebras

Zebras, 52, 144, 145

* Indicates an activity related to this topic.

Credits

Researchers, Inc.; (tl) C Squared Studios/Getty Images; (tr) V&A Images/Alamy; (tcr) Stockbyte Silver/Alamy; (br) Royalty-Free/Corbis. 276: (l) Bob Krist/Corbis; (r) Colin Cuthbert/Photo Researchers, Inc. 276-277: Stocktrek/Brand X Pictures/Alamy. 277: C Squared Studios/Getty Images. 278: PhotoDisc/Getty Images. 279: (t) Stockbyte Silver/Alamy; (c) Colin Cuthbert/Photo Researchers, Inc. 280: Photo by Denis Finnin. Copyright American Museum of Natural History. 280-281: NOAO / AURA / NSF / Photo Researchers, Inc. 282: Royalty-Free/Corbis. 283: Andrew Syred/Photo Researchers, Inc. 284-285: (bkgd) BananaStock/Punchstock; (inset) Richard Ransier/Index Stock/Alamy. 286-287: LMR Group/Alamy. 287: (l) John Hartman/Stock Connection Distribution/Alamy; (tr) C Squared Studios/Getty Images; (br) Macduff Everton/CORBIS. 288: (t) D. Hurst/Alamy; (c) Design Pics/age footstock; (b) D. Hurst/Alamy. 289: (l) Lew Robertson/FoodPix/Getty Images; (c) Madeline Polss/Envision; (r) Ian O'Leary/DK Images. 290: (t) PhotoLink/Getty Images; (c) John T. Fowler/Alamy. 291: (t) John Hartman/Stock Connection Distribution/Alamy; (c) Design Pics/age footstock; (b) PhotoLink/Getty Images. 294: (t) David Wall/Alamy; (c) Robert Slade/Alamy; (b) BananaStock/Punchstock; (inset) Richard Ransier/Index Stock/Alamy. 295: (t) Design Pics/age footstock; (b) Royalty-Free/Corbis. 296: (tl) D. Hurst/Alamy; (tr) V&A Images/Alamy; (c) Mauritius/age footstock; (b) Royalty-free/Corbis. 298-299: Terje Rakke/The Image Bannk/Getty Images. 299: (t) Peter Gridley/Stock Connection Distribution/Alamy; (c) Mike Dobel/Alamy; (b) Matthias Breiter/Minden Pictures. 300-301: Brian Lawrence/ImageState/Alamy. 302-303: Peter Gridley/Stock Connection Distribution/Alamy. 304-305: age fotostock/SuperStock. 306: (t) TPH/allOver photography/Alamy; (tc) James Schnepf/The Image Bank/Getty Images; (b) Peter Brogden/Alamy; (bc) Tomas del Amo/Alamy. 308: Tom Brakefield/Stock Connection Blue/Alamy. 309: (t) blickwinkel/Alamy; (b) Masterfile (Royalty-Free Div.). 310: (t) Alaska Stock LLC/Alamy; (b) Martin Hanke/Bildagentur Franz Waldhaeusl/Alamy. 311: (t) age fotostock/SuperStock; (c) TPH/allOver photography/Alamy; (b) Tom Brakefield/Stock Connection Blue/Alamy. 312: Neil McAllister/Alamy. 314-315: Mike Dobel/Alalmy. 316: ImageState Royalty Free/Alamy. 317: (t) Photodisc/Getty Images; (b) Jim Olive/Peter Arnold, Inc./Alamy. 318: Kelly Redinger/Design Pics Inc./Alamy. 319: Brian Pieters/Masterfile. 320: (t) Paul Barton/Corbis; (b) SuperStock/Alamy. 321: (tl) Jim Olive/Peter Arnold, Inc./Alamy; (cl) Kelly Redinger/Design Pics Inc./Alamy; (bl) Paul Barton/Corbis. 322: (bl) Wisconsin Historical Society; (br) Klaus Guldbrandsen / Photo Researchers, Inc. 322-323: Cristina Pedrazzini / Photo Researchers, Inc. 323: (bl) Tommaso Guicciardini/Photo Researchers, Inc.; (br) Warren Gretz/NREL/US Department of Energy/Science Photo Library. 324: (t) BananaStock/PunchStock; (bl) Dave Mager/IndexStock; (br) Jose Carillo/PhotoEdit Inc. 325: Royalty-Free/Corbis. 326-327: Matthias Breiter/Minden Pictures. 328-329: Alan Thornton/Stone/Getty Images. 329: (l) BananaStock/Alamy; (b) Comstock Images/Alamy. 330-331: Surfpix/Alamy. 332: David Gregs/Alamy. 333: sciencephotos/Alamy. 334: (t) Steve Allen/Brand X Pictures/Alamy; (c) Steve Allen/Brand X Pictures/Alamy; (b) B.A.E. Inc./Alamy. 335: (t) Bananastock/Alamy; (b) Steve Allen/Brand X Pictures/Alamy. 338: (t) Peter Gridley/Stock Connection Distribution/Alamy; (c) Mike Dobel/Alalmy; (b) Matthias Breiter/Minden Pictures. 339: (tl) Alaska Stock LLC/Alamy; (bl) ImageState Royalty Free / Alamy; (tr) Kelly Redinger/Design Pics Inc./Alamy. 340: (l) Getty Images; (tr) TPH/allOver photography/Alamy; (cr) Alan Thornton/Stone/Getty Images; (br) Tomas del Amo/Alamy. 342-333: Jesus Rodriguez /Alamy. 343: (t) Ben Hays/Alamy; (c) Ilja Hulinsky/Alamy; (b) Bo Zanders/Corbis. 344-345: David Young-Wolff /Alamy. 346-347: Ben Hays/Alamy. 348: (l) G. P. Bowater/Alamy; (c) Eric Kamp/Index Stock; (r) Ted Kinsman/Photo Researchers,

Inc. 349: (l) Park Street/PhotoEdit Inc.; (c) Russ Widstrand/Alamy; (r) ImageState/Alamy. 350: (t) Terry Oakley/Alamy; (b) Yoav Levy / Phototake. 350-351: (t) Andrew Lambert/Leslie Garland Picture Library/Alamy; (b) Richard Hutchings/PhotoEdit Inc. 352: David Muench/CORBIS. 353: (t) Russ Widstrand/Alamy; (c) Andrew Lambert/Leslie Garland Picture Library/Alamy; (b) David Muench/Corbis. 354: Chad Ehlers/Stock Connection Distribution/Alamy. 356-357: Ilja Hulinsky/Alamy. 359: PhotoStockFile/Alamy. 360: Alfred Pasieka/Photo Researchers, Inc. 360-361: David Olsen/Photo Resource Hawaii/Alamy. 361: (l) David Fischer/Photodisc Red/Getty Images; (r) Lisa Barber/Photonica/Getty Images. 362: C Squared Studios/Getty Images. 363: (t) David Fischer/Photodisc Red/Getty Images; (c) David Olsen/Photo Resource Hawaii/Alamy; (b) C Squared Studios/Getty Images. 364: Rich LaSalle/Getty Images. 364-365: Kurt Coste/Getty Images. 368-369: Bo Zanders/Corbis. 370: Jim Cummins/Taxi/Getty Images. 371: (t) David Keaton/Corbis; (b) Michael Keller/Index Stock. 372: (t) Stockbyte/PictureQuest; (b) Liane Cary/AGE footstock. 373: Ingram Publishing/Alamy. 374: Susan Van Etten/PhotoEdit Inc. 375: (t) Michael Keller/Index Stock; (c) Liane Cary/AGE footstock; (b) Susan Van Etten/PhotoEdit Inc. 376: Yoav Levy/Phototake Inc./Alamy. 377: Anthony Dunn/Alamy. 378: (t) Ben Hays/Alamy; (c) Ilja Hulinsky/Alamy; (b) Bo Zanders/Corbis. 379: (l) PhotoStockFile/Alamy; (b) Jesus Rodriguez /Alamy. 380: (t) Michael Keller/Index Stock; (tc) Susan Van Etten/PhotoEdit Inc. 382-383: Richard T. Nowitz / Photo Researchers, Inc. 383: (t) George Grall/National Geographic Image Collection; (r) Hans Reinhard/Bruce Coleman Inc. 384: (t) Adam Woolfitt/Corbis; (b) Michael Newman/PhotoEdit. 388: (tl) David Young-Wolff/Photo Edit; (bl) Randy Faris/Corbis; (c) Getty Images; (cr) Ingram Publishing; (br) PhotoLink/Getty Images. 389: (r) BananaStock/PunchStock. 391: (l) Creatas/PunchStock; (c) Amos Morgan/Getty Images. 393: (b) Stockbyte/PunchStock. 394: (b) Rim Light/PhotoLink/Getty Images. 397: (l) image100 Ltd; (r) Getty Images. 398: TRBfoto/Getty Images. 398-399: (b) Tony Watson/Alamy. 400-401: (c) Stockbyte/PunchStock; (b) Siede Preis/Getty Images.

Acknowledgments

"Crystal Vision" by Lawrence Schimel. Copyright © 1999 by Lawrence Schimel. Used by permission of the author, who controls all rights.

"Dragons of the Seas" by Elizabeth Schleichert from *Ranger Rick*. Copyright © 2005 by The National Wildlife Federation. Published by The National Wildlife Federation.

"Freezing Rain" from *Chill in the Air* by John Frank. Copyright © 2003 by John Frank. Published by Simon & Schuster Books for Young Readers.

"Giant Sequoias" from *Iguanas in the Snow* by Francisco X. Alarcón. Poems copyright © 2001 by Francisco X. Alarcón. Published by Children's Book Press. All rights reserved.

"Peregrine Falcons" from *Can We Save Them?* by David Dobson. Text Copyright © 1997 by David Dobson. Published by Charlesbridge Publishing. All rights reserved.

"Tehachapi Pass" from *Wind Power* by Christine Petersen. Copyright © 2004 by Scholastic, Inc. Published by Children's Press, a division of Scholastic, Inc.

"The Sun and the Moon" by Elaine Laron from *Free to Be You and Me* by Marlo Thomas and Associates. Copyright © 1974 by Free to Be Foundation, Inc. Used by Permission of Bantam Books, a division of Bantam Doubleday Dell Publishing Group. Inc.

"To Space and Back" by Sally Ride with Susan Okie. Copyright © 1986 by Sally Ride and Susan Okie. Published by Lothrop, Lee & Shepard Books, a division of William Morrow & Company, Inc.